Webster: The Tragedies

Strode's College
Library

822
WEB

This book is to be returned on or before the
date stamped above.

ANALYSING TEXTS

General Editor: Nicholas Marsh

Published

Chaucer: *The Canterbury Tales*   Gail Ashton

Webster: The Tragedies   *Kate Aughterson*

Shakespeare: The Comedies   *R. P. Draper*

Charlotte Brontë: The Novels   *Mike Edwards*

Shakespeare: The Tragedies   *Nicholas Marsh*

Jane Austen: The Novels   *Nicholas Marsh*

Emily Brontë: *Wuthering Heights*   *Nicholas Marsh*

Virginia Woolf: The Novels   *Nicholas Marsh*

D. H. Lawrence: The Novels   *Nicholas Marsh*

John Donne: The Poems   *Joe Nutt*

Analysing Texts
Series Standing Order ISBN 0–333–73260–X
(*outside North America only*)

You can receive future titles in this series as they are published by placing a standing order. Please contact your bookseller or, in case of difficulty, write to us at the address below with your name and address, the title of the series and the ISBN quoted above.

Customer Services Department, Macmillan Distribution Ltd
Houndmills, Basingstoke, Hampshire RG21 6XS, England

Webster:
The Tragedies

KATE AUGHTERSON

First published 2001 by
PALGRAVE
Houndmills, Basingstoke, Hampshire RG21 6XS and
175 Fifth Avenue, New York, N.Y. 10010
Companies and representatives throughout the world

PALGRAVE was formerly Macmillan Press Ltd and St. Martin's Press
Scholarly and Reference Division.

ISBN 0–333–80129–6 hardback
ISBN 0–333–80130–X paperback

This book is printed on paper suitable for recycling and
made from fully managed and sustained forest sources.

A catalogue record for this book is available
from the British Library.

Library of Congress Cataloging-in-Publication Data
Aughterson, Kate, 1961–
     Webster : the tragedies / Kate Aughterson.
        p. cm. – (Analysing texts)
     Includes bibliographical references.
     ISBN 0–333–80129–6 — ISBN 0–333–80130–X (pbk.)
        1. Webster, John, 1580?–1634—Criticism and interpretation.
     2. Webster, John, 1580?–1634—Examinations—Study guides.
     3. Tragedy—Examinations—Study guides. I. Title. II. Series.

PR3187 A9 2000
822'.3–dc21   00-062614

10 9 8 7 6 5 4 3 2 1
10 09 08 07 06 05 04 03 02 01

Printed in China

For Elizabeth

Contents

General Editor's Preface

This series is dedicated to one clear belief: that we can all enjoy, understand and analyse literature for ourselves, provided we know how to do it. How can we build on close understanding of a short passage, and develop our insight into the whole work? What features do we expect to find in a text? Why do we study style in so much detail? In demystifying the study of literature, these are only some of the questions the *Analysing Texts* series addresses and answers.

The books in this series will not do all the work for you, but will provide you with the tools, and show you how to use them. Here, you will find samples of close, detailed analysis, with an explanation of the analytical techniques utilised. At the end of each chapter there are useful suggestions for further work you can do to practise, develop and hone the skills demonstrated and build confidence in your own analytical ability.

An author's individuality shows in the way they write: every work they produce bears the hallmark of that writer's personal 'style'. In the main part of each book we concentrate therefore on analysing the particular flavour and concerns of one author's work, and explain the features of their writing in connection with major themes. In Part 2 there are chapters about the author's life and work, assessing their contribution to developments in literature; and a sample of critics' views are summarised and discussed in comparison with each other. Some suggestions for further reading provide a bridge towards further critical research.

Analysing Texts is designed to stimulate and encourage your critical and analytic faculty, to develop your personal insight into the author's work and individual style, and to provide you with the skills and techniques to enjoy at first hand the excitement of discovering the richness of the text.

NICHOLAS MARSH

A Note on Editions

References to act, scene and line numbers in both of Webster's tragedies in this book are to the Revels Student Editions, published by Manchester University Press, and both edited by John Russell Brown. *The White Devil* was published in 1996, and *The Duchess of Malfi* in 1997. Square brackets are used to indicate editorial stage directions.

Introduction

Analysing Webster's Plays

This book aims to enable students to approach and understand Webster's plays without being hindered by a surplus of technical and theoretical terminology. Nevertheless, when we read a four-hundred-years-old play, the verbal, literary and social conventions to which it adheres are necessarily alien to us. So, before we plunge into the play, it is useful to outline some of the analytical terms which we shall be using in our analyses in this book. These may be divided into three areas: the linguistic form; imagery; and dramatic form and performance.

Language

Verse, metre, rhythm and rhyme

These plays use a combination of verse and prose. The former is usually what is called **blank verse**. Blank verse is unrhymed and consists of a ten-beat (or ten-syllable) line, in which there are five stressed syllables, and five syllables which are not stressed (de *dum*, de *dum*, de *dum*, de *dum*, de *dum*). Each 'de dum', the combined stressed and unstressed syllable, is called a **foot**. A ten-beat line with five stresses is called a **pentameter** (from the Greek, meaning 'five feet'). Where those stresses fall regularly in an alternating beat, the line is called an **iambic pentameter**, which is often said to be the 'natural' rhythm of the English language. 'Hello' stresses the second syllable, and not the first. Webster's blank verse rarely conforms precisely to a regular iambic pentameter, but there are key occasions where it does so, and we draw attention to these in our analysis.

He uses at least three variations on a ten-syllable line. We may see an example of all these variations in one speech: that by the Duchess to Antonio as she woos him (1, i, 440–59). First, Webster often use lines which contain five stressed syllables, but twelve syllables altogether: 'I hope/ 'twill mul/tiply/ love there./ You do/ tremble' (l. 450). In this line, the first four feet each contain one stressed syllable. The final four beats place the stress on the first syllable of tremble, giving a line with five stresses but twelve feet.

Secondly, if you read a line out-loud which looks as though it contains more than ten syllables, when read aloud some of the syllables are elided, giving a ten-beat line with five stresses to the ear: 'You have left me heartless – mine is in your bosom' (l. 439). If we speak this aloud it looks something like this: 'You'have left/ me heart/less – mine's/ in your/ bosom/', the delivered sound is a regular iambic pentameter.

Thirdly, he may use an eleven-beat line, with the final foot consisting of three beats, where the last beat has no stress ('We are/ forced to/ woo bec/ause none/ dare woo us', *The Duchess of Malfi* 1. i. 442). In the final foot the emphasis is on 'dare woo'. A foot with two stressed syllables followed by an unstressed one is called an **anapestic foot**. This line contains six stresses.

Each of these variations enables Webster to write verse which sounds varied and responsive to situation and character, whilst maintaining an overall structural elegance.

Pauses, stops and continuous speech are an integral part of the way rhythm works. In this book, I have used common descriptive terms for these phenomena. Where a pause falls midline, we use the term **caesura**, an easy short-hand term for 'pause-in-the-middle-of-a-line'. Where a line's end coincides with the end of a sentence or speech, we have termed such a line **end-stopped**, and where the end of a line does not mark the end of the sentence or sense, it is termed a **run-on** line.

Webster frequently makes two adjacent lines rhyme. The pairs of lines are referred to as **rhyming couplets**. These occur at various key points in scenes: such as at the end, or at the exit of a major character. Webster additionally uses them to make emphatic points, for example, many proverbial phrases are given as a rhyming couplet. In all these examples, the effect of the couplet is the appearance and sound of a summative statement. The natural symmetry of a couplet, in which two lines are balanced against each other, enables two paradoxical ideas to be expressed neatly together, creating an ironic closure to a scene or a character's speech. Webster also uses **prose**, either for whole scenes or for parts of scenes. It is important to note where he does this, because it is a good indicator of a change of pace, tone and emotion. Prose was usually used by Webster and his contemporary dramatists for the lower social ranks, although this is not always the case. Try to be aware of when such linguistic shifts happen and why.

Imagery

Throughout this book, we will comment on and analyse the imagery in particular extracts, and in Chapter 8, we devote much of the chapter to patterns of imagery. It is important that we define what 'imagery' is, as well as some of the terms we use in the book to analyse how it works. Imagery is a word, or group of words, which self-consciously creates an image or picture for the purposes of comparison to something else. Flamineo says to the dying Vittoria: 'seas do laugh, show white, when rocks are near' (5. vi. 251). He is not really talking about the ocean, but using this as a comparison to describe how prosperity can deceive us.

There are several different kinds of imagery which we point to in this book. The first two listed here are used most frequently. The first is **metaphor**. A metaphor is an image which claims identity, rather than just comparison, with the idea, thing or concept to which it is referring. The example I have just cited is a metaphor: Flamineo cites it as a parallel way of thinking about prosperity, without telling us that this is precisely what he is doing. When we analyse how metaphors work we look at both the literal meaning which is conveyed by the image (the stormy, rough sea) and the concept or thing to which it refers or compares (prosperity). These two parts of a metaphor are called the **vehicle** (the actual image of the metaphor) and **tenor** (the meaning of the metaphor), respectively.

The second kind of image is a **simile**. A simile is an image which explicitly compares itself to something else, using 'like' or 'as' to signal the comparison. When Vittoria is dying she says to Flamineo: 'My soul, like to a ship in a black storm' (5. vi. 248): this is a simile because she makes the nature of the comparison explicit. In a simile, both vehicle and tenor are present: in a metaphor the vehicle is what we see, and we have to intuit the tenor from the surrounding context.

The third type of image which we refer to is **metonymy**. A metonymy is a particular kind of metaphor, where the vehicle is linked by sense to the tenor. One example is the use of 'sail' to refer to a whole ship.

Drama and Performance

You will notice as you read through this book that we talk about the play text both as a dramatic structure and as a performance, trying to envisage it in three dimensions on the stage. There are a few analytical and technical terms we have used, which are defined below.

Peripateia is a Greek term from Aristotle's *Poetics*, meaning the reversal right at the end of the play which precipitates the final end. It is used slightly more broadly here to mean a 'turning point' in the plot, narrative or action, after which the fortunes of an individual character, or a particular course of action, are irretrievably changed. We discuss this at greater length in Chapter 3.

Blocking is the arrangement of characters on and about the stage during a scene.

Theatricality is used to denote Webster's self-conscious usage of the devices and machinery of the theatre as an integral part of the play.

Meta-theatrical literally means 'above' or 'beyond' the theatre, and is used to describe plays which incorporate a sense of their own theatrical or fictional status within the action, dialogue or structure of the play. This will become much clearer in Chapter 7.

PART 1

ANALYSING
WEBSTER'S TRAGEDIES

1

Openings

Renaissance public performances of plays usually began with music, which like overtures for concerts, or modern theatres' dimming of the lights, gave forewarning that the important part was about to start. The dramatist and performers want us to pay attention from the very first words, to be plunged into their fictional world and space with all our senses alert. The openings can tell us more about Webster's intentions than any other single part of the play. They focus our attention on a new world and its concerns, and demand our attention.

When we are studying a text out of its immediate theatrical context, it is a good idea to continue to imagine it as if it were being performed, or to read it out loud with a group of like-minded friends. This helps remind us that drama is a three-dimensional art, in which words on the page are only part of the overall meaning of a text. We must consider consciously how these words work in a theatrical space. How do the actors move about the stage as they speak, or don't speak? How does costume and lighting affect our interpretation, and are these indicated in stage directions and by the content of the dialogue? What is the relationship between audience and actors and how does this affect our thinking about the play? How is the relationship between characters visualised on the stage? How do our answers to these questions help us to understand the play as a whole?

This chapter will look at the openings of two of Webster's plays. We shall analyse the text, focusing on the content, style and performance, to produce some preliminary answers to these questions. Webster's dramatic talent sketches his fictional world clearly and resonantly in these short openings.

*   *   *

Here is the opening of *The White Devil*:

[Act 1, Scene i]
      Enter Count LODOVICO, ANTONELLI and GASPARO.
Lodovico.   Banished?
Antonelli.   It grieved me much to hear the sentence.
Lodovico.   Ha, ha, O Democritus thy Gods
           That govern the whole world! Courtly reward,
           And punishment! Fortune's a right whore.
           If she give aught, she deals it in small parcels,   5
           That she may take away all at one swoop.
           This 'tis to have great enemies, God quite them.
           Your wolf no longer seems to be a wolf
           Than when she's hungry.
Gasparo.   You term those enemies
           Are men of princely rank.
Lodovico.   O, I pray for them.   10
           The violent thunder is adored by those
           Are pashed in pieces by it.
Antonelli.   Come, my lord
           You are justly doomed; look but a little back
           Into your former life: you have in three years
           Ruined the noblest earldom –
Gasparo.   Your followers   15
           Have swallowed you like mummia, and being sick
           With such unnatural and horrid physic
           Vomit you up i'th'kennel –
Antonelli.   All the damnable degrees
           Of drinking have you staggered through – one citizen
           Is lord of two fair manors, called you master   20
           Only for caviare.
Gasparo.   Those noblemen

Which were invited to your prodigal feasts,
Wherein the phoenix scarce could 'scape your throats,
Laugh at your misery, as fore-deeming you
An idle meteor which drawn forth the earth   25
Would be soon lost i'th'air.

Antonelli.   Jest upon you,
And say you were begotten in an earthquake,
You have ruined such fair lordships.

Lodovico.   Very good. –
This well goes with two buckets; I must tend
The pouring out of either.

Gasparo.   Worse than these,   30
You have acted certain murders here in Rome,
Bloody and full of horror.

Lodovico.   'Las, they were flea-bitings.
Why took they not my head then?

Gasparo.   O my lord,
The law doth sometimes mediate, thinks it good
Not ever to steep violent sins in blood.   35
This gentle penance may both end your crimes,
And in the example better these bad times.

Lodovico.   So, – but I wonder then some great men 'scape
This banishment. There's Paulo Giordano Orsini,
The Duke of Bracciano, now lives in Rome,   40
And by close pandarism seeks to prostitute
The honour of Vittoria Corombona –
Vittoria, she that might have got my pardon
For one kiss to the duke.

Antonelli. Have a full man within you.   45
We see that trees bear no such pleasant fruit
There where they grew first as where they are new set.
Perfumes the more they are chafed the more they render
Their pleasing scents, and so affliction
Expresseth virtue, fully, whether true,   50
Or else adulterate.

Lodovico.   Leave your painted comforts.

                    I'll make Italian cut-works in their guts
                    If ever I return.
Gasparo.   O sir.
Lodovico.   I am patient.
          I have seen some ready to be executed
          Give pleasant looks, and money, and grown familiar   55
          With the knave hangman, so do I, – I thank them,
          And would account them nobly merciful
          Would they dispatch me quickly.
Antonelli.   Fare you well.
          We shall find time I doubt not to repeal
          Your banishment.
Lodovico.   I am ever bound to you.
                                        A sennet sounds.   60
          This is the great world's alms – pray make use of it –
        ⎧ Great men sell sheep, thus to be cut in pieces,
        ⎨ When first they have shorn them bare and sold their
        ⎩   fleeces.
                                               Exeunt.
                              (*The White Devil,* 1, i, 1–63)

What is the dramatic effect of this scene? The play begins with a
question ('Banished?'), which in tone, mode and content tells us
about Lodovico's response to his sentence. We imagine the three
friends are in an antechamber to the place of political and judicial
decisions: they speak from the margins of power and bring news
about decisions taken elsewhere which affect the individuals on
stage. The interrogative opening word immediately establishes both
Lodovico's outlawed status and his disbelief that his political masters
have abandoned him. The men are on friendly and equal terms, and
are able to speak the truth to each other. This is a quick-moving
scene. Lodovico is being hurried away before the violence he
threatens erupts, and we sense his resentment flaring and building as
the scene progresses. We don't know whether to believe his outbursts
against those in power, or the account of his fall by his friends.
Swift-moving political events, deals done in side-rooms, political

corruption and resentment are the dominant topics in this scene. The sounding of the sennet during Lodovico's departing speech contributes to the atmosphere of intrigue: events here are propelled by orders and events from elsewhere. This scene plays quickly: there is one brief pause at line 38, when Lodovico appears to consider Gasparo's advice ('So – '). However, overall, quick action and reaction are the key motifs.

Up until now we have visualised the opening short scene, focusing on its atmosphere and effect in performance. Let us now approach it in a more conventional, 'literary' way. We shall find that this reinforces and deepens our physical impressions of the imagined performance. One of the most important features of a dramatic text is the rhythm of the dialogue. The courtiers never speak more than a couple of sentences at a time, and interrupt each other frequently. Webster divides many lines between two, and at one point three, speakers. The longest individual speech is Lodovico's opening diatribe of eight lines. Most lines are irregular iambic pentameters, ranging between 10 and 12 beats, with the anapestic foot often falling in the final foot. This reinforces a sense of an overall regular rhythm, whilst enabling flexibility. With the exception of the two opening lines and Lodovico's speech at line 38, no speaker begins on a new line. This creates a sense of intimate, quick, responsive and forward-moving dialogue. There are two sets of rhyming couplets in the scene: two together at lines 34–7, spoken by Gasparo, and one at the end, spoken by Lodovico. Couplets are used in the first example to emphasise a generality (about crime and punishment) and its relevance to Lodovico. The final couplet is a conventional scenic closure. It functions proverbially, reverberating into the next scene and the play as a whole.

Gasparo's double couplet is followed by the only pause and Lodovico beginning a new line. These three coinciding linguistic shifts together indicate a turning point in the scene, allowing the actors to slow, and asking the audience to pay attention to the content rather than the fast-paced dialogue. For the first time we are told explicitly about the wider world of the play and the names of new characters.

What do all these first impressions tell us? The tone of the scene is conversational, informal, and friendly. The casual, run-on lines, punctuated only by the two sets of couplets, create an atmosphere of confidences shared. But this style is set against the content of the scene, in which Lodovico is informed of his banishment for murder, and in which the three courtiers display their involvement in the general corruption of political life. The juxtaposition of an informal style with the serious content introduces us to the paradox of a public political world where private desires predominate over serious political or judicial purpose. In addition, both the place of this scene (an antechamber) and its informal style reinforce our impression of characters buffeted by larger political and judicial decisions, which we do not see. This analysis tells us much about the tragic world which Webster creates. All the individuals are enmeshed in their private worlds of desire, revenge and frustration, which conflict with the judicial and moral order. Any sense of public order is fragile: only Gasparo gives voice to it, and his contribution, whilst a crucial one, is evidently a minority one in the scene.

The structure of the overall scene also tells us how to interpret its meaning. The conversation has several turning points, where Lodovico's dominant status is wounded, but from which he tries to rebound. The first is where Antonelli reminds him of the justice of his sentence ('Come my lord / You are justly doomed'). Lodovico is silent while they outline the reasons for fourteen lines. They revel in the details of corruption: but Lodovico retains superiority in the exchange. His silence does not signify defeat and he dismisses their gleeful account of his fall with disdain: 'Very good. – / This well goes with two buckets: I must tend / The pouring out of either.' This elicits the second attempt by his friends to get him to admit the justice of the sentence ('Worse than these, / You have enacted certain murders'). Lodovico's retort reveals much about his view of murder ('Las they were flea-bitings'), but also a deflation of his confidence with a straight question: 'Why took they not my head then?' This new sense of realism invokes the third turn of the conversation, in which Lodovico's resentment focuses on Bracciano and Vittoria for failing to gain him a pardon and becomes a vividly violent threat of revenge ('I'll make Italian cut-works in their guts / If ever I return'). This structure helps inform us about the characters. The subject matter, the way the scene is structured and the physical staging of the characters circle around Lodovico. He is still potentially powerful. Gasparo's reasoned moderation, by contrast is represented as secondary. These insights have emerged from an analysis of the dramatic effect and structure of these opening lines. Let us now turn to the content and language of the scene. What is extraordinarily noticeable about this scene is the number of separate and successive metaphors. Of the total sixty-two lines, only thirty-three are literal and advance the plot (lines 1–4, 9–10, 13–14, 18–19, 30–4, 36–45, and 53–60), whilst the remainder are metaphorical. There are fifteen distinct metaphors. On a formal level it is clear that these courtiers prefer to articulate their ideas through analogy and indirection: and this communicative style invokes a political atmosphere in which plain speaking has little place.

But the metaphors function as more than formal indices of verbal indirection. This is clear if we list the metaphors.

1. Fortune as whore (l. 4)
2. Fortune as card dealer (ll. 5–6)
3. Great men as she-wolves (ll. 7–9)
4. Justice as unpredictable and destructive thunder (ll. 11–12)
5. Courtly sycophancy as emetic poison (ll. 14–17)
6. Caviar and the phoenix as metonyms for festive excess (ll. 21–4)
7. Lodovico's career and birth paralleled to two natural disasters: a meteor and an earthquake (ll. 24–8)
8. Courtiers' advice likened to the mechanical workings of a well with two buckets (ll. 29–30)
9. Murder as 'flea-biting' (l. 32)
10. Sin is 'steeped' in blood (l. 35)
11. Political affliction as transplanting (ll. 46–7)
12. And as perfumery (ll. 48–51)
13. Murder euphemised as tailoring (l. 51)
14. Advice described as 'alms' (l. 60)
15. Political patronage analogised to both shearing and butchering sheep (ll. 61–2)

With the exception of example 10, a conventional description, these metaphors paint vivid and disturbing pictures. Some describe nature as violently abused, twisted and torn from its usual patterns (examples 4, 7, 11, and 12). Others delineate political corruption and instability as poison, unique excess, and economic exploitation (examples 5, 6, and 15), and the severe lack of political reward (examples 14 and 15). Capital crime and sin are taken out of a moral context by metaphoric diminutions (examples 9 and 13). Female sexuality is used to signify aberrance (examples 1, 2 and 3). Fate and fortune are seen to dominate life and action (examples 1 and 2). Finally, the language of religious charity is twisted to apply to cynical political advice (example 14).

The metaphors share common features and subject matter. The most prominent is the twisting and inversion of natural events: disturbed feasts, physic as poison, earthquakes and meteors, which together construct an atmosphere of a disordered, violent and corrupt political environment. The cumulative effect of these metaphors gives a feel for the characters' sense of displacement and rootlessness and adds to our sense of an oppressive political and judicial regime. From the opening lines this rootlessness and corruption are intimately linked, via the metaphors, to transgressive female sexuality. These images and themes are not accidental: they are precisely echoed in the rest of the play's action, plot and language, as we shall see in subsequent chapters. The Italianate setting is emphasised in the outline of the main characters and their origins. The Jacobean audience would have understood this setting to symbolise a decadent political world, linked directly to the views of Machiavelli. Finally, Lodovico constructs Bracciano's and Vittoria's characters before we meet them: but Webster has also made us sceptical about Lodovico's accounts. So, we are eager to move on to discover how this brief explosive slant on themes, events and characters will play out in the rest of the drama.

*   *   *

This close textual analysis of the first scene of *The White Devil* has produced a surprising number of critical and dramatic insights. Now let us read through the opening lines of *The Duchess of Malfi* in a similar vein:

[Act 1, Scene i]

Enter ANTONIO *and* DELIO

Delio.   You are welcome to your country, dear Antonio;
You have been long in France, and you return
A very formal Frenchman in your habit.
How do you like the French court?

Antonio.   I admire it –
In seeking to reduce both state and people   5
To a fixed order, their judicious king
Begins at home: quits first his royal palace
Of flatt'ring sycophants, of dissolute
And infamous persons, which he sweetly terms
His master's masterpiece, the work of heaven,   10
Consid'ring duly that a prince's court
Is like a common fountain, whence should flow
Pure silver drops in general; but if't chance
Some cursed example poison't near the head,
Death and diseases through the whole land spread.   15
And what is't makes this blessed government
But a most provident council, who dare freely
Inform him the corruption of the times?
Though some o'th'court hold it presumption
To instruct princes what they ought to do,   20
It is a noble duty to inform them
What they ought to foresee.

Enter BOSOLA

                    Here comes Bosola,
The only court-gall: – yet I observe his railing
Is not for simple love of piety;
Indeed he rails at those things which he wants,   25
Would be as lecherous, covetous, or proud,
Bloody or envious, as any man,
If he had means to be so.

Enter CARDINAL

                    Here's the Cardinal

Bosola.   I do haunt you still.
Cardinal.   So.

Bosola.   I have done you
          Better service than to be slighted thus.   30
          Miserable age, where only the reward
          Of doing well is the doing of it.
Cardinal.   You enforce your merit too much.
Bosola.   I fell into the galleys in your service, where for two
     years together, I wore two towels instead of a shirt, with   35
     a knot on the shoulder, after the fashion of a Roman
     mantle. Slighted thus? I will thrive some way: black-
     birds fatten best in hard weather; why not I, in these dog-days?
Cardinal.   Would you could become honest.
Bosola.   With all your divinity, do but direct me the way to it – 40
     [*Exit Cardinal*]. I have known many travel far for it, and
     yet return as arrant knaves as they went forth, because
     they carried themselves always along with them; – Are
     you gone? Some fellows, they say, are possessed with the
     devil, but this great fellow were able to possess the great-   45
     est devil, and make him worse.
Antonio.   He hath denied thee some suit?
Bosola.   He and his brother are like plum-trees, that grow
     crooked over standing pools; they are rich and o'erladen
     with fruit, but none but crows, pies and caterpillars feed   50
     on them. Could I be one of their flattering panders, I
     would hang on their ears like a horse-leech till I were full,
     and then drop off: – I pray leave me.
          Who would rely upon these miserable dependences, in
     expectation to be advanced tomorrow? What creature   55
     ever fed worse than hoping Tantalus? Nor ever died any
     man more fearfully than he that hoped for a pardon.
     There are rewards for hawks and dogs, and whores when they
     have done us service; but for a soldier that hazards his limbs
     in a battle, nothing but a kind of geometry is his last support- 60
     ation.
Delio.   Geometry?
Bosola.   Ay, to hang in a fair pair of slings, take his latter swing in
     the world upon an honourable pair of crutches, from hos-

pital to hospital. Fare ye well sir. And yet do not you   65
scorn us, for places in the court are but like beds in the
hospital, where this man's head lies at that man's foot, and
so lower and lower.

[*Exit*]
(*The Duchess of Malfi*, 1, i, 1–68)

What happens on stage? The whole of Act 1 is a succession of
semi-private conversations on the public stage of a Duchess's court:
men and women exit and enter relatively informally, with the exception of the Duchess's public entrance later in the scene. The juxtaposition of private dialogues with the public setting of these
conversations is also used in the opening of *The White Devil*. The
technique can foster different audience responses. In these opening
lines, it aids our sense of an intimate and confident friendship
between Antonio and Delio, who must stand towards the front of
the stage while the political business of the presence-chamber begins
around and behind them. Parts of their conversation act as stage
directions ('Here comes Bosola', l. 22, and 'Here's the Cardinal', l.
28). We hence see these two characters as commentators on the
action, and this helps us view the content of their dialogue as a commentary as well. Their position at the edge of the stage also links
them to us, because they are physically closer to us. They observe
Bosola and the Cardinal conversing, although they cannot hear their
conversation: we are in a more privileged position, observing the
observers and privy to the content of all conversations.

By contrast, Bosola and the Cardinal are partly distanced from the
audience, both physically and emotionally, because Antonio and
Delio are nearer to us and comment on them. This distancing is partially reduced as Bosola joins in the dialogue with Antonio and
Delio in the later part of this extract, but Bosola alone moves
between the two positions. This helps place him physically as an
ambiguous character. This ambiguity is reinforced by the content of
his dialogue with the Cardinal.

Antonio speaks for much of the first thirty lines, and Bosola for
most of the last thirty, Antonio in verse and Bosola mainly in prose.
This sets up a clear parallel for the audience between the two men,

which is reinforced by the similar content of their speeches. Nevertheless, Antonio is clearly figured as superior to Bosola: first through his positioning as commentator for the audience, secondly through Bosola's corrupt links with the Cardinal, and thirdly through the device of allocating him the baser language of prose, except when he converses with the Cardinal. The Cardinal's short time on the stage (13 lines), and brief words, reinforces our sense that the stage itself and the characters now speaking are on the outskirts of power. The text gives no reason for the Cardinal's entrance and exit: it is part of the unexplained business of state.

Bosola's speeches, after the Cardinal's departure, are delivered part-distractedly, to himself and to the audience. He continues speaking for nearly four lines before he notices the Cardinal's departure ('Are you gone?' l. 44). He does not converse with Antonio and Delio, indeed he barely acknowledges them. Antonio overhears his complaints and asks a question, which initiates the description of the brothers. Bosola does not actually answer the question and says, 'I pray leave me' (l. 53). He commands the stage and action here: it is evident that he is pacing the stage as he speaks, because Antonio and Delio overhear only parts of his speech. He dismisses the courtiers, and moves off to muse aloud on political patronage. When Delio interrupts with another question, he is quickly answered before a further dismissal ('fare ye well sir'), pulled back for a word of warning, before Bosola walks off. What we see here is that both the physical stage and the conversation are dominated and controlled by Bosola. He may speak in prose, and be base-born, but he is more powerful than either Antonio or Delio. Although he is evidently a paid servant, he is able to dismiss the courtiers with impunity, and commands a greater range of the stage space at this point. By contrast, Delio and Antonio seem to be static commentators for much of this scene.

All these insights have emerged from a consideration of the staging of the opening lines, using the clues given to us from the text about the placing and relationship of characters on the stage and within the scene. What about the language in this extract? We have already noticed that Antonio and Delio speak in verse, whilst Bosola uses prose. The dialogue is slower than that of the opening of *The*

White Devil: no speaker interrupts another, and most speeches start at the beginning of a line. The conversation between Bosola and the Cardinal is the one exception to this. Bosola's abrupt greeting, the Cardinal's grunted and ambiguous 'So,' and Bosola's come-back are all delivered in a single iambic pentameter of monosyllabic words (l. 29). The short, quick-fire exchange is in marked opposition to Antonio's deliberative verse in the previous twenty-eight lines. This formal contrast adds urgency and a sense of a surreptitious exchange to the words between Bosola and the Cardinal.

Antonio's language is a discursive, semi-philosophical narration about the French political system, and about his ideal political state. Although he begins his account with a personal comment, 'I admire it' (l. 4), the remainder of the speech is third-person descriptive. Most of the lines are run-on and we have a sense of an easy, flowing narrative. The rhythm is regular, and this encourages a sense of deliberation and easiness. The only rhyming couplet in this extract is midway through this speech, acting as both a natural pause and an emphatic proverb: 'Some cursed example poison't near the head, / Death and diseases through the whole land spread' (ll. 14–15). When Antonio comments directly on Bosola, his language is more abrupt; there is only one run-on line, a line with a distinct caesura (l. 23), and each of the other lines contains a separate point about Bosola's character. This stylistic shift slows the pace of his verbal delivery and reinforces the sense of intimacy. It also suggests that he pauses for thought to find the words to describe Bosola's political behaviour. Antonio and Delio speak lucidly and frankly.

By contrast, the Cardinal's style is pointedly short and ambiguous. His opening word, 'So,' could be an interrogative ('So?'), an emphatic dismissal ('So what?') or an acquiescent affirmative ('Indeed'). There is no clear indication in the text which way to play this. The delivery is wholly up to the actor and director, and will depend on their interpretation of the character in the play as a whole. The ambiguity of the Cardinal's character is established with that single opening word.

Bosola's style is earthy and direct: his language illustrating the character of 'court-gall' constructed by Antonio in line 23. Bosola's plain claim for recognition and reward appears to have the merit of justification: 'I have done you / Better service than to be slighted thus' (ll. 29–30). His forthright and detailed account of his punishment in the galleys for work done on behalf of the Cardinal contrasts with the Cardinal's short answers and brief presence on the stage. We sympathise more with Bosola's discontent as a result of the Cardinal's abrupt behaviour.

Bosola's self-characterisation is conveyed in a continually ironic tone and in displays of wit. For example, he mockingly aggrandises his punishment in the galleys by comparing his prison uniform to a Roman toga (ll. 35–7). Once the listener has latched on to his irony, we are able to pick up his scornful attitude to those in power. His response to the Cardinal's 'Would you could become honest' is barely polite, clearly ironic, and goes un-rebuked ('With all your divinity, do but direct me the way to it', l. 40). His unchecked plain speaking and familiarity with a Cardinal, combined with his reminder that his previous service resulted in slave punishment, tell us from the very beginning that the Cardinal is corrupt. His descriptions of political chicanery and of the characters of the Cardinal and his brother are vivid and physical, in contrast to Antonio's more stilted language.

Both Bosola and Antonio use imagery to denote similar attitudes to the political situation and philosophy. At first glance, as we have seen, Antonio appears to use more 'poetic' language: he speaks eloquently and fluently in verse, whilst Bosola speaks abruptly and earthily in prose. Nevertheless, Antonio uses only two metaphors, one of which is arguably extended into a third. By contrast, most of Bosola's statements are metaphorical, and he uses at least ten different ones. This manner of speaking has two paradoxical effects. It enables us to see his points visually, but it also conveys a culture of circumlocution: nobody here says quite what they mean. Antonio's metaphoric vehicles ('His master's masterpiece' and 'court / Is like a common fountain, whence should flow / Pure silver drops') conjure holiness and purity and are used to represent political integrity and order. His extension of the image of the fountain into a negative example (what happens if it should be poisoned) forewarns us of later images of disease, poison and disorder, and coincides with the only rhyming couplet. These images of disease are used negatively by

Antonio, and deliberately emphasised through the use of the couplet. Images of disease also dominate Bosola's imagery in his description of the court.

Bosola uses twelve separate metaphors in forty lines. These are:

1. 'I do *haunt* thee still' (l. 29)
2. 'Blackbirds fatten best in hard weather' (l. 38)
3. 'in these dog-days' (l. 38)
4. Journeying as self discovery (ll. 41–3)
5. Possession by the devil analogised to political patronage (ll. 45–6)
6. Crooked plum trees, fed upon by caterpillars and crows, used to denote Ferdinand and Cardinal (ll. 48–51)
7. Horse-leeches denote political sycophancy (ll. 52–3)
8. Tantalus as an analogy of the hopelessness of political reward (ll. 55–6)
9. Condemned man awaiting pardon, as signifier of continual political fear (ll. 56–7)
10. Soldiers' service valued negatively, compared with hunting animals (ll. 59–61)
11. Soldiers' service metonymically represented by a pair of crutches (ll. 61–4)
12. Crowded hospital denotes court (ll. 64–8)

What do these metaphors have in common? Most share several features: the world which Bosola describes is one in which the natural has become unnatural or inverted, in which the basest animals (leeches, caterpillars and crows) dominate, or in which disease is rife. The common referent is the court and political order (or disorder). In these packed forty lines we view a picture of courtly life which is diseased, rotting, crowded, animalistic, disordered and corrupt. But it is remarkable that Bosola says none of these things directly, nor do we experience them directly, at this stage. Our impression has been created solely by imagery. Many of Bosola's images leave lasting impressions on our minds. The image of a crowded hospital, with heads and feet lying intertwined, graphically conveys putrefaction, crowding, disease, smell, and death, as well as Bosola's own distaste and bitterness at the courtly politics. His imagery conveys the general atmosphere of the court, but it also establishes his character. He is a man of bitter resentment and eager willingness, and this lends credibility to his political criticisms, as well as depth to his characterisation.

Finally, what can we say about the way this opening section is structured? The opening sixty-nine-line section falls into three parts, each acting as a kind of commentary upon the others. First we have Antonio's and Delio's conversation about how a good state should be run; secondly, Bosola's conversation with the Cardinal; and thirdly Bosola's near-monologue, with short interjections from Antonio and Delio. These three parts are contrasted in stage position, style and content. In the first part, as we have seen, Antonio and Delio stand at the front of the stage; Bosola's conversation with the Cardinal must happen further back, so the two courtiers can comment on it; and Bosola's monologues must be delivered as he is walking up and down the stage. Physically, then, the contrast between these three parts is crucial: it shows us that Antonio and Delio are marginal to the main action, that Bosola is equally at home on all parts of the stage, and that the Cardinal controls his own time and actions. Stylistically, as we have seen, the three parts are different also. The first part is slow and discursive; the second, abrupt and ambiguous; the third, vivid railing prose. Within sixty-nine lines we are given three different perspectives on the court and its life, and each acts as a stylistic contrast to the others.

The content of the three parts is also juxtaposed. Delio and Antonio frame the play by talking specifically about the French court and how to run an ideal political state: to exile sycophants, foster good political advisers, and lead by active example. This makes an implicit contrast with the present Italian courts we are about to meet and discover. We are immediately shown an encounter between two members of this political world: the powerful Cardinal and Bosola. Their verbal ambiguity highlights their clandestine relationship, and Bosola explicitly demands political rewards for past illegal services. This is the only part of these opening lines which advances the action of the plot. Thus it is clear that political ambition and corruption will drive the plot, not political virtue. But it is also clear that, whilst such ambition and corruption dominate the stage (and therefore the play), a clear space for moral commentary on that action is made by Webster through the placing and characters of Antonio and Delio, and their juxtapositional advocacy of an ideal political state.

The final part, in which Bosola rails against the political world he inhabits, suggests through both form and content that Webster does not set up a simple black-and-white opposition in his play. As we have seen, the first forty-two lines establish a clear opposition between an ideal and a fallen political world, one of which is theoretically expounded and one of which we observe in practice. The third part acts as a partial bridge between these two oppositions, both physically and thematically. Physically, Bosola moves between the two sets of characters who represent the twin poles of the good/bad opposition. Thematically, he shares Antonio's disgust at political corruption, and the audience feel his anger and visualise that corruption through his words and his vision. Nevertheless, he is clearly also part of that corruption, effectively blackmailing the Cardinal by reminding him of his previous service. The tri-partite structure of these opening lines, then, acts to destabilise a clear-cut moral judgement on this political world.

By using contrasting and shifting perspectives, Webster promotes a suspension of judgement in his audience, at the same time as he engenders a thinking response. What, we ask, is the point of Bosola's shifting allegiances? Why are Antonio and Delio so marginal? Does effective political life demand a more complex philosophy than that articulated by Antonio? These questions are ones Webster raises through character and staging contrasts: and he wants us to continue to ask them throughout the performance of his play.

Conclusions

It is clear that the openings of these plays can lead us to some far-reaching conclusions about how Webster's stagecraft functions and constructs his tragic world from the opening moments.

1. We have discovered that Webster's dramatic political worlds are full of private intrigue, instability and uncertainty. Political power is located tantalisingly just out of reach. Characters express this view both as opponents of political corruption and as eager participants in it. At this stage in both plays, the characters are certain of their views and their place in the world. It is the audience who is made uncomfortable with their morality. In *The White Devil* one courtier is legally banished for participation in such corruption, generating an ambivalent sense of political change for the audience. By contrast, in *The Duchess of Malfi*, Bosola makes it clear that corruption is prevalent from the beginning.

But, as we have seen, our close textual and dramatic analyses have enabled us to expand and deepen these insights. We are able to see how and why these political worlds are corrupted and how Webster creates our perceptions. In each play he shows us characters representing conflicting views about political morality, but he places these characters in different relationships to the audience. This both sets up a debate and a potential for conflict and offers the audience the opportunity to make moral judgements. He also shows us characters, for the most part, with no absolute control over their own destinies: power is located elsewhere. The amorphous source of power, as well as its unreliability, is a constant theme in his work. Thus, in these scenes, he constructs a vivid feeling of intense political struggle and intrigue, simultaneously with an overarching sense of powerlessness. He conveys this sense dramatically by stage positioning (blocking of characters): for example in *The Duchess of Malfi*, in which characters at the front of the stage comment on the morality of those elsewhere on the stage. But this marginal position, whilst producing a moral commentary on political corruption, is simultaneously a self-confessedly impotent position. Moral judgement is thus iconically rendered as powerless. Stylistic shifts coincide with characters' moral and social positions, and act as markers of each for the audience: the contrast between Antonio and Bosola is the clearest example of this. Finally, those with the most power (for example, the Cardinal) are either invisibly off stage, or speak most tersely.

There is a linguistic contrast between silent power and the verbosity of anxious courtiers. This is particularly noticeable in the intensity of the courtiers' metaphoric images, striving to articulate their sense of a world which neither recognises nor ranks them. The most commonly expressed view, even by the corrupt courtiers, is that the world is twisted and unnatural.

We can thus provisionally conclude that Webster constructs a recognisably corrupt world, where we also see the necessity of a moral perspective. In each play this moral perspective is acknowledged, but judged as impotent. Equally ambiguous are the location and morality of those in power themselves. These ambiguities are ones which we shall examine and discuss in later chapters.

2. In both tragedies, Webster uses the margins of the stage, closest to the audience, to represent the corridors just outside the location of central power. Thus, he uses stage space to indicate an iconic divide between private plotting and public politics and events. At this early point we have no sense of the nature of the wider public political world: Webster introduces us first to the courtiers' private worlds within the larger political world. This thematic divide, between private desires and public demands or duty, forms the central conflict of both tragedies. Through close textual and dramatic analysis of the opening lines, we can see and understand that this conflict is constructed through three-dimensional staging as well as the character oppositions and the language. Our visual understanding deepens our response and involvement. A further and crucial effect of this spatial manipulation is that Webster empowers his audience as critical interpreters. By showing us diverging interpretative positions on the stage, he acknowledges that the audience themselves can be sceptical about the events and characters depicted.

3. Both plays are introduced by characters who are on the fringes not only of the main political power, but also of the lives of the central characters. We are given their views on these central characters. This has several, divergent effects. It makes us eager to meet the main players in this world, and it makes us want to 'place' the new characters in the moral debate which has already

been established. Nevertheless, we already know that we cannot trust everything such characters tell us. Thus, when Lodovico constructs Vittoria's character, we note, but do not necessarily accept, it. The reputations of female characters are constructed by male courtiers, a structural feature of Webster's plays to which we shall return repeatedly.

4. We find a character in each play who articulates a philosophy of political expediency: Lodovico and Bosola. Each character is both participant in and commentator on the corrupt political world: observing it, only to use it. This latter political philosophy was characterised by the Italian writer Machiavelli. Webster's political analysis continually returns to a consideration of the political issues raised by Machiavelli: what kind of compromises do we have to make with morality in political life? Should a prince lie for the common good? How are private desires controlled or encompassed by the public good? Is absolutism possible or desirable?

The presence in each play of a Machiavellian character enables Webster to give a three-dimensional view of these political questions, and to show the consequences of some answers. We shall return to these characters in Chapter 5, and to questions of society and politics in Chapter 6.

5. Webster's language is overtly metaphorical, as we have seen. These metaphors portray a world of cut-throat and unprincipled competition between men at court: but they do so by using images which suggest to the audience a world out of kilter. By using images of a twisted and inverted nature to portray the political world, Webster simultaneously conveys a vivid portrait and a moral view on it. Language helps us both to envision the minute details of the society and to recognise its disordered nature. Metaphoric language has a paradoxical effect in Webster's plays: it conveys vivid meaning and images, but it also conveys a world of circumlocution. Why does no-one speak plainly?

6. Finally, Webster uses juxtapositional contrasts to render dramatic and philosophical debates more complex. We have already noted that he uses the margins of the stage, in conjunction with oppositions between characters, to set up a conflict between public and private demands. He also uses this contrasting technique between

different dialogues, juxtaposing the first third of our extract from *The Duchess of Malfi*, with the second, and then the second with the third. This establishes fast-moving scenes, but it also asks the audience to make comparisons between each new dialogue, and to measure them against each other. The result of this, then, is to construct an active audience who quickly gain a multiple perspective on the politics of this particular society. Yet, as we shall see in subsequent chapters, the creation of shifting perspectives does not mean that we are absolved from coming to judgement.

Methods of Analysis

The following analytical approaches have been applied to the extracts in this chapter, and are the best way of beginning to analyse a play:

1. **The text as drama.** When you first read a play, imagine how it plays on the stage. Think about what effect it will have on an audience. Where are the characters placed on the stage and why? How does their positioning give an indication of their relationship to the audience? How do they move around, and in what ways does this affect our interpretation? Our consideration of these factors illuminates understanding of themes, debates and characters. Thus, without conceiving of the text as drama, we might think that Bosola's monologue was actually a dialogue with Antonio and Delio. As we have seen, this reading would fundamentally misunderstand their relationship.

2. **Visuals.** What does the stage look like? Where are the characters placed on the stage and how does their visual relationship help construct meaning? Iconic meanings are a crucial part of Webster's stagecraft.

3. **Language.** Are there any key words or phrases? Do specific responses stand out in any way? Why are they predominant? How do they link in with each other? What do they have in common? Do different characters speak in different ways? Why? Why is prose used at certain points?

4. **Imagery.** Look at who uses images, and at both what they mean and the way in which it is expressed. What do the images have in common? What is the significance of any recurrence? Are there sets of images which inter-relate?

5. **Poetry.** Webster's plays mingle prose and poetry, and his poetic metre is less regular than that found in Shakespeare's tragedies. Look at which characters use poetry and why. Look for broken lines, regular metre and couplets: what is the effect of these?

6. **Rhythm.** Look for changes in rhythm, both by speaking the lines out loud and in relation to the character. Look for short or broken lines, for punctuated caesurae, or pauses, and consider the effect of these rhythmic shifts.

7. **Scenic structure.** Look at the way the scene is divided up, both thematically and between characters. Decide why it is divided in this way. Are there any turning points in the scene? What is the effect of these?

8. **Sentences.** Look closely at the sentences: are they long or short? What does their structure tell us? How does this close analysis illuminate the character speaking?

9. **Subject matter.** What are the characters actually saying? What is the whole scene about? It is remarkable how often we concentrate on smaller issues, such as imagery and character, and forget how the scene as a whole is part of the overall plot and story. So, in *The Duchess of Malfi*, we must not forget that Antonio's return from France precipitates the Duchess's own eventual downfall, through their private marriage.

This list looks rather mechanical: and to start with, as you begin to analyse your text using this list, it may feel 'bitty'. However, you will soon find that each approach feeds into the next, and that all are inter-related. In combination, they contribute to your overall analysis of the play. In addition, each approach supplements the next: stage placing, style and character intersect and coincide, and in combination deepen our sense of dramatic conflict and life.

Use this list to help in the suggested work below to continue your analysis of the openings of Webster's plays.

Suggested Work

In order to build on our analysis and insights from this chapter, look at the rest of the opening acts in each play.

The White Devil
Look at Act 1, Scene ii. This is a long scene for close analysis, but a worthwhile one, because it illustrates Webster's dramatic technique. It is a deliberate contrast to Act 1, Scene i. Analyse the scene using the above list, concentrating first on how characters move around the stage, who is grouped with whom and when, and who takes part in the dialogues. Divide the scene into parts, and decide where its key moments lie. What is the relationship between each section of the scene? Examine the creation of a private space between Vittoria and Bracciano and compare it with the Duchess and Antonio's in Act 1 of *The Duchess of Malfi*. How does the setting of each differ, and in each case what does it convey symbolically? For example, Vittoria and Bracciano meet in a garden setting. What is the effect of both couples' privacy being overlooked by other characters? Look at how audience expectation and judgement shifts and is manipulated throughout the scene.

The Duchess of Malfi
Look at the whole of Act 1, as the various characters arrive and depart in the antechamber, revolving around the Duchess. Examine the continuing conflict between public and private identity. How is it figured on stage and in the language? How is our view of the Duchess different from that of her courtiers and brothers? Why does Webster set up opposing views of her? Look at when, how and why she speaks. In what ways does the scene as a whole prepare for the subsequent one? Does the scene change our opinions or our views in any way?

These analyses will further illuminate the kinds of things we have found in the opening lines of the plays. You will find that suddenly small parts of the scene, which you might have passed over before as unimportant, have gained in significance. You should be starting to find it easier to visualise the scene as if it was on a stage, and to recognise how this deepens and strengthens your understanding of the meanings of the play.

2

Endings

The endings of plays, particularly when we have seen them on stage, remain in our memories and imaginations for many years. They coalesce and distil all the emotions, plot-lines, conflicts and themes in a final show-down. The nature of the show-down (who dies, who is married, who feasts and who does not) tells us much about the play's dramatic intent. Does the ending resolve conflict or perpetuate it? Is the ending idealistic, if so why is this? Is the ending darkly pragmatic? Does it answer all our questions, or not? The answers to these broader questions can be found through close analysis of the closing moments of any play. Let us turn, then, to the ending of *The White Devil*.

[Act 5, Scene vi]

Vittoria.	My soul, like to a ship in a black storm,
	Is driven I know not whither.
Flamineo.	Then cast anchor,

Prosperity doth bewitch men seeming clear,   250
But seas do laugh, show white, when rocks are near.
We cease to grieve, cease to be Fortune's slaves,
Nay, cease to die by dying. Art thou gone,
And thou so near the bottom? – False report
Which says that women vie with the nine Muses   255

	For nine tough durable lives. I do not look	
	Who went before, nor who shall follow me;	
	No, at myself I will begin and end:	
	While we look up to heaven we confound	
	Knowledge with knowledge. O, I am in a mist.	260

Vittoria.   O happy they that never saw the court,
Nor ever knew great man but by report.
          Vittoria dies.

Flamineo.   I recover like a spent taper for a flash
  And instantly go out.
  Let all that belong to great men remember th'old wives'   265
  tradition, to be like the lions i'th'Tower on Candlemas
  Day to mourn if the sun shine, for fear of the pitiful
  remainder of winter to come.
  'Tis well yet there's some goodness in my death,
  My life was a black charnel. I have caught   270
  An everlasting cold. I have lost my voice
  Most irrecoverably. Farewell, glorious villains;
  This busy trade of life appears most vain,
  Since rest breeds rest, where all seek pain by pain.
  Let no harsh flattering bells resound my knell,   275
  Strike thunder, and strike loud to my farewell.   *Dies.*

English Amb.   This way, this way, break ope the doors, this way.

Lodovico.   Ha, are we betrayed? –
          Why then let's constantly die all together,
          And having finished this most noble deed,   280
          Defy the worst of fate, not fear to bleed.
              Enter Ambassadors, *and* GIOVANNI.

English Amb.   Keep back the prince. Shoot, shoot!

Lodovico   O, I am wounded.
  I fear I shall be ta'en.

Giovanni.   You bloody villains,
  By what authority have you committed
  This massacre?

Lodovico.   By thine.

Giovanni.	Mine?
Lodovico.	Yes, thy uncle 285

Which is part of thee, enjoined us to't.
Thou know'st me, I am sure, I am Count Lodowick,
And thy most noble uncle in disguise
Was last night in thy court.

Giovanni.	Ha!
Lodovico.	Yes, that Moor

Thy father chose his pensioner.

Giovanni.	He turned murderer? 290

Away with them to prison, and to torture;
All that have hands in this shall taste our justice,
As I hope heaven.

Lodovico.	I do glory yet

That I can call this act mine own. For my part,
The rack, the gallows and the torturing wheel   295
Shall be but sound sleeps to me. Here's my rest,
I limbed this night-piece and it was my best.

Giovanni.   Remove the bodies. See, my honoured lord,
What use you ought to make of their punishment.
Let guilty men remember their black deeds   300
Do lean on crutches, made of slender reeds.

          (*The White Devil*, 5, vi, 248–301)

What we see in these last moments of the play replicates what we expect at the end of a tragedy. The bodies of the two dominant malefactors, and of Zanche the maid, are displayed on stage. The new prince has entered and pronounced judgement and punishment on the two notorious henchmen, Lodovico and Gasparo. Nevertheless, despite the signals of a new political order symbolised both by the punishment of wrong-doers and by the accession of Isabella's and Bracciano's son, two figures who have secretly dominated the action are absent from the closing moments: Monticelso, in Rome as Pope, and Francisco, advised to be absent by Lodovico in the previous scene. The audience's sense of completed action consequently remains suspended: we alone know that those holding highest office have corruptly contributed to much of the disorder, killing and deceit that has been so much part of the action of the play. Despite the very visible conventional tragic punishments and arrival of a new political order, we recognise that nothing has fundamentally changed. The absence of Monticelso and Francisco at the close of the play leaves us with a sense that corruption is endemic to the political process. These primary insights emerge clearly by a simple body count of the characters at the end.

If we analyse further the way in which these final moments are physically organised on the stage, it is clear that Webster points to these conclusions. The scene takes place in a private chamber, beginning with Flamineo's 'What, are you at your prayers?' (5, vi, 1) to Vittoria. Their conversation throughout the scene is also intensely private, playing out an argument between brother and sister that has been one of the central conflicts of the drama. Flamineo first attempts to get Vittoria to kill herself in a joint suicide pact, and she, pretending to do so, tries to precipitate his death first. Their private fight is interrupted by the arrival of Gasparo and Lodovico, who are revenging the divorce and death of Isabella, on behalf of the absent Francisco. They bind Flamineo to a pillar (l. 183), and stab him along with Zanche and Vittoria. It is at this point that the above extract begins. Flamineo is still bound to the pillar as he speaks his dying words. Zanche must be dead, for, although no stage direction indicates the moment, she does not speak again. Vittoria's body is prone, and Flamineo dies. For a moment the revengers must stand above the prone and bleeding bodies, signalling iconically the triumph of private revenge within this private space. However, it is only momentary: Flamineo's dying call for thunder is echoed by the banging on the doors by the ambassadors and Giovanni. Private revenge and chamber are literally disrupted by the arrival of representatives of international law and the rightful political heir. But the men of the new order are undermined, both by the confusion of their entrance and gun shots, and by Lodovico's claim that Giovanni's uncles ordered the killings. Giovanni's disbelief ('Mine?' and 'Ha!') underlines his political innocence and confirms the audience's suspicion that corruption will not be excised. The text indicates that Giovanni is still very young: he is called a 'prince', and the ambassadors give the initial orders: 'Keep back the prince. Shoot, shoot!' (l. 282). His small size, the ambassadors' physical dominance and Giovanni's failure to take Lodovico seriously, visually underline his impotence. Setting, circumstances, and physical size reinforce our perception of an ambiguous closure. Giovanni is no match for the shadowy figures of his absent, plotting and unpunished uncles. The play ends as it began, in a private space in which events are propelled by decisions made at the centre of power, which always appears to lie elsewhere.

Only two characters speak directly to the audience: Flamineo as he is dying, and Giovanni at the close of the play. Direct address to the audience emphasises the speeches' contents. Both are moral, Christian commentaries on the consequences of evil actions in this world, in rhyming couplets. Direct speech allows the Christian message to stand aside from the action of the play, and effectively act as a commentary both on the political content and on the closure. In this way, despite the darkness of the ending, a moral position beyond that political world is articulated.

The pace and rhythm of this whole scene tells us much about its meaning. It is slower than that of the opening scene, allowing space for a developing dialogue between Flamineo and Vittoria. The pace speeds up when the ambassadors and Giovanni arrive. This extract falls clearly into two parts, with different rhythms and dramatic directions. In the first part, as Vittoria and Flamineo are dying, slowness of pace predominates, creating an intimate atmosphere, both between themselves and with the audience. During these speeches, Lodovico and Gasparo remain silent. Perhaps they draw to one side, conferring about their subsequent plan of action. The sentences in the first thirty lines are of medium length, allowing a sense of reflection and response between the siblings. They do not interrupt each other, and Flamineo, for example, echoes Vittoria's metaphor of a soul at sea, in order to help reassure her as she dies. The rhythm is very regular, with the exception of the first few lines of Flamineo's soliloquy after Vittoria dies. There he both pauses (at line 264) and speaks prose (ll. 265–8), followed by his final eight lines in regular iambic pentameters.

Many of these lines are run on, occasionally juxtaposed with a short observation, such as 'O, I am in a mist' and 'I have caught an everlasting cold', which change the pace, aiding the sense of intimacy, and of self-revelation. The switch to prose, when Vittoria dies, occurring after the only pause, conveys Flamineo's loss of some of his cocky self-regard. He does not express grief directly. However, this change of rhythm, combined with his curious analogy of the mourning lions, signals a powerful distress which is echoed in the subsequent eight lines, addressed to the audience. His words are self-revelatory and intimate a moral outcome from his death, and self-knowledge about his devilish status. Their rhythm builds to the climax of the two final rhyming couplets. The first four lines (ll. 269–73) are run-on, and contain four sentences, each unconnected logically to the former, creating a sense of a man dying in fear. This contrasts markedly with his earlier speech to Vittoria. There each sentence logically followed from the former, he claimed death was nothing to fear, and he defended a self-creating secularism. His two speeches, before and after her death, are contrasts in rhythm, tone and content: from being outward looking and reassuring, he becomes introspective. His final four lines sound out his own funeral oration, in a dirge-like rhythm, echoed and reinforced by the sententious rhyming couplets.

The placing, timing and effect of the rhyming couplets aids the sense of pace and rhythm, as well as the meaning of the end. There are six couplets, and thus twelve rhyming lines, in the final fifty-three lines. This is quite a high proportion, in comparison with other parts of the play. Three of the couplets coincide with the dying words of a character: those of Vittoria and Flamineo (ll. 261–2, and 273–6). Two of the other couplets are spoken by Lodovico, first as he stands to fight the ambassadors, and then as he is led off for punishment. In each case the couplet acts as a summary of his position. The final couplet conventionally closes the play, and is spoken by Giovanni. The overall effect of the number of couplets is to give the scene a formal, almost funereal feeling. In addition, the rhymes echo in the audience's aural memory: court/report; vain/pain; knell/farewell; deed/bleed; rest/best; and deeds/reeds. The list summarises the thematic concerns of the play, particularly the concern with the politics of reputation and the links between immoral deeds and their consequences. The final rhyme tries to mark the conventional, moralised and proverbial closure to a tragedy: 'Let guilty men remember their black deeds / Do lean on crutches, made of slender reeds' (ll. 280–1). However, because it echoes Lodovico's earlier deed/bleed, the audience still hear the resonance of the silent echo 'bleeds' behind Giovanni's words. The effect is to undermine any complete sense of closure. Thus rhymes help construct, almost without our realising it, our sense that everything is not quite as black and white as Giovanni believes.

The action of the second part of this extract speeds up, and the rhythm echoes this. The regular poetic closure to Flamineo's speech is juxtaposed to the shouting of the Ambassador's short monosyllabic instructions, and to Lodovico's panicked 'Ha, are we betrayed?' A pause follows this line, providing space for the actor playing Lodovico to check that they really are trapped, or register their betrayal. His following three lines revert to a regular iambic pentameter, with a final heroic couplet, as he takes on the role and discourse of a noble courtier, prepared to face his fate. The subsequent rapid-fire dialogue between him and Giovanni echoes the actual sound of shooting. The speedy conclusion and the absence of Francisco and Monticelso paradoxically show us that the new order is both partial and too hasty. Lodovico is able to reassert his self-interested Faustian creed ('I do glory yet / That I can call this act mine own', ll. 293–7), using half a line more than Giovanni's own four-line judgemental summary. Their two speeches mirror but contrast each other, both ending on a summative couplet. Giovanni does not dominate linguistically: for example, he allows Lodovico to have his say, and he does not directly contradict him.

Thus, throughout this short extract, physical, iconic and verbal means are manipulated by Webster to reinforce an ambiguous conclusion: do we believe that corruption and evil have been obliterated? The opposition between good and evil is thus compromised. Webster's tragic closure is left partly open-ended and resonates into our world.

The scene's structural organisation echoes this interpretation. We have already noted its two parts, which contrast rhythmically, spatially and in terms of content. Each part acts as a commentary on the other: thus Vittoria and Francisco's deaths, in fear and self-knowledge, contrast and thereby comment on Lodovico's unrepentant bluster. These contrasts are reinforced and extended by the three sets of juxtaposed characters within this extract. They are, first, the opposition between Vittoria and Flamineo, on the one hand, and Lodovico and Gasparo in the other, which, as we have seen is underlined by the bi-partite scenic structure. The second opposition between sets of characters is that between those who are dead, dying, or condemned to die, and those who will live and take on power. The third opposition is between those who are present on the stage, and those who are absent. In seeing the organisation of characters in this way, we can understand that Webster shows us that *on stage* virtue conventionally triumphs over corruption. Nevertheless, we are always made aware that real power resides *off stage*, and that it is the absent characters in the third opposition who are the true victors. Representatives of virtue are thereby visually and structurally undermined and marginalised in the closing moments of the play.

In what ways does the language and imagery of the closing moments enhance our understanding of these issues? One of the most immediately obvious linguistic features of this extract is the repetition of the word 'black' by three different characters. Vittoria describes her soul as like a ship in a black storm (l. 248), Flamineo his life as a 'black charnel' (l. 270), and Giovanni the actions of the play as 'black deeds' (l. 300). Repetition links the moral perceptions of these characters with their actions, and posits a Christian message in which the disordered and private politics of the play are damned. This is reinforced by a whole semantic field of metaphors which link light and sun to life, and evil to night and black, implicit in the paradoxical title of *The White Devil*. Here it is extended in, for example, Flamineo's description of his life as a spent taper, his analogy of winter's lack of sun with fear, death and mourning; and Lodovico's description of his revenge plots as a 'night-piece'. Ostensibly, in these final fifty-four lines, blackness is posited as both evil and self-evident, particularly in Giovanni's final words. However, as we have seen, his belief in the self-evidence of evil deeds is completely undermined by the action, structure, rhymes, character placings and contrasts of this final scene. Blackness may conventionally symbolise evil: however, the play has made us sceptical of equating black and white to moral realities. Those responsible for black deeds are absent and, in the case of Monticelso, clothed in the Papal white dress.

The other dominant metaphor in the closing moments is that of self-conscious theatricality. Flamineo's dying words draw attention to his actions as *enacted*, and to his character as an actor playing a role. Both his 'farewell *glorious villains*' and 'strike thunder' invoke his self-conscious participation in the roles and stage business of the conventional vice character in a tragedy. Lodovico, the other villain slain, also invokes a theatrical metaphor to summarise his actions: 'I *limbed* this night-piece'. He puns on the Jacobean term for painting ('limn'), analogising his plotting to artistic creation and simultaneously delineating the literal result in the dead 'limbs' which lie around the stage. Theatricality becomes associated with villainy, plotting, false appearances, and finally death. We shall return to these issues in Chapter 7.

What do the rest of the metaphors here tell us? In the first half of this extract (ll. 248–76), of the twenty-eight lines, only ten lines are non-metaphoric, and two of those are Vittoria's dying *sententia* ('O happy they that never saw the court, / Nor ever knew great man but by report.') By contrast, the second half (the final 33 lines) is remarkably metaphor-free, with only one and a half lines using two separate metaphors. This aids our sense of a quiet closure after the high emotional intensity of the two deaths. The first metaphor is Lodovico's morbid pun, 'I limbed this night-piece'. Even under the shadow of the gallows, Lodovico's wit underlines his unrepentant, celebratory Machiavellianism. The second metaphor is Giovanni's final line, which, as we have noted, echoes ironically and differently than apparently intended. We are left with an image of men hobbling forward on crutches. Rhyme, rhythm, content and action point towards a sense of a false resolution, so his words sound naively trite. As in the opening scene, metaphor acts as a displacement of political truth. By contrast, metaphor is used very differently in the first half of our extract, to which we shall now turn.

The dominance of metaphor here does not create that sense of indirection. Instead, because it is combined with the dying moments of two main characters, and their attempts to articulate and find some comfort in death, it invokes pathos in evoking a sense of incomprehension and loss. Flamineo, as we saw, echoes and expands Vittoria's metaphor of the soul lost at sea. This metaphor is a conventional Christian one, and hints at Vittoria's repentance. Flamineo's response to her is reassuring, and conventionally Christian: 'cast anchor, / . . . We . . . cease to die by dying' (ll. 249–53). However, once he believes she has died ('Art thou gone?'), he rejects Christian imagery quite self-consciously. His first reference is to a pagan myth (ll. 254–6), but he moves swiftly to direct speech to the audience, eschewing metaphor. Here he articulates a philosophy of stark secular individualism: 'I do not look / Who went before, nor who shall follow me; / No, at myself I will begin and end: / While we look up to heaven we confound / Knowledge with knowledge' (ll. 256–60). He here clearly rejects Christian 'knowledge', on the grounds that empirical knowledge (looking up at the heavens) places knowledge of God in doubt. Flamineo explicitly illustrates and gives voice to early seventeenth-century fears that the new secularism would breed atheism.

In the subsequent sentences, he alternates between two subjects: the cold and fear gripping his body, and warnings to the audience on the morally corrupt world of politics. But the metaphors reveal more than their literal content and his state of mind: for he is acting as the audience's commentator on the action and morality. His first metaphor is the parable-like analogy of the lions in the tower, to remind all hangers-on of great men to 'mourn if the sun shine, for fear of the pitiful . . . winter to come'. His second, third and fourth all describe his physical life or feelings, and judge them in Christian moral terms. His life was 'a black charnel', he has 'caught / An everlasting cold', and 'lost my voice / Most irrevocably' (ll. 270–2). The metaphors function, as did those Vittoria used, to suggest a moral self-knowledge, if not repentance ('yet there's some goodness in my death'), and a consciousness of hell. His final metaphor comments on political life, but again carries conventional Christian overtones. 'This busy trade of life appears most vain, / Since rest breeds rest, where all seek pain by pain,' acknowledges ambition as a purely self-regarding secular trait entailing damnation. Each sibling's final couplets structurally echo each other: formally, in their non-metaphorical address, and in their functions as epitaphs. Vittoria's words are a general proverbial warning to others. Flamineo's reflect his dual outlook, to the political world and to his own fate, echoing a simultaneous disgust at the sycophantic political world with a bleak acknowledgement of his own damnation: 'Let no harsh flattering bells resound my knell, / Strike thunder, and strike loud to my farewell'. The literal action of the theatrical performance, as the ambassadors break down the doors, reinforces the metaphorical and moralised meanings explicit in Flamineo's final words.

*   *   *

Now let us turn to the closing moments of Webster's other tragedy.

[Act 5, Scene v]

Bosola.	Now my revenge is perfect: *He kills Ferdinand.*
	Sink, thou main cause
	Of my undoing! The last part of my life
	Hath done me best service. 65
Ferdinand.	Give me some wet hay; I am broken-winded.
	I do account this world but a dog-kennel:
	I will vault credit, and affect high pleasure
	Beyond death.
Bosola.	He seems to come to himself;
	Now he's so near the bottom. 70
Ferdinand.	My sister! O, my sister! There's the cause on't:
	Whether we fall by ambition, blood, or lust,
	Like diamonds, we are cut with our own dust. [*Dies.*]
Cardinal.	Thou hast thy payment too.
Bosola.	Yes, I hold my weary soul in my teeth; 75
	'Tis ready to part from me. I do glory
	That thou, which stood'st like a huge pyramid
	Begun upon a large and ample base,
	Shalt end in a little point, a kind of nothing.
	[Enter PESCARA, MALATESTE, RODERIGO, and GRISOLAN]
Pescara.	How now, my lord?

Malateste.	O, sad disaster!
Roderigo.	How comes this? 80
Bosola.	Revenge, for the Duchess of Malfi, murdered

By th'Aragonian brethren; for Antonio
Slain by this hand; for lustful Julia,
Poisoned by this man; and lastly for myself,
That was an actor in the main of all   85
Much 'gainst mine own good nature, yet i'th'end
Neglected.

Pescara. [*To Cardinal*]   How now my, Lord?

Cardinal.   Look to my brother.

He gave us these large wounds, as we were struggling
Here i'th'rushes. And now, I pray, let me
Be laid by, and never thought of.   [*Dies.*]   90

Pescara.   How fatally, it seems, he did withstand
His own rescue!

Malateste. [*To Bosola*]   Thou wretched thing of blood,
How came Antonio by his death?

Bosola.   In a mist: I know not how –
Such a mistake as I have often seen   95
In a play. O, I am gone!
We are only like dead walls, or vaulted graves,
That, ruined, yields no echo. Fare you well.
It may be pain, but no harm to me to die
In so good a quarrel. O, this gloomy world!   100
In what a shadow, or deep pit of darkness,
Doth womanish and fearful mankind live!
Let worthy minds ne'er stagger in distrust
To suffer death or shame for what is just –
Mine is another voyage.   [*Dies.*]   105

Pescara.   The noble Delio, as I came to th'palace
Told me of Antonio's being here, and showed me
A pretty gentleman, his son and heir.

          Enter DELIO [*with* Antonio's son].

Malateste.   O, sir, you come too late!

Delio.   I heard so, and

Was armed for't ere I came. Let us make noble use   110
Of this great ruin, and join all our force
To establish this young, hopeful gentleman
In's mother's right. These wretched eminent things
Leave no more fame behind'em than should one
Fall in a frost, and leave his prints in snow;   115
As soon as the sun shines, it ever melts,
Both form and matter. – I have ever thought
Nature doth nothing so great, for great men,
As when she's pleased to make them lords of truth:
Integrity of life is fame's best friend,   120
Which nobly, beyond death, shall crown the end.

                                              Exeunt.
                    (*The Duchess of Malfi*, 5, v, 63–121)

What does the end of the play look and feel like? In the closing lines, the evidence of the fifth Act's rapid and confused events lies literally about the stage. At the very beginning of the scene, the bodies of Julia and Antonio already lie dead in the chamber; by the end there are four more, those of the servant, the Cardinal, Ferdinand and Bosola. In these final fifty-nine lines we witness three of those deaths. The arrival of Pescara and Malateste does not alter the course of the action; they maintain their characteristic, self-interested blind eye to political corruption. The audience is unsure about the outcome until Delio's entrance with the Duchess's and Antonio's son, whose ambiguous horoscope suggested an early death. But Delio's arrival and final speech spell out the redemptive symbolic nature of the 'young, hopeful gentleman', although the young heir is silent. This contrasts with *The White Devil*, where the young prince does speak. However, here all characters are a part of the final reckoning. The play's moral closure asks us to believe, if tentatively, in the new order. Is this conclusion reinforced by other dramatic techniques?

The visual, physical appearance of the setting is an important indicator. Six bodies lie variously placed around the stage, while six living men stand above them. The audience is relatively sure of the political credibility of Delio (who, despite his links with Julia, the Cardinal's mistress, has remained Antonio's staunch friend) and the Duchess's son, but less so of the four courtiers, who have only now shifted allegiance to the new order. The courtiers' numerical and physical superiority over Delio and the young heir iconically suggests simultaneously the new order's hope and its fragility. The heir is very young, small and vulnerable amidst the carnage on stage. Many productions dress him in white, so that his size and colour distinguish him from the spilled blood and the courtiers' black clothes. Our sympathies lie with his youth, his vulnerability, and his orphaned status.

The atmosphere is intimate: as with *The White Devil*, the denouement is set in private rooms, in the dark. The feelings of intimacy, claustrophobia and confusion generated by the setting are intensified by Bosola's murder of the servant, blocking entrances and exits, to prevent him going for help ("cause you shall not unbarricade the door', l. 35). Justice is achieved behind locked doors. Once private justice is breached by innocent men, the closeted atmosphere is dispersed. Space becomes symbolic of political openness.

Another way in which a feeling of a new order is established is through the transformation of the character of Bosola. As this extract opens he explicitly takes on a new dramatic function, which is fused with what we know and feel about his changed character: 'Now my revenge is perfect' (l. 63). The revenger figure in Jacobean drama usually takes on the task of retribution to revenge what they and the audience see as a terrible wrong which cannot be redressed by legal means in a corrupt political world. They tend to have the audience's sympathies, until they themselves become corrupted by their actions. Bosola self-consciously places himself on the side of the audience and of moral action. Our belief in the rightness of his action is reinforced by the timing of his conversion. Bosola's journey to revenge has been a reverse of other Jacobean characters, who take on the role at the beginning of the play. By assuming the role late in the plot, the retributory and judicial functions dominate. Bosola's voice thence becomes the play's moral conscience, a position he has gradually assumed since the Duchess's death. Both his function as revenger and his character conversion give moral credibility to his

words: for example, his attack on the moral status of a cardinal
('thou . . . / Shalt end in a little point, a kind of nothing', l. 79) and
his defence of his revenge of the murders of the Duchess, Antonio
and Julia. His dying speech (ll. 95–105) thence evokes a pathos
which, had he died an Act earlier, he would not have garnered. We
shall return to a discussion of his heroic status in Chapter 5. It is
clear that his conversion to support the Duchess and her family
helps the audience believe in her redemptive function and consequently that of her son as credible heir. Those who committed evil
have been vanquished, and those who have the power to act ethically
in a political environment have triumphed. Nevertheless, this
triumph is achieved through Bosola's actions.

The play's end clearly echoes the beginning: Delio's words open
and close the action. The end reminds us of his opening conversation with Antonio on the reforming French government. This
reminder of a heritage of ethical and legal politics gives added credibility to the new order. Delio's summary: 'Let us make noble use /
Of this great ruin' (ll. 110–11) invokes the play's action as a moral
lesson for both actors and audience.

The structure of these final moments contributes towards our
feeling that this is a redemptive ending. It falls into three clear parts:
first, Bosola's killing of Ferdinand and conversation with the
Cardinal; secondly, the arrival of Pescara, Malateste and others to
support the Cardinal, and their conversation with Bosola as he dies;
and thirdly, the arrival of Delio and the Duchess's son. In seeing the
action as a tri-partite structure, we can understand how Webster uses
character entrances to shift the meaning of the ending. In the first
part, the private world of the brothers and Bosola plays out to its
conclusion. The arrival of the courtiers opens that world out to a
wider moral scrutiny, although still within the brothers' political
world, and it is to their courtiers that Bosola states his legalistic case
for revenge. Finally, the arrival of Delio signals the ending of political chicanery, and triumph over the sycophantic political culture.
The plot is thus echoed by the internal dramatic structure of the last
lines, moving from action, to the setting forth of evidence and
judgement, to resolution and rebirth. By understanding scenic structure, and the way in which the presence and absence of characters

constructs meaning and contributes to a scene's structure, it is possible to visualise and appreciate dramatic meaning.

Webster's use of metre, language and imagery in these lines helps reinforce the audience's sense of a satisfactory resolution. The rhythm of the scene is actually quite slow: there is time for killing and for repentance. No character interrupts another, and this aids our attention to the content of their conversations, which clarify motives, feelings and moral outlook. The only line which speeds up the pace is where the courtiers burst in, and each ask an abrupt question, within the compass of a single pentameter (l. 80). But their arrival does not change the outcome of the action, since the subsequent pace does not change, and none of the characters change their views or actions as a result of their entrance.

There are three rhyming couplets in the extract, one in each of the three parts, and predictably coinciding with the close of the play and the deaths of characters. However, Webster's allocation of the couplets is interesting. Ferdinand dies on a proverbial couplet, which acts as a summative epitaph of his life: '*Whether we fall by ambition, blood, or lust, / Like diamonds, we are cut with our own dust*' (ll. 72–3). The emphasis created by the rhymes (lust/dust) both acts as an unconscious commentary on his motives throughout the play, and places them within political ('ambition'), sexual ('lust') and personal ('blood') contexts. The couplet intensifies the moment of his death by slowing down the rhythms of the run-on lines for a moment: so we concentrate both on his words and on his death. In the second part of this extract, both the Cardinal and Bosola die. However, the Cardinal's death is completely overshadowed by Bosola's, both in terms of the number of lines each speaks (three and a half, and eighteen respectively), and in the fact only Bosola has a couplet. The Cardinal's words end on a falling rhythm and an incomplete pentameter: 'And now, I pray, let me / Be laid by, and never thought of' (ll. 89–90). By contrast, Bosola speaks a couplet on which the audience can pause, and then a final half-line commentary before he dies. His couplet ('Let worthy minds ne'er stagger in distrust / To suffer death or shame for what is just') ostensibly proclaims his belief in and acceptance of a just universal moral order. But there are two counterweights to this. The first is the echo of the rhyme (distrust/just), which invokes suspicion of the possibility of justice. The second is his appended half-line to that couplet: 'Mine is another voyage', an acknowledgement of his continued moral isolation, even marginalisation.

His use of the term 'worthy' acts as a triple ironic commentary on the status-obsessed and murdering brothers. First, it invokes an economic sense of value, and their refusal to reward Bosola's worth for his actions on their behalf throughout the play. Secondly, worth implies desert: and the brothers' evil worth has been matched by Bosola's revenge. Finally, it conveys the idea of a nobility of mind that transcends economic and social status. Bosola's (finally) 'worthy mind', albeit in a base body, becomes the bearer of truth and the means whereby the new order is established. Delio's final couplet echoes Bosola's words. Delio redefines nobility and worth as '*Integrity of life*' (l. 120), echoing Bosola's philosophy on behalf of the Duchess's son and her memory ('*Which nobly, beyond death, shall crown the end*'). Suitably closing on the word 'end', the play carries a dual message. The rightful heir has been restored: intimating social and political continuity. But that genealogical continuity is articulated through a new order based on ethical distinctions of worth, and 'in's mother's right' (l. 113), rather than the conventional patrilinear succession.

Metaphors sustain and help construct the atmosphere of the final moments. Over half the total lines are plain-spoken. Delio, for example, has always been a straight-talker, and continues to maintain that linguistic and ethical status in his final words. His metaphor, then, strikes the audience as an unusual mode of speech for him. His analogy is an extended metaphor (ll. 114–17) comparing fame and footprints melting in snow. The length of the analogy, combined with his uncharacteristic metaphoric usage, ensure that the pace of delivery is slowed, and that the audience take note of both how and what he speaks. It makes his words gently, but finally, elegiac in the context of the actions of the three dead men, and the image hangs in the air after he has spoken, intensifying the audience's sense of loss.

The way in which Bosola and Ferdinand use metaphoric language tells us how to interpret their characters as they die. Ferdinand's

'Give me some wet hay' and his description of the world as a 'dog-kennel' echo the link between his character and the animal world. Metaphor clarifies that Ferdinand's character has not changed. By contrast, Bosola appears to use imagery quite self-consciously. His explicit use of simile (where one thing is said to be *like* something else) as opposed to metaphor (where one thing is said to be *the same as* something else) displays a character making rational judgements, and using language as a polemical tool. He compares the Cardinal to a pyramid to attack his political corruption and eventual ineffectiveness (ll. 77–9), using this huge monument as an inverted image to suggest the Cardinal's inconsequence. Similes delineate ineffective mortality: 'We are only like dead walls, or vaulted graves, / That, ruined, yields no echo' (ll. 97–8). Where he uses metaphor, he does so in two areas: first in his assumption of theatrical analogies (ll. 85 and 96) and secondly in his description of his physical state as he dies. The theatrical analogies enhance our sense that Bosola's views act as a commentary for us on the actions of the main players. In highlighting his own fictional status (as an actor), the actor playing this character partly steps aside from involvement in the fiction, and draws the audience's attention to the content of his words, which gain credibility. We have already seen that his self-conscious status as a revenger figure also places his character closer to the audience's sympathies: his theatrical metaphors further this. His other metaphors all describe his physical condition using words evoking absence of sight and a loss of perceived manliness: 'In a mist', 'O, this gloomy world! / In what a shadow, or deep pit of darkness, / Doth womanish and fearful mankind live!' (ll. 94 and 100–2). These images invoke Bosola's misogyny, but also conventional Christian conceptions of the mortal world and hell. Bosola's dying words do not mention light at all (in contrast to Flamineo's in *The White Devil*), and we are left with a sense of the dreadful self-knowledge of a damned man. Given that the audience has shifted some allegiance to Bosola, this death carries nearly as much pathos as the Duchess's.

Conclusions

1. Webster's tragedies end conventionally with the defeat and punishment of the forces of corruption, disorder and evil, the conclusion of all the intrigues we have witnessed within the plot, and
   with the appearance on stage of a new political order. The major
   characters die and acknowledge the errors or evil of their actions.
   However, Webster's tragic closures complicate the apparently
   black and white outcome of the endings in several ways. For
   example, the representatives of the new order are, in each case,
   vulnerable young boys. Their youth can be seen as a symbol of
   rebirth and hope. But, in both plays, Webster deepens and questions such symbolism, showing the audience that youth often
   means political naivety, a lack of pragmatism (in the case of
   Giovanni), and/or being in the shadow of adult political figures.
   Webster's endings are deliberately ambiguous in this respect,
   forcing the audience to ask themselves a set of questions. Is political naivety or idealism a bad thing? Should political accession
   depend on blood, interest, or ability? What is the nature of political corruption?

   The tragic closure of *The White Devil* is unusual in the absence
   of key characters. Monticelso and Francisco remain untouched
   by the law, despite their abuse of civic and theological law. Their
   orders arrive from off-stage, but direct the action and events in
   both opening and ending. Giovanni refuses to believe his uncles'
   culpability. The play ends unresolved: disorder, corruption and
   abuse remain unpunished. This ending forces us to ask big political questions. Should the Church be above the civil law? Does
   political power always depend on cabals? Is power always open to
   abuse?

   In each play the character most physically involved in the plots
   (Flamineo and Bosola) dies invoking images of hell. Both characters have held an ambiguous relationship with the audience. They
   often speak directly to us, are both resentful and desirous of
   power: middle-men who did the dirty work of those more powerful. Their deaths are seen to be morally necessary: but their
   manner of dying, the self-knowledge displayed, and their belated

acknowledgement of alternative ethical courses of action, engender our sympathy. Once again, this complicates the finality of the closure, forcing us to reconsider where responsibility lies.

2. Political corruption is seen to be endemic and ongoing. The aristocratic politics of privilege and unaccountability are shown to be particularly flawed and dangerous. Private worlds and private interest are demonstrated to be corruptible, sick, and obsessive, but directly linked to the abuse of power in families, courts and the Church. The endings are not hopeful about eliminating such abuses. The tragedies encourage us to think about political pragmatism within an ethical and legal framework.

3. The endings share an atmosphere of darkness, fear, and blindness in the dying characters. None of the characters ask for forgiveness, nor do they repent. Instead, they anticipate punishment and give voice to perceptions which echo the conventional dramatic and literary trappings linked with hell: thunder, darkness, cold, pits and shadows. The characters' self-perceived hellish punishments begin as they die: and their belief in retribution implies a Christian framework. However, no *spiritual* counterpoint to sin and punishment is represented in the closing moments of the plays.

4. This links to another feature of Webster's endings: their self-conscious theatricality. Key actors express awareness of their fictional status, and of the dramatic conventions in which they operate, rendering such conventions visible. Theatricality makes us think objectively about the conditions in which the characters are placed and the nature of the conflict in a broader way.

On a thematic level, theatricality, or playing a part, is associated in Webster's plays with the temporal world. This metaphor was a common one in Webster's time ('all the world's a stage'): but Webster's usage suggests that the mortal world alone is conceivable, whatever lies beyond is unimaginable, whether heaven or hell. His self-conscious theatrical imagery thus names both the corrupted and partial nature of this fallen world and the limits of his own, or anyone's, art.

Finally, Delio's last speech ('Let us make noble *use* / Of this great ruin') proclaims the didactic importance of theatre: there is a moral lesson for an audience in this story.

5. The women of the plays do not have a major physical presence in the closing moments of the plays: but their absence lingers, symbolic of what has been lost through the plays' patriarchal politics. In each case, the young son of a woman who has been the victim of masculine politics, inherits power. The gendered abuse of power is criticised, since the heirs of the good women inherit power at the end. However, the heir to power is figured as masculine. In *The Duchess of Malfi* the perceived dangers of feminine power, which the play as a whole exposes, are resolved only through the accession of a son at the end. The masculine gendering of the new order qualifies any optimism an audience may feel about the possibilities of political or gender change.

6. The cumulative effect of these conclusions is an image in which individual men and women are trapped by decisions of those more powerful, and by power structures over which they have no influence. This feeling of powerlessness, lack of agency and claustrophobia is generated by the plot, in the staging and setting of the final moments, and in *The White Devil*, by the fact that real power lies elsewhere than on the stage.

7. Webster structures his plays so that individual scenic units are important interpretative indicators. Each play begins and ends with the same characters on stage, conveying a sense of completion, and a reminder of the opening's key issues. In *The White Devil* Lodovico's reappearance serves to underline again the absence of his powerful and corrupt masters. In *The Duchess of Malfi* the symmetry reminds us of Delio's and Antonio's political ethical philosophy, expressed at the beginning. We have observed how internal scenic structure creates individual units of meaning, which are then juxtaposed, as though in dialogue, with the next scenic unit. As we noted in our chapter on openings, Webster characteristically sets up debates between characters and ideas in this way. This dramatic method encourages a responsive, thinking audience.

8. Imagery, both verbal and visual, is a key indicator of emotion and meaning in Webster's plays. Imagery is used here to fuse with the feelings of a character and so deepen characterisation; in conventional religious imagery to suggest spiritual redemption or damnation; as a reminder of previous events and or feelings in

the play; and as a rhetoric which signals one's ethical political position. Plain speaking equates with ethical integrity and truth, for example, in Bosola's plainly delivered summary of the motives for his revenge killings.

Methods of Analysis

This chapter has built on the methods of analysis we used in chapter one in the following ways.

1. We have used our understanding of the text as drama as an integrated part of our analysis of language, character and themes to deepen our account of the meanings of the endings. We have seen drama as a complex physical, visual, three-dimensional *and* linguistic form. The more you practise this kind of analysis, the more natural it will feel.

2. We have explicitly used and tested the conclusions we reached in the first chapter. This is both a methodological and an analytical point. Where our analysis of endings produces conclusions differing from those about the openings, this will tell us something about the structure and meaning of the play. For example, Bosola's character seemed unredeemable in the opening of *The Duchess of Malfi*, but his shifted position as effective revenger at the end, tells us how the play asks us to judge the influence of the Duchess herself. In *The White Devil* our perception that action on the stage was marginal to the source of real power, partly clouds our judgement of the danger of Lodovico. Looking at both the openings and endings, and their structural and thematic relationship to each other, enables us to make sophisticated judgements about the play.

3. We have begun to learn about the way in which tragedy constructs debates about political and social issues, through analysis of genre, character placing, key iconic moments and staging issues. Without an understanding of such *dramatic* method, we would tend to see such debates as theoretical: in drama we see them embodied.

Suggested Work

It is clear that we can best understand how the closing moments come about dramatically, and what they mean, if we consider the whole denouement. A good way of doing this is to use a table of columns showing what happens when, who is present at key moments, where different scenes happen, and in what order, and noting any authorial stage directions, and the presence of themes. Such tables enable us to see how scenes and parts of scenes work in juxtaposition. Draw up a table for each play's final act.

Why do you think the endings are so drawn out? What is the significance of the settings in different scenes, and of the time they happen? Is there a turning point in each scene? How does each scene relate to the one before and the one after? How and where do our sympathies with key characters change? Does the pace of each scene contrast with or echo the previous and subsequent ones? What is the effect of continuity or shifts of pace?

Your answers to these questions will deepen your analysis. They will also help you see how the plays will look on stage. This sense of a three-dimensional text should also help you understand how drama makes political and philosophical debate come alive. We are beginning to see how a dramatist can manipulate and inter-relate scenes, setting, character blocking, and dialogue to fuse into a complex 'moving-picture-story'. When we see these individual dramatic elements as part of a whole performed text, we are closest to beginning to understand what Webster's tragedies are doing.

3

Turning Points

Plays often feature a central dramatic turning point: prior to this we remain unsure of how the story will unfold; afterwards, inevitable conclusions hurtle towards their finale. Webster's tragedies are no exception, and a good understanding of his pivotal scenes helps us see, feel and understand the crises which lead to the final tragic moments we discussed in Chapter 2.

Let us look now at such a scene in *The White Devil.*

[Act 3, Scene ii]

Vittoria.	Grant I was tempted;
	Temptation to lust proves not the act.
	Casta est quam nemo rogavit; 200
	You read his hot love to me, but you want
	My frosty answer.
Monticelso.	Frost i'th'dog days! Strange!
Vittoria.	Condemn you me for that the duke did love me?
	So may you blame some fair and crystal river
	For that some melancholic distracted man 205
	Hath drowned himself in't.
Monticelso.	Truly, drowned indeed.
Vittoria.	Sum up my faults, I pray, and you shall find
	That beauty and gay clothes, a merry heart,
	And a good stomach to a feast, are all,

	All the poor crimes that you can charge me with.	210
	In faith, my lord, you might go pistol flies;	
	That sport would be more noble.	

Monticelso.   Very good.

Vittoria.   But take you your course; it seems you have
                   beggared me first
               And now would fain undo me. I have houses,
               Jewels, and a poor remnant of crusadoes;   215
               Would those would make you charitable.

Monticelso.   If the devil
               Did ever take good shape, behold his picture.

Vittoria.   You have one virtue left:
               You will not flatter me.

Francisco.   Who brought this letter?

Vittoria.   I am not compelled to tell you.   220

Monticelso.   My lord duke sent to you a thousand ducats,
               The twelfth of August.

Vittoria.   'Twas to keep your cousin
               From prison; I paid use for't.

Monticelso.   I rather think
               'Twas interest for his lust.

Vittoria.   Who says so but yourself? If you be my accuser,   225
               Pray cease to be my judge; come from the bench;
               Give in your evidence 'gainst me, and let these
               Be moderators. My lord cardinal,
               Were your intelligencing ears as long
               As to my thoughts, had you an honest tongue,   230
               I would not care though you proclaimed
                   them all.

Monticelso.   Go to, go to.
               After your godly and vainglorious banquet,
               I'll give you a choke-pear.

Vittoria.   A' your own grafting?

Monticelso.   You were born in Venice, honourably
                   descended   235
               From the Vitelli; 'twas my cousin's fate –

	Ill may I name the hour – to marry you;
	He bought you of your father.
Vittoria.	Ha?
Monticelso.	He spent there in six months
	Twelve thousand ducats, and to my
	acquaintance 240
	Received in dowry with you not one julio;
	'Twas a hard penny-worth, the ware being so light.
	I yet but draw the curtain; now to your picture.
	You came from thence a most notorious strumpet,
	And so you have continued.
Vittoria.	My lord –
Monticelso.	Nay hear me, 245
	You shall have time to prate. My Lord Bracciano –
	Alas, I make but repetition
	Of what is ordinary and Rialto talk,
	And ballated, and would be played a'th'stage,
	But that vice many times finds such loud
	friends 250
	That preachers are charmed silent. –
	You gentlemen, Flamineo and Marcello,
	The court hath nothing now to charge you with,
	Only you must remain upon your sureties
	For your appearance.
Francisco.	I stand for Marcello. 255
Flamineo.	And my lord duke for me.
Monticelso.	For you Vittoria, your public fault,
	Joined to th'condition of the present time,
	Takes from you all the fruits of noble pity.
	Such a corrupted trial have you made 260
	Both of your life and beauty, and been styled
	No less in ominous fate than blazing stars
	To princes; here's your sentence: you are confined
	Unto a house of convertites, and your bawd –
Flamineo.	Who, I?
Monticelso.	The moor.

Flamineo.	O, I am a sound man again. 265
Vittoria.	A house of convertites, what's that?
Monticelso.	A house
	Of penitent whores.
Vittoria.	Do the noblemen in Rome
	Erect it for their wives, that I am sent
	To lodge there?
Francisco.	You must have patience.
Vittoria.	I must first have vengeance. 270
	I fain would know if you have your salvation
	By patent, that you proceed thus.
Monticelso.	Away with her.
	Take her hence.
Vittoria.	A rape, a rape!
Monticelso.	How?
Vittoria.	Yes, you have ravished justice,
	Forced her to do your pleasure.
Monticelso.	Fie, she's mad – 275
Vittoria.	Die with those pills in your most cursed maw
	Should bring you health, or, while you sit
	a'th'bench,
	Let your own spittle choke you.
Monticelso.	She's turned Fury.
Vittoria.	That the last day of judgement may so find you,
	And leave you the same devil you were before. 280
	Instruct me some good horse-leech to speak
	treason,
	For, since you cannot take my life for deeds,
	Take it for words. O woman's poor revenge
	Which dwells but in the tongue! I will not weep,
	No I do not scorn to call up one poor tear 285
	To fawn on your injustice. Bear me hence,
	Unto this house of – what's your mitigating title?
Monticelso.	Of convertites.
Vittoria.	It shall not be a house of convertites;

My mind shall make it honester to me   290
Than the Pope's palace, and more peaceable
Than thy soul, though thou art a cardinal.
Know this, and let it somewhat raise your spite:
Through darkness diamonds spread their
   richest light.

Exit Vittoria.
(*The White Devil,* 3, ii, 198–294)

This scene is a key turning point in the action, in characterisation, and in the marshalling of the audience's sympathies. Turning points are scenes where divergent plot-lines meet and clash; a temporary solution is achieved, although conflict remains; and which precipitate the final resolution. Some turning points are signalled, others are only clear retrospectively. This scene belongs to the former category. In the original published play, it was headed 'The arraignment of Vittoria', drawing explicit textual attention to its formality. Divergent plots are here drawn together. Vittoria's and Bracciano's private actions are called to public and judicial account, and the theological and judicial systems triumph over private will. However, the audience has already learned to distrust Monticelso and Francisco. So we await the outcome of the scene with interest. Who will win? Will it be conclusive?

Let us first consider setting, characterisation and internal structure. Setting is central to the meaning and self-consciously pivotal nature of this scene. It is a court of ecclesiastical law. At the beginning we watch the formal entrance of Francisco, Monticelso, six ambassadors, Flamineo and lawyer, and Vittoria and Zanche guarded. The combined visual formality of procession, robes, prisoner and judge symbolises solemnity, and engenders awe, and is established via silent stage business. We know that Vittoria may lose her life or property. The scene's subsequent action and the players' roles act as counterpoints to the first visual and physical setting. We judge their behaviour and actions by the standards established by the setting: of a legal process in which truth and the objective testing of evidence should triumph. The audience fulfils the jury's role.

The characters' formal positioning on stage reflects their power in the proceedings. Bracciano can come and go as he pleases. Vittoria is in the dock: Monticelso above her as judge.

Setting develops and refines characterisation. The formality of the legal surroundings and process emphasises Monticelso's status as a Cardinal with judicial power over men and women. However, in abusing that role his character exposes the legal process as corruptible. Bracciano's ability to walk away from the court and to threaten the judge with impunity, emphasises both his own political power and his scorn for the law. Within the legal forum Vittoria is the only character who does not step out of her assigned role (as accused). However, guarded in the dock, she has no physical power to do so. Her physical restraint, her conformity with the court's rule and her accused status, contrast markedly with the behaviour of all the other main players. The ambassadors function as neutral (but powerless) observers. We perceive Vittoria as literally subject to the abuse of a political and judicial system by corrupt men. The setting and enacted roles, thence, deepen the general philosophical and political issues raised by the play; clarify and extend characterisation; and emphasise the central significance of the turning-point scene.

Turning-point scenes engender incertitude. Their internal structure consists of peripateia which shift power and audience sympathies. Such scenes are not simple bridges to another part of the plot, or a report of off-stage action, but central to the meaning, action and conflict of the play. If we were to draw a diagram of the way tension rises and subsequent action is determined in the play, this scene would be the crest of the peak. Let us look closely at the way this is achieved internally, before discussing how it is placed in the play as a whole.

This whole scene falls clearly into two halves, Bracciano's exit, at line 179, marking the division. As the murderer of Camillo, he was a key character at the trial, yet he is silent until he gives Vittoria's alibi, immediately departing on a threatening note: '*nemo me impunit lacessit*' [no-one injures me with impunity], words which echo through our extract. In the Renaissance, formal public jousts between knights to test male prowess were popular courtly entertainments. Knights wore a chivalric latinate motto, and would nominally protect a lady's honour. Bracciano's phrase invokes that world of competition *between* men, *for* women. Monticelso's words on Bracciano's departure acknowledge the discursive framework in which the men operate: 'your *champion's* gone' (l. 180).

This extract is the second part of the scene, and clearly falls into three parts. The first part (ll. 198–235) shows Vittoria dominating the exchange and the court. In the second part (ll. 236–67) Monticelso takes the advantage; whilst in the final part (ll. 268–94) Vittoria again dominates. The formal structure of the scene echoes the rhythms of a physical battle: first one side, then the other, struggling for victory. The rhythm of the internal scenic structure establishes a sense of tension, and ensures our investment in the trial's outcome, echoing the content. Let us analyse how this tension and audience involvement are achieved.

Vittoria dominates the action for the first thirty-four lines, in the content and manner of her speech. Most speeches end in the middle of a line. This creates a sense of lively debate, in which characters appear to respond immediately to another's words. However, where Monticelso completes Vittoria's lines he comments sarcastically upon what she has said, and repeats some of her very words, demonstrating Vittoria's linguistic dominance (ll. 202 and 206). By contrast, where Vittoria's words comment on what is said (for example, lines 199–200), she speaks directly and responsively. Vittoria's more direct speech in conjunction with her physical imprisonment help engender sympathy.

Where she completes Monticelso's lines these run on into subsequent lines, moving the debate forward. They are intellectual engagements with the prosecutorial system in the court of law. Her first interruption, ('Grant I was tempted; / Temptation to lust proves not the act' (l. 198–9), acknowledges his evidence, but denies his interpretation of it and provides an alternative explanation. In addition, she does so in both the language of the law ('proves not') and in a Latin quotation ('Casta est . . . '). Her usage of these two conventionally masculine linguistic domains (the Latinate and legal) could be seen as transgressive: a woman using the rhetoric of male worlds.

But the scene asks the audience to question this in a number of ways. First, her Latin tag is a quotation from Ovid's *Amores*, and translates as: 'she is chaste whom no man has solicited'. Ovid's poem was frequently cited by and for young men as a handbook for achieving sexual fulfilment and encouraging sexual predatoriness. It suggested that chastity in women, but not for men, was a prerequisite for marriage; and that women's overt sexual lure was the cause of sexual propositions. Vittoria's citation is therefore critical: she intends it ironically, given that it contradicts her previous sentence. Thus, she exposes both the double sexual standard and the court's partial and inequitable view of sexuality. The audience see her trapped in a world where perception and belief about female behaviour are dominated and constrained by a masculine ideology.

The second way in which this scene lends dramatic credibility to Vittoria, is that she alone speaks within the framework and the language of the rule of law, and is the character through whom Monticelso's abuse is exposed. Her access to and use of legal language proclaims a proud equity with men and a concomitant belief in the rule of law. She continually uses the language of equity here, marshalling metaphors for both rhetorical proofs ('Condemn you me . . . / So may you blame some fair and crystal river', ll. 203–4) and emphatic rebuttals ('you might go pistol flies; / That sport would be more noble', ll. 211–12). She uses the language of legal rights ('I am not *compelled* to tell you', l. 220); she challenges conceptual paradigms ('Condemn you me for that the duke did love me?', l. 203), and Monticelso's transgression of the rule of law ('Who says so but yourself? If you be my accuser / Pray cease to be my judge', ll. 225–6).

Webster gives her dominance through intellectual, linguistic and physical manipulation of her position as the accused, and through the marshalling of audience sympathy. Her character is given moral strength by contrast with Monticelso. His anger at her rational responses, evident both in his sarcastic comments and in his threats ('I'll give you a choke-pear', l. 234), transgresses his status as objective judge through his emotionalism.

This all changes over the next thirty lines, in which the balance of linguistic power shifts completely away from Vittoria. The shift is signalled by a rhythmic change in her responses to Monticelso's attacks. Instead of completing his lines, and moving on to make new points or refute his charges using legal language, her responses are now a short, reactive monosyllable ('Ha?', l. 238) and an interrupted plea ('My lord –', l. 245), followed by complete silence. Monticelso's sudden dominance emerges both from his surprise information about her marriage ('He bought you of your father'); and from his swift move to judgement. His re-appropriation of the judge's role lends him physical dominance, which is now seen as an arbitrary abuse of power. His use of legal language contrasts with Vittoria's in the previous section: hers was appropriate to her situation, his is an abuse. His judgement is also clearly inequitable: he allows the men freedom, as long as their masters can vouch for them, whilst Vittoria is condemned. Both court and men have linguistic, physical and legal dominance over her life and body. This is a moment of intense defeat for Vittoria: it is the key turning point of the scene and of the play. Judgement should preface the closure of a play: leading to the restoration of political and social order. Here judgement is paradoxically used to illustrate the inversion of such order.

There are two dramatic means whereby this is displayed. The first is that Monticelso has been exposed as a force of disorder: so his victory here posits only the success of corruption. Second, and equally important, is what is predicated by a further turning point. Vittoria comes to dominate the proceedings even as she is condemned, establishing a credible moral critique of Monticelso.

Her reassertion of dominance comes through linguistic interruptions, questionings and re-definitions. She exposes the status of a 'house of convertites' as a convenient male construction, 'Do the noblemen in Rome / Erect it for their wives?' (ll. 267–9). She shouts out threats, 'Die with those pills in your most cursed maw' (l. 276); and accusations, 'A rape, a rape!' (l. 274), intimating Monticelso's abuse of sexual power involved in the travesty of justice. She demands vengeance. She invokes both legal and religious moral law: claiming that he has 'ravished justice' (l. 274); that 'the last day of judgement may so find you' (l. 279); and sarcastically questioning whether his salvation is 'by patent' (ll. 271–2). She becomes the voice of ethical criticism, despite her own ambiguous morality. She commands her own departure, denying that power to the judge and simultaneously exposing his specious abuse of language: '– what's your mitigating title?' (l. 287). Her final words are delivered more quietly, contrasting her earlier distress and anger, and carry eerily into the auditorium with moral and prophetic resonance: 'My mind shall make it honester to me / Than the Pope's palace, and more peaceable / Than thy soul' (ll. 290–1). Honesty is figured as an internal virtue found in seclusion, in women, and away from both politics and the Church. Her departing proverbial couplet is typically a challenge and an assertion of her innocence: 'Know this, and let it somewhat raise your spite: / Through darkness diamonds spread their richest light' (ll. 293–4), intimating both current corruption and the inevitable final judgement. The turning-point scene is thus one in which ethical considerations become linked with the voice and actions of Vittoria, and where abuse of power is unveiled as evil.

The audience is a key player here. We are privy observers of the shifting and differential power relationships, of the exploding anger and distress, and are exhausted by action and reaction. We are also encouraged to be the jury: judgement is invoked and Vittoria's words are key signals of both an absent ethical order and an appeal to the listeners to provide that order.

It is not only the internal structure of the scene which engenders this critical perspective. Let us now turn to ask how the play constructs the whole scene as a turning point and as a means of converting us to Vittoria's perspective.

There are four ways in which this critical perspective is achieved: first, the clear establishment of binary oppositions; secondly, scenic juxtapositions; thirdly, the interlinking of structural crisis points with clarifications in characterisation and characters' self-awareness; and finally Webster's use of visual icons which echo or contrast verbal themes. We shall discuss each of these briefly.

We have already observed in our analysis of the play's opening that a thematic opposition is set up between private and public worlds. This is also true in this scene: but here Monticelso uses the public machinery of law and theology to achieve his own personal ends. By contrast, Vittoria acknowledges her acquiescence to the public functions of a court, and is condemned in public for her assertion of private will, which is ironically termed a 'public fault'

(l. 257). The contrast between these two characters reinforces the sense of a gender disparity in the opposition of private and public. This helps inform our understanding of another key opposition in the play, that between women and the institutions of power run by men: marriage, the Church, and political life. Thematically, each of these institutions is raised in this scene's action, characterisation, and in what is said. Sympathy for Vittoria reinforces our perception of this thematic opposition, helping us conceptualise a critique of the play's patriarchy.

Another opposition in which Vittoria is the key actor is that between individual freedom and the authoritarian law. We see her isolation, we feel her imprisonment, and the injustice with which the trial's legal mechanisms are abused. In dramatising an abusive system, Webster turns our sympathies to the individual. These oppositions invoke broader debates: between justice and truth, and *realpolitik*; between inner and outer; reality and appearance. The characterisation of Monticelso in this extract illustrates these oppositions. He is dressed formally as a Cardinal, probably in red, the colour of officialdom. However, in allowing personal fury to dominate, he transgresses the role and duty of both cleric and judge, an observation endorsed by Vittoria and the English Ambassador earlier in the scene. Each thematic opposition is symbolically represented through the characterisation and actions of Vittoria and Monticelso. In each case Vittoria represents the opposite of corruption, abuse, and patriarchal power. This scene therefore clarifies Vittoria's role. She clearly acts as a symbol of criticism, however flawed she may be personally, against larger manipulative and corrupt political and religious institutions.

The second way we recognise this as a turning point and sympathise with Vittoria is through scenic juxtaposition: what scenes come just before and just after, and how do they help us interpret this scene? The most obvious way in which scenic juxtaposition helps construct our interpretation is by contrast with the previous scene (3, i). In that scene we observe Francisco and Monticelso discussing the case prior to trial, acknowledging they have no proof to charge her with her husband's murder, and therefore agreeing to blacken her name. We are witnesses to a display of how the law is travestied by those who are supposed to uphold it and are made sceptical of its ability to deliver objective judgement and justice.

Thirdly, we recognise this as a structural turning point through crises in characterisation. The scene clarifies the dramatic function and strength of all major characters. This is another way in which a turning-point scene should work: it should be a testing moment for all main characters, and help us come to firmer conclusions. Bracciano is tested, and abandons Vittoria to a trial by leaving the stage. Flamineo fails to stand up for his sister. Francisco acts as flatterer and as pander to Monticelso. Monticelso gets so angry that he abandons and then abuses his role as judge. Vittoria is cool under pressure, acts within a legal framework and emerges with a greater sense of self-knowledge: it is her turning point, as well as the play's. Moments of self-revelation are a key aspect of a good turning-point scene, for several reasons. They help us to sympathise with, or pity, such characters, to feel involved in the action, and consequently to mind about the outcome of the scene. It is dramatically economical to ensure that crisis points in the structure coincide with turning-points for characters. It also sustains the fiction that character is dependent upon and developed by events, fostering good characterisation, realism, and our suspension of disbelief.

Finally, in turning-point scenes many visual and verbal themes coalesce, ensuring a memorable dramatic and visual display. This is, of course, created foremost by the action and setting which we have already discussed. But let us note a few of those central themes. The first is that of the devil: a word of mutual accusation between Monticelso and Vittoria (l. 216, and l. 280). This is linked to the colour black, invoked literally by Francisco before this extract opens (l. 183), and in Vittoria's final couplet, figuring herself as a diamond shining through the darkness. The colour symbolism of black and white, conventionally linked to evil and good, is used by all the characters, and is frequently reflected in the colours of their clothes. The titular 'white devil' posits one whose appearance is deceptive: this scene invokes that paradoxical title by the integration of colour symbolism with the action, characterisation and emotion of this scene. Is the white devil Monticelso or Vittoria?

Similarly, the use of animal metaphors (ll. 211–12), of poison

(l. 234), of excessive banqueting (ll. 233–4), of rape (l. 274), and acting (ll. 249–50), all continue to invoke a fallen world in which nature's excesses are given full rein, in which appearance provides a deceptive mask on reality, and in which civic law and truth have no place. This is the first scene in which we see the fruition of such themes as action: the corrupt trial literally enacts such a world. Successful and believable turning-point scenes must achieve this conjunction of theme and action in order to carry their audience.

*   *   *

Let us now look at another turning-point scene: the key one in *The Duchess of Malfi* is also the second scene of the third act.

[Act 3, Scene ii]

<table>
<tr><td></td><td colspan="2">*Enter* Duchess, ANTONIO *and* CARIOLA</td></tr>
<tr><td>*Duchess.*</td><td>Bring me the casket hither, and the glass. –</td><td></td></tr>
<tr><td></td><td>You get no lodging here tonight, my lord.</td><td></td></tr>
<tr><td>*Antonio.*</td><td>Indeed, I must persuade one.</td><td></td></tr>
<tr><td>*Duchess.*</td><td>Very good:</td><td></td></tr>
<tr><td></td><td>I hope in time 'twill grow into a custom</td><td></td></tr>
<tr><td></td><td>That noblemen shall come with cap and knee</td><td>5</td></tr>
<tr><td></td><td>To purchase a night's lodging of their wives.</td><td></td></tr>
<tr><td>*Antonio.*</td><td>I must lie here.</td><td></td></tr>
<tr><td>*Duchess.*</td><td>Must? You are a lord of mis-rule.</td><td></td></tr>
<tr><td>*Antonio.*</td><td>Indeed, my rule is only in the night.</td><td></td></tr>
<tr><td>*Duchess.*</td><td>To what use will you put me?</td><td></td></tr>
<tr><td>*Antonio.*</td><td>We'll sleep together.</td><td></td></tr>
<tr><td>*Duchess.*</td><td>Alas, what pleasure can two lovers find in sleep?</td><td>10</td></tr>
<tr><td>*Cariola.*</td><td>My lord, I lie with her often, and I know</td><td></td></tr>
<tr><td></td><td>She'll much disquiet you –</td><td></td></tr>
<tr><td>*Antonio.*</td><td>See, you are complained of.</td><td></td></tr>
<tr><td>*Cariola.*</td><td>For she's the sprawling'st bedfellow.</td><td></td></tr>
<tr><td>*Antonio.*</td><td>I shall like her the better for that.</td><td></td></tr>
<tr><td>*Cariola.*</td><td>Sir, shall I ask you a question?</td><td>15</td></tr>
<tr><td>*Antonio.*</td><td>I pray thee, Cariola.</td><td></td></tr>
<tr><td>*Cariola.*</td><td>Wherefore still when you lie with my lady</td><td></td></tr>
</table>

	Do you rise so early?	
Antonio.	Labouring men	
	Count the clock oft'nest, Cariola,	
	Are glad when their task's ended.	
Duchess.	I'll stop your mouth.	20
Antonio.	Nay, that's but one. Venus had two soft doves	
	To draw her chariot; I must have another.	
	When wilt thou marry, Cariola?	
Cariola.	Never, my lord.	
Antonio.	O, fie upon this single life! Forgo it!	
	We read how Daphne, for her peevish flight,	25
	Became a fruitless bay tree, Syrinx turned	
	To the pale empty reed, Anaxerete	
	Was frozen into marble; whereas those	
	Which married, or proved kind unto their friends,	
	Were by a gracious influence transshaped	30
	Into the olive, pomegranate, mulberry;	
	Became flow'rs, precious stones, or eminent stars.	
Cariola.	This is a vain poetry. But I pray you, tell me,	
	If there were proposed me wisdom, riches, and beauty,	
	In three several young men, which should I	
	choose?	35
Antonio.	'Tis a hard question. This was Paris' case,	
	And he was blind in't, and there was great cause;	
	For how was't possible he could judge right,	
	Having three amorous goddesses in view,	
	And they stark naked? 'Twas a motion	40
	Were able to benight the apprehension	
	Of the severest counsellor of Europe.	
	Now I look on both your faces so well formed,	
	It puts me in mind of a question I would ask.	
Cariola.	What is 't?	
Antonio.	I do wonder why hard-favoured ladies,	45
	For the most part, keep worse-favoured waiting	

	women	
	To attend them, and cannot endure fair ones.	
Duchess.	O, that's soon answered.	
	Did you ever in your life know an ill painter	
	Desire to have his dwelling next door to the shop	50
	Of an excellent picture-maker? 'Twould disgrace	
	His face-making, and undo him. I prithee,	
	When were we so merry? – My hair tangles.	
Antonio.	Pray thee, Cariola, let's steal forth the room	
	And let her talk to herself; I have divers times	55
	Served her the like, when she hath chafed extremely:	
	I love to see her angry. Softly, Cariola.	

Exit with Cariola.

Duchess.	Doth not the colour of my hair 'gin to change?	
	When I wax grey, I shall have all the court	
	Powder their hair with arras, to be like me.	60
	You have cause to love me; I entered you into my	
	heart	
	Before you would vouchsafe to call for the keys.	

Enter FERDINAND.

	We shall one day have my brothers take you	
	napping:	
	Methinks his presence, being now in court,	
	Should make you keep your own bed. – But, you'll	
	say,	65
	Love mixed with fear is sweetest. I'll assure you	
	You shall get no more children till my brothers	
	Consent to be your gossips. Have you lost your	
	tongue?	
	'Tis welcome;	
	For know, whether I am doomed to live or die,	70
	I can do both like a prince.	

Ferdinand gives her a poniard.

Ferdinand.	Die then, quickly!	
	Virtue, where art thou hid? What hideous thing	
	Is it that doth eclipse thee?	

Duchess.	Pray sir, hear me!
Ferdinand.	Or is it true, thou art but a bare name,
	And no essential thing?
Duchess.	Sir –
Ferdinand.	Do not speak.
Duchess.	No, sir: 75

I will plant my soul in mine ears to hear you.

Ferdinand. O most imperfect light of human reason,
Thou mak'st us so unhappy, to foresee
What we can least prevent! Pursue thy wishes,
And glory in them; there's in shame no comfort   80
But to be past all bounds and sense of shame.

Duchess. I pray sir, hear me: I am married.

Ferdinand.   So.

Duchess. Happily, not to your liking; but for that,
Alas, your shears do come untimely now
To clip the bird's wings that's already flown!   85
Will you see my husband?

Ferdinand.   Yes, if I could change
Eyes with a basilisk.

Duchess.   Sure, you came hither
By his confederacy.

Ferdinand.   The howling of a wolf
Is music to thee, screech-owl. Prithee, peace!
Whate'er thou art, that hast enjoyed my sister –   90
For I am sure thou hear'st me – for thine own sake
Let me not know thee. I came hither prepared
To work thy discovery, yet am now persuaded
It would beget such violent effects
As would damn us both. I would not for ten
     millions   95
I had beheld thee; therefore use all means
I never may have knowledge of thy name;
Enjoy thy lust still, and a wretched life,
On that condition. And for thee, vile woman,
If thou do wish thy lecher may grow old   100

In thy embracements, I would have thee build
Such a room for him as our anchorites
To holier use inhabit. Let not the sun
Shine on him till he's dead. Let dogs and monkeys
Only converse with him, and such dumb things   105
To whom nature denies use to sound his name.
Do not keep a paraquito, lest she learn it.
If thou do love him, cut out thine own tongue
Lest it bewray him.

Duchess.   Why might not I marry?
I have not gone about, in this, to create   110
Any new world, or custom.

Ferdinand.   Thou art undone;
And thou hast ta'en that massy sheet of lead
That hid thy husband's bones, and folded it
About my heart.

Duchess.   Mine bleeds for't.

Ferdinand.   Thine? Thy heart?
What should I name't, unless a hollow bullet   115
Filled with unquenchable wildfire?

Duchess.   You are, in this,
Too strict; and, were you not my princely brother,
I would say too wilful. My reputation is safe.

Ferdinand. Dost thou know what reputation is?
I'll tell thee – to small purpose, since th'instruction   120
Comes now too late.
Upon a time, Reputation, Love and Death
Would travel o'er the world; and it was concluded
That they should part, and take three several ways.
Death told them they should find him in great
        battles,   125
Or cities plagued with plagues. Love gives them
        counsel
To inquire for him 'mongst unambitious shepherds,
Where dowries were not talked of, and sometimes

'Mongst quiet kindred that had nothing left
By their dead parents. 'Stay', quoth Reputation, 130
'Do not forsake me; for it is my nature
If once I part from any man I meet
I am never found again.' And so, for you:
You have shook hands with Reputation,
And made him invisible. So, fare you well. 135
I will never see you more.

Duchess. Why should only I,
Of all the other princes of the world,
Be cased up, like a holy relic? I have youth,
And a little beauty.

Ferdinand. So you have some virgins 140
That are witches. – I will never see thee more.

Exit.

(*The Duchess of Malfi*, 3, ii, 1–141)

This extract opens and closes in the intimate and private setting of
the Duchess's bedroom. It falls clearly into two parts, which act as
contrasting halves. In the first half she converses with her husband
and maid, in the second with her brother. In both cases the dialogue
is between intimates, and the setting, atmosphere, character
blocking and movement, and the rhythms of the language reflect
and help construct this intimacy and an intensity of feeling and
exchange. It is the first, and only, scene in the play where we see
Antonio and the Duchess together as a married couple. It reinforces
and echoes the end of the opening act, where the Duchess and
Antonio, with Cariola present, first court each other and then
perform a private marriage ceremony. Their privacy in that scene
was hard won, and quickly superseded by the demands of both
public life and the Duchess's brothers' views about her status. This
scene echoes the opening scene in reverse: rather than beginning
with public discussion and ending in privacy, it commences in
domesticity, and opens out involuntarily to admit her brother, and
later Bosola. Scenic symmetry thereby marks this scene as the end of
one phase of the play: a turning point.

We have not seen the Duchess on stage since the beginning of Act

2, when Bosola gave her the apricots, inducing the birth of her first child. We heard her cries in childbirth in 2, ii, but have only heard *about* her since then. In the immediately preceding scene, we observe the growing arrogance of Antonio about the success of their deception; the arrival of Ferdinand at the Duchess's court; the ongoing reports from Bosola, his spy; and Ferdinand's decision to hide himself in the Duchess's bedroom that night.

Thus the structural tension established by the narrative and emotions of the play climaxes in this extract. Questions about the course of private desires and their public consequences coincide, and are answered by the events of the scene. When will the Duchess's marriage be discovered by her brothers? What will they do? When will we see the couple together? Tension is relieved, in the sense that the truth is in the open; but then re-established, in that action is postponed. This turning point has similarities with that of Act 3, Scene ii in *The White Devil*. Key plot-lines meet in an anticipated dramatic conflict: but their resolution provides only temporary relief. Nevertheless, their resolution also marks the beginning of the end: from here on the Duchess is on a downward trajectory. Tragic closure is now inevitable. It is less obviously a set-piece than the trial in *The White Devil*; although, as a 'bed room scene', it carries connotations and expectations of a major event. (Think of the bedroom scene in *Othello* or *Cymbeline*.)

Let us analyse the situation as the scene opens, to determine how this turning-point scene works. We know that Ferdinand is hidden on stage: in some performances the audience are able to see him. So, we are immediately presented with an impossible and unbearable situation, of which the main protagonists on stage are unaware. This kind of situation is often described as 'dramatic irony', but the effect and function of such a situation is not simply a rhetorical ploy. By allowing the audience to know more than the characters on stage, Webster involves us in its outcomes, and asks us to judge them. Paradoxically, then, the technique both involves our emotions and distances us through our judgement.

The scene proceeds with a rising sense of poignancy and tension: we feel pity and empathy for the three on stage, and dread Ferdinand's appearance. Ferdinand himself has already displayed violent and unpredictable characteristics, threatening the Duchess in the opening scene with his poniard: so we anticipate violence.

Ferdinand remains hidden until line 63, and leaves the stage at line 141, hidden for almost exactly half his time on stage. His emergence structures the scene: both heightening the dramatic tension, and releasing it, as he threatens, but does not enact, violence. Real consequences are postponed for a few scenes. Internal peripateia (turning points) help construct and identify the whole scene as a turning point: we hang on the outcome, and are buffeted by the changes in dramatic direction.

The two halves of this part of the scene clearly act as counterpoints to each other, in tone, tension, characters present, and rhythm. The setting of the first half is intimate and domestic: a husband and wife, in their bedroom, with their maid. The situation is also informal: it is night-time, and they are getting ready for bed. The Duchess asks for a mirror and cabinet (l. 1). We visualise her sitting before the mirror, removing jewellery, and make-up, worrying about going grey (l. 58), and brushing her hair (l. 53). Cariola may be preparing the bed, and helping the Duchess undress. Antonio may be lounging on the bed, and around the room. He is clearly observing the nightly ritual with pleasure. The tone echoes the setting: their banter is playful, intimate and sexual. The speed of these sixty-two lines is measured and slow, echoing the situation, but also feeding the building dramatic tension.

The Duchess dominates this first part, even though she actually speaks far less than we feel when we watch it. Up to the point where Antonio and Cariola sneak out (l. 57), she speaks only fourteen lines to Antonio's thirty-five and Cariola's nine. Her dominance of the scene actually comes from her relative silence, and the circling of her dependants about her, a dominance also displayed in Act 1. So, despite the fact that she is theoretically vulnerable: undressed, without the badges of her status, such as jewellery and clothing; seated at a mirror (the Renaissance symbol of earthly vanity); and relatively quiet, she maintains a physical presence over the action and dialogue. Her teasing relationship to Antonio, making explicit their sexual pleasure in each other (ll. 9 and 10), reinforces her centrality. She introduces sexual banter, which Antonio and Cariola then pick up for ten lines. Their playfulness, jestingly competing for the best story about her bed behaviour, ensures our attention remains focused on her actions more than their words. Despite her silence, Antonio addresses one of his lines directly to her (l. 12), and she is clearly their audience. The Duchess's 'I'll stop your mouth' intervenes: we imagine she has risen from her mirror briefly to claim the kiss. Once again she, not the man, initiates sexual behaviour, repeating the pattern of her wooing in Act 1. After the kiss, she is silent for a further twenty-seven lines: but this silence serves to render Antonio's and Cariola's chatter as noisy irrelevance. Their lively insouciance raises the dramatic tension again: it reinforces our sense of their folly in thinking that their privacy is a protection against public discovery. Her second interruption, in answer to a jesting question from Antonio to her and Cariola, continues the light-hearted and playful dialogue, acknowledged in her 'I prithee, / When were we so merry?' (ll. 52–3).

This thematic reiteration of playfulness and inversion is also continuous throughout these sixty lines, and explicit here and in the Duchess's first two addresses to Antonio: that noblemen should come and beg a night's lodging of their wives, and that Antonio is 'a lord of misrule'. The 'normal' patriarchal marital order is explicitly acknowledged as inverted. This is not a marriage in which the husband is head and the wife obedient and subservient. Their playfulness is placed in a theatrical context. The lord of misrule was licensed to invert traditional hierarchies for a limited time, either a single performance, or for several festival days, such as Christmas, New Year, or Carnival time. Afterwards, the conventional hierarchies and the social and political status quo were re-established. The Duchess's analogy is spoken playfully, but the audience perceive its darker implications, for two reasons. First, because Ferdinand is hidden and about to pounce. Secondly, because Ferdinand has previously used such terminology to damn her behaviour as disordered: 'I would have you to give o'er these chargeable revels; / A visor and a mask are whispering rooms' (1, i, 333–4). Revelry, masking, jesting, playing are follies which invert the proper political and social order. The two brothers continually return to dramatic metaphors to signal their disapproval of the Duchess's transgressions of patriarchal order.

Here, she and Antonio use these metaphors, and it helps foster an almost unbearable, simultaneous sense both of their pleasures and of her brothers' inevitable retribution.

Antonio's final jest, his departure with Cariola to trick the Duchess, precipitates Ferdinand's confrontation with her. Antonio's absence protects his identity, but prolongs Ferdinand's search for him. The Duchess is left alone, without any physical support: had Antonio not played the jest, they could have faced public shame together. This turning point, initiated unknowingly by a simple jest, leads to tragedy. Ferdinand is able to confront her violently, catapulting her sexuality into the public domain. Additionally, her continued insistence on the privacy of her marriage, and the secret identity of her husband, leads her to confide in Bosola, precipitating the final tragedy. Playing and jesting thus come to signify something different for the audience. To us, it signals an absence from public responsibility and awareness. By maintaining the distinctness of her private life, she jettisons potential public support due to her as a prince. This choice leads inevitably to flight, defeat, and death. Jesting thus becomes endangerment. This internal turning point is clear only to the audience.

The informal language and rhythms of the first sixty lines are crucial to the scene's resonance: short, run-on lines, and interruptions, convey a sense of intimacy and informality. For the most part conventional poetic metre is eschewed, and with few exceptions, characters begin or end speaking in the middle of a line. There are no rhyming couplets. There is little overt metaphor other than of the lord of misrule. Antonio's diversion on Ovid's *Metamorphoses* (the references to Daphne and others, ll. 24–33) asserts a natural image for marital bliss (transformation to the olive and mulberry). However, this reminds us that Ovid's metamorphoses are all deaths arising from the private pursuit and fulfilment of love. With the exception of Antonio's disquisition, then, these straight forward and informal linguistic lines help create a slow, happy pace in establishing a model of private domestic bliss. Both the atmosphere and the language change in the subsequent engagement with Ferdinand, to which we shall now turn.

In this second half, the rhythms and tone change more frequently:

it is similar to the discursive battle between Monticelso and Vittoria in *The White Devil*. This part of the scene has several internal peripateia, each marking a shift in power. The first is when the Duchess sees Ferdinand (l. 69); the second when he gives her a dagger (l. 71); and the third when the Duchess tells him she is married (l. 82). These peripateia structure the second half of the extract into four parts: lines 58–69, lines 69–71, lines 71–82, and lines 83–142. At each turning point, their relationship and roles shift, ensuring a forward-moving plot, real conflict, and our engagement in the outcome. In the first part Ferdinand dominates visually; in the second the Duchess dominates through language; in the third Ferdinand, by violence; and in the last the Duchess, through reason. Let us analyse each part in turn.

Once Cariola and Antonio depart, the Duchess is visually isolated: in the dark, and in front of her mirror, she engages in both physical and philosophical self-reflection. Ferdinand stands out of sight: but visible to the audience. Her thought in lines 58–68 moves from personal observations about her hair, a joking suggestion about setting a fashion at court for grey hair, to musings about the security of Antonio's love and worries about discovery. Her delivery is in measured pentameters. Her demand, 'Have you lost your tongue?' (l. 68) is a stage-cue to turn around from her mirror. Thinking to find Antonio, she confronts Ferdinand instead. The regular pentameters break up for a moment: the short line ''Tis welcome' (l. 69) is usually printed as the beginning of a line: but the pause must surely come before she speaks. The pause marks the first dramatic turning point. We do not know what the outcome of this encounter will be. Will she capitulate or resist?

Her recovery is quick, when she recommences speaking, it is with self-conscious formality: ''Tis welcome; / For know, whether I am doomed to live or die / I can do both like a prince.' She appropriates the heroic language and role of a public leader, hers by birthright and position. For a brief moment she holds herself regally in front of Ferdinand. However, power shifts again as he thrusts his poniard at her. For the next eleven lines she tries to interrupt him, but is allowed only short monosyllabic interruptions (ll. 73, 75), or quiescent responses (ll. 75–6). Ferdinand's violence dominates. When he thrusts his dagger at her (albeit for her to use on herself), this is echoed in his linguistic dominance. He refuses to allow her to speak: for example, his interruption of her in line 75. The tone and content of his words is one of high moral outrage: using rhetorical questions (ll. 72–3 and 74–5); exclamatory phrases (ll. 78–80); and moralised sententiae (ll. 80–1). However, although the exaggerated rhetoric allows him to dominate the Duchess, it registers with the audience as nigh-hysterical excess.

This is emphasised by its tonal contrast with the next turning point, as the Duchess finally gets a word in. Her statement is lucid, courteous, and blunt: 'I pray sir, hear me: I am married' (l. 82). From this point on, until Ferdinand departs, the Duchess is in control of herself, in contrast to the ranting Ferdinand. Her defence of her independent status is represented in clear, rational language. Her questions, contrasting Ferdinand's earlier rhetorical ones, are straightforward requests: 'Will you see my husband?' (l. 86); 'Why might not I marry?' (l. 109); and 'Why should only I . . . / Be cased up, like a holy relic?' (ll. 137–9). She uses no metaphors. Her one simile ('cased up like a holy relic') invokes simultaneous pathos for her and criticism of Ferdinand's patriarchal views on sibling marriages (l. 139). Her plain speaking displays moral heroism in contrast to Ferdinand's dramatic invasion and linguistic excess. She counters each of his charges with reason, answering his accusations with reasoned questions, a logical statement ('I have not gone about, in this, to create / Any new world, or custom', ll. 110–11), or sympathy ('Mine bleeds for't', l. 114). Her dominance here is then both rational and rhetorical. Whilst denying her brother any right to intervene in her life, she continues to speak to him with affection.

Ferdinand's linguistic excess is extraordinary here. First, he speaks about three-quarters of the total number of lines. Secondly his exaggerated analogies imply violent actions: he wishes Antonio a basilisk and banished to solitary confinement; and he implicitly accuses the Duchess of witchcraft through a series of invocations to animals associated with devilry and witchcraft (ll. 88–9, and 140–1). Thirdly, his long-winded story about Death, Love and Reputation does not illustrate or substantiate his argument, and his lack of logic provides us with an image of a character whose rational thoughts are out of control. Fourthly, his metaphors all invoke aberrations of nature or death. Fifthly he continually uses superlatives and absolutes: '*most* imperfect light' (l. 77); 'to be *past all* bounds' (l. 81); 'I would not *for ten millions*' (l. 95); 'therefore use *all means*' (l. 96); 'I will *never* see you more' (l. 136). Sixthly, he persistently uses rhetorical questions, adding to the hysterical tone. Seventhly, where he does speak directly, the contrast with the rest of his language places an eerie emphasis on the direct words. Such direct words are always threats 'If thou do love him, cut out thine own tongue / Lest it bewray him' (ll. 108–9); curses (ll. 97–9); or the twice spoken 'I will never see you more' (ll. 136 and 141).

The rhythms of this final part of the scene, and Webster's use of poetic metre, are telling. For the most part, the whole exchange is conveyed in iambic pentameters. The opening line of this section (l. 82) gives nine syllables to the Duchess's announcement, and the tenth is Ferdinand's single-syllabic response, 'So' (l. 82). This emphatic monosyllable is drawn out, into a hiss-like, sibilant sound, conveying both distress and self-satisfaction at the confirmation of suspicion. Sibilant sounds recur in his next statement ('Eyes with a basilisk', l. 87). The exceptions to regularity are noticeable, and slow down the pace. The first, Ferdinand's 'Comes now too late' (l. 121), is only four syllables, engendering a pause before his 'story', and allowing time for a tangible pathos to be experienced by brother, sister and audience. The two other short lines (ll. 136 and 137) may be two halves of an irregular 12-beat line, which Webster uses elsewhere. However, editorial convention concurs in setting them, as the original quarto did, as two short lines. This again emphasises pathos and atmosphere: 'I will never see you more' echoes with Ferdinand's anger and sorrow. Whilst the Duchess's short line ('Why should only I') emphasises her solitary and abandoned status. By keeping such pauses to a minimum, Webster gives them individual resonance and significance: in each case they deepen our sense of tragedy by underlining the emotional engagement and responses of the characters. Such emotional intensity is another successful feature of turning-point scenes.

The final point to note about this extract is the stage business. The two props which are referred to by dialogue and stage directions are the dagger and the mirror. Both are effective props because they are integrated into the narrative plot; they feature at the very moment of each internal peripateia; and have symbolic functions. The dagger is symbolic in several ways: it had been brandished at the Duchess in 1, i by Ferdinand as a symbol of their dead father's honour, and metonymically his masculinity. Its shape also functions as a phallic symbol of masculinity. Ferdinand's attack on the Duchess is thus visually seen to be both about family honour and about Ferdinand's own jealous guarding of his sister's sexuality. It iconically images forth his violent entrance into her private chamber, itself a spatial metaphor of his invasion into her sexual life.

The mirror, as we have noted, symbolised vanity: and the Duchess's own words in front of it illustrate this vice. However, it also symbolised self-knowledge and discovery: both enacted here. Stage props in this scene thus coalesce into single visual icons, insights into character and plot, and link these visually and structurally with the very moments of the internal scenic turning points. Such icons, then, resonate throughout the play. We shall return to this issue in Chapter 8.

Conclusions

1. Webster's theatrical skills are particularly evident in turning-point scenes. These scenes are characterised by the following: previously disparate plot-lines meet, clash, and move into a new arena; characters are tested and judged by the crisis; setting, plot and characterisation are mutually integrated to deepen significance; the audience is encouraged to formulate a moral position, through characters who are themselves morally ambiguous; stage business prior to the turning-point scene gives the audience privileged knowledge; they contain several internal peripateia, generating an atmosphere of crisis-in-progress; and imagery and iconography coalesce verbal and iconic themes into action. These dramatic skills illustrate Webster's theatrical control over his drama.

2. Webster characteristically uses set-piece scenes, which combine the visual and verbal to intensify the audience's emotional and intellectual responses. This analysis shows that, like modern

cinema, Webster's drama works simultaneously with multiple dramatic means on multiple sensory levels (visual, emotional, aural, intellectual, visceral), to give depth to narrative, character and conflict. In some cases these multiple means reinforce the verbal text, but in many cases cited here, they make our interpretation much more ambiguous. For example, the dagger is used to suggest both honour (of the family name) and dishonour (Ferdinand's sexual desire, and wish to kill his sister). It thus complicates our perception of Ferdinand's motives. The mirror illustrates both the Duchess's vanity and her self-knowledge: we have hitherto seen her solely as heroic and noble.

3. Key thematic issues are clarified through binary oppositions, developed and illustrated in characterisation, language and action. Oppositions include public versus private; woman versus patriarchal institutions; individual freedom versus custom and law; truth versus politics; and inner versus outer. The audience's sympathy in each opposition is drawn to the first term, and against the second, which nevertheless triumphs. Tragic closure is precipitated through the conflict between these oppositions.

4. The observable inequity between genders is demonstrated by the outcome of each turning-point scene, and dramatically asks the audience to see masculinity as abusively corrupt.

5. Structural crisis points are linked to characters' self-awareness of entrapment.

6. Key visual and verbal icons reappear in each turning-point or set-piece scene.

7. Silence is used by Webster as a key dramatic signifier of political and dramatic power.

8. In Webster's tragedies his key turning point comes almost exactly in the middle of the play: Act 3, Scene ii.

Methods of Analysis

This chapter has continued to use the methods of analysis we discussed in Chapter 1. However, we have explicitly introduced approaches to drama as theatre.

1. We have deliberately thought about the overall structure of the plays, using the terms 'turning points' and 'peripateia' interchangeably. We analysed the play's moment of crisis, asking how it is achieved and what effect it has on the outcome of the narrative, the characters, and audience judgement. We have begun to think about the play as a dramatic whole.

2. We have analysed the *internal* structure of scenes, considering character dominance, linguistic and rhythmic patterns, and action. Internal peripateia are essential to an effective dramatic turning-point scene, because they help us focus on the issues at stake, they engender emotion, and maintain dramatic tension.

3. We have also introduced the term 'scenic juxtaposition', to describe how each scene acts as a signifying unit in juxtaposition to the former and subsequent ones. We have discussed how the *external* scenic structure is used to give the audience more information than is available to the main protagonists, and thence to ask us to come to interpretative judgements.

4. We have considered metaphor, thematic oppositions, setting and stage props as integrated parts of a visual and dramatic narrative unit. By comparing the plays to film, we can illuminate Webster's dramaturgy. His drama, like film, uses quickly changing points of view, mise-en-scène, and contrasting scenes.

Suggested Work

There is much in these scenes that we have not had time or space to discuss here.

- What themes are present in the extract from *The Duchess of Malfi*? What kinds of binary oppositions are set up in it?
- Analyse each scene as a whole, examining its internal structure. How do the central characters, the language and themes in the rest of the scene conform with our analysis of these extracts? Look at characters' blocking, entrances and exits. Are there other turning points in these scenes?
- Look at the scenes surrounding the central one. How do they

comment on, or help prepare us for, the central scene? Do they contribute towards the crisis? In what ways do they encourage the audience to make a judgement, and what is that judgement?

- Identify other turning points in the play as a whole. What are their characteristics? How important are they to the plot and characterisation? We shall turn to other 'set-piece' scenes in the chapter on theatricality, and many of your answers to these questions are addressed in that chapter.

4

Tragic Heroines

Webster's central characters are women. What makes his tragic heroines distinctive? How does he generate a sense of tragedy around them? How central are women to his idea of dramatic tragedy? We shall examine in detail two speeches, or participation in key dialogue, by Vittoria and the Duchess of Malfi. This chapter does not intend to summarise the central characters' place within the play, but uses a couple of speeches as starting points from which you can build a broader analysis. We have already noticed how the play establishes a sense of gender conflict through structural, character and linguistic contrasts. To what extent does this conflict inform the female heroines? We have also noted the conflict between corrupt political institutions and behaviour, and the needs, or rights, of the individual. What place does a tragic heroine have within that conflict? In addition, we have commented on the moral ambiguity of the central characters: to what extent is their downfall created by their own folly, and to what extent is it caused by the circumstances into which they are forced by others? These are the kinds of questions we should keep in mind over the next few chapters.

*   *   *

In the following extract Vittoria engages in dialogue with Monticelso in court. Monticelso has accused her of being a whore. In a public forum she explicitly behaves contrary to the ideal, submissive woman.

[Act 3, Scene ii]

Monticelso.	And look upon this creature was his wife.
	She comes not like a widow; she comes armed 120
	With scorn and impudence. Is this a mourning
	habit?
Vittoria.	Had I foreknown his death as you suggest,
	I would have bespoke my mourning.
Monticelso.	O, you are cunning.
Vittoria.	You shame your wit and judgement 125
	To call it so; what, is my just defence
	By him that is my judge called impudence?
	Let me appeal then from this Christian court
	To the uncivil tartar.
Monticelso.	See, my lords,
	She scandals our proceedings.
Vittoria.	Humbly thus, 130
	Thus low, to the most worthy and respected
	Lieger ambassadors, my modesty
	And womanhood I tender; but withal
	So entangled in a cursed accusation
	That my defence, of force like Perseus, 135
	Must personate masculine virtue. To the point:
	Find me but guilty, sever head from body,
	We'll part good friends; I scorn to hold my life
	At yours or any man's entreaty, sir.
English Amb.	She hath a brave spirit. 140
Monticelso.	Well, well, such counterfeit jewels
	Make true ones oft suspected.
Vittoria.	You are deceived;
	For know that all your strict-combined heads,
	Which strike against this mine of diamonds,
	Shall prove but glassen hammers; they shall
	break, – 145
	These are but feigned shadows of my evils.
	Terrify babes, my lord, with painted devils;
	I am past such needless palsy. For your names
	Of whore and murd'ress, they proceed from you,

> As if a man should spit against the wind,   150
> The filth returns in's face.
>
> *Monticelso.*   Pray you, mistress, satisfy me one question:
> Who lodged beneath your roof that fatal night
> Your husband brake his neck?
>
>   (*The White Devil*, 3, ii, 119–54)

One of the noticeable features of Webster's heroines is that they never address the audience directly. They have no soliloquies, unlike Shakespeare's tragic heroes, or Webster's villains. So the way we learn about their character is generally from dialogue, and the more lengthy 'set' speeches they give at moments of crisis. In fact, the lack of soliloquies is not a hindrance to characterisation, but illustrates how Webster constructs character through dramatic action: we learn about their ideas and feelings through dialogue and plot advancement, and not from direct address. Thus we must always contextualise dialogue and speeches, and not analyse them in isolation.

In this short extract Vittoria clearly displays the characteristics which she retains for the rest of the play. She is proud, intelligent, logical and rational. She speaks out for what she believes are her rights. The setting and the characters present in this extract are exemplary for clarifying this: she appeals directly to the ambassadors as a wider court of opinion and judgement about the irregular legal process. The judge acts as prosecutor, in detailed dialogue with the accused, thereby violating his objective and independent function. Setting and dialogue thus establish Vittoria as both victim and resistant heroine. The contrast between Monticelso and Vittoria is a crucial dramatic means by which Webster does this, and is a contrast we have seen throughout the scene as a whole, in which Monticelso has slightly more lines, but both have far more than any other character. Each contribution to their dialogue acts as a counterpoint to the subsequent one. In this exchange they each speak four times, Monticelso's shorter responsive statement to Vittoria's words (a total seven and a half lines to her twenty-five and a half) shows her dominance. The exception to this model is Monticelso's final question, where the balance of power shifts back towards Monticelso. Let us examine the exchange in detail, and consider how it illuminates how Webster constructs character.

Vittoria resists Monticelso's accusations in four distinctive movements, each response illustrating an additional point about her character, establishing a resistance to the theological law of the court,
and displacing any argument about her own wrong-doing onto a
discussion about the legality of the court and its processes.

In her first response Vittoria opens with a logical counter-argu-
ment to Monticelso's sarcasm, using the rhetoric of legal refutation
as proof of her innocence: 'Had I foreknown his death, as you
suggest / I would have bespoke my mourning' (ll. 122–3). Although
this does not actually 'prove' her innocence, we recognise it as witty,
plausible, and acceptable argument in a court of law where the
burden of proof is on the prosecution. Monticelso uses personal
insults in response, rather than legal engagement: 'O, you are
cunning' (l. 124). He personalises their exchange until his final question, which shifts back to the inquisitorial, a personal language
which opposes her public linguistic usage, replicated in her appeal to
the public court of the ambassadors' opinions. Vittoria remains conscious of her role as accused, of the need to refute his false proofs,
and does not get distracted by personal insults. Her calm and intelligent poise under attack is clearly established by situation, setting,
and her linguistic and logical control of the dialogue.

Vittoria's second response is to make a direct attack on his misuse
of the law ('You shame your wit and judgement', l. 125), with a
rhetorical question in illustration ('what, is my just defence / By him
that is my judge called impudence?', ll. 126–7). Her language here is
balanced and logical, in both sense and structure. 'Just defence' balances in line position, rhyme and syllabic count with 'impudence'.
She rhetorically contrasts her legal rights and her account of events
('just defence') with his earlier use of a shameful title ('impudence').
The rhyme places an emphatic and sceptical pause on the word
'impudence'. This word carried connotations of female sexual
impropriety in Early Modern England, denoting both a transgressive
outspokenness, and sexual shamelessness. Her delivery of this final
word in the couplet is necessarily slowed by the rhythm of the line,
but it is also slowed by the intent. She dangles the final words before
the court, 'By him that is my judge called [pause] impudence?'
Line, rhythm, rhyme and delivery converge to underline

Monticelso's prejudicial and partial account of her character and of events and his lack of legal evidence. Vittoria uses her control and knowledge of legal process and argument to put the court itself on trial. This reversal of ordinary process posits her as a heroine, fighting against injustice. The manner in which she does so invokes both admiration and sympathy. Having done all this, she then makes a grand rhetorical gesture: 'Let me appeal then from this Christian court / To the uncivil tartar' (ll. 128–9). Her sarcasm is ripe and bitter: the 'uncivil' East is implicitly more civil than Monticelso's court. Both her sarcasm and bitterness are vocal, and mesh with the audience's own perceptions of a justified response to the handling of her trial.

Her third speech is crucial to an understanding of Vittoria's actions and character, paradigmatic of her complexity. It has four parts to it: the humble submission; the proud defence of her apparently transgressive 'masculine' acting; an acknowledgement of the power of the court and its judgement alongside a defiant claim to a clear conscience; and finally a refusal to plead for her life. Let us look closely at each of those parts. The speech is addressed first to the ambassadors, and implies a physical gesture of humility towards them: 'Humbly *thus*, / *Thus low*' (ll. 130–1). She has shown no such respect for any other officials of, or participants in, the court. Is her humility part of a wider, self-conscious role-playing, through which she tries to manipulate the independence of a court to her own ends? Many Vittorias have played the role in precisely this way. However, as we have seen, Monticelso himself is compromised by his abuse of the court, and the audience's sympathies are demonstrably drawn to Vittoria by the scene's dramaturgy and rhetoric. Webster has altered our judgements of Vittoria from those of Act 1, Scene ii. Her language to the ambassadors differs from that addressed to Monticelso. It humbly acknowledges their status and her own ('my modesty / and womanhood I tender', ll. 132–3). Her switch of roles, from proud resister to humble petitioner, alerts us to her ability to act. But although this helps create a sceptical audience, we remain sympathetic to her because of both the force of her arguments and the corruption of the other characters.

The rest of this speech is also crucial in garnering our respect for her actions and role-playing. She continues her logical argument as she moves into the second part of this speech: 'but withal' (l. 133). Her situation requires her to move from humility to an active defence, necessitating role-playing: 'So entangled in a cursed accusation / That my defence, *of force*, like Perseus, / Must personate masculine virtue' (ll. 134–6; 'personate' means to 'act'). Her explanatory defence of a masculine use of legal language and outspokenness is clear: it both disarms the audience from any criticism of her role-playing, and indirectly denies the transgressive 'impudence' of which Monticelso accused her. She thus effectively turns the tables on Monticelso's accusation of gender transgression, disarming her listeners by drawing attention to the context in which she speaks and the circumstances which force her to act in a particular way.

The third part of this speech, submitting to the court's legal right to take her life, simultaneously claims a clear conscience: 'To the point: / Find me but guilty, sever head from body, / We'll part good friends' (ll. 136–8). Though condemned to death, her soul and body will remain friends, intimating that she will not be damned. She acquiesces in temporal and spiritual judgement, still claiming her innocence. She thus constructs herself indirectly as a martyr: a blatant rhetorical strategy, which nevertheless still effectively engenders our sympathy. The final, and fourth, part of this short speech asserts heroic determination in the face of death: she refuses to beg for her life. This heroism, the apex of her speech, is explicitly commended by the English Ambassador ('She hath a brave spirit', l. 140). This commendation, by the character to whom the original English audience would have been closest, further signals that Webster asks us to admire Vittoria.

There are two contrasting responses to her speech: this first from the ambassador, and the second from Monticelso. His sarcastic comment begins with a mock-plaudit ('Well, well'), and draws attention to her unreliable theatricality (counterfeit jewels are so realistic they make us suspicious of real ones). The audience recognises the truth of what he says: Vittoria *is* a convincing actor, and we are perhaps not quite sure when and where she is telling the truth. However, the balance of the scene, and Monticelso's corrupting and abusive influence, lead the audience to decide more for Vittoria than against her.

Vittoria's fourth speech is partly addressed to Monticelso, and partly to the court as a whole. Because it has that broader audience, it is the closest she comes to a soliloquy, although it is firmly contextualised in the ongoing dialogue. It is an extended metaphor, which anticipates her final words as she leaves the court after her conviction (l. 294). Both the extension of the metaphor, and its later repetition indicate its significance as an articulation of her self-perceived character. She characterises her head as 'diamonds', signifying determination, hardness and brightness. She then reverses the theatrical metaphor which Monticelso used against her, claiming that his account is as 'feigned shadows' (l. 146) and 'painted devils' (l. 147), implicitly positing herself as truthful. The English Church attacked Roman Catholicism in these terms during the Reformation: arguing that worship of icons was idolatrous and blasphemous. Vittoria's use of this language links her to the Jacobean audience against the Catholic Church, here represented by Monticelso. Her final words sound triumphantly resistant, and resonate truthfully to the audience: his story of events and his definitions are seen to be partial and subjective. Vittoria succeeds in demonstrating that he is abusing the court of law, but she does so by descending to insult: 'As if a man should spit against the wind, / The filth returns in's face' (ll. 150–1). The words prove the catalyst for him to return to his interrogative and inquisitorial function. The overall conflict in this scene never allows her to dominate the action completely, so that even though she appears to have justice and the audience on her side, the corrupt court triumphs. By becoming the victim in this way, she ascends to heroic and tragic status, conscious of doing so.

*   *   *

[Act 4, Scene ii]

Bracciano. That hand, that cursed hand, which I have wearied
         With doting kisses! O my sweetest duchess,
         How lovely thou art now! Thy loose thoughts   100
         Scatter like quicksilver; I was bewitched;
         For all the world speaks ill of thee.

Vittoria.   No matter.
         I'll live so now I'll make that world recant

	And change her speeches. You did name your duchess.	
Bracciano.	Whose death God pardon.	
Vittoria.	Whose death God	

revenge   105
On thee, most godless Duke.

Flamineo.	Now for two whirlwinds.	
Vittoria.	What have I gained by thee but infamy?	

Thou hast stained the spotless honour of my house,
And frighted thence noble society,
Like those which, sick o'th'palsy, and retain   110
Ill-scenting foxes 'bout them, are still shunned
By those of choicer nostrils.
What do you call this house?
Is this your palace? Did not the judge style it
A house of penitent whores? Who sent me to it?   115
Who hath the honour to advance Vittoria
To this incontinent college? Is't not you?
Is't not your high preferment? Go, go brag
How many ladies you have undone, like me.
Fare you well, sir; let me hear no more of you.   120
I had a limb corrupted to an ulcer,
But I have cut it off; and now I'll go
Weeping to heaven on crutches. For your gifts,
I will return them all; and I do wish
That I could make you full executor   125
To all my sins. – O that I could toss myself
Into a grave as quickly! For all thou art worth
I'll not shed one tear more; I'll burst first.
         She throws herself upon a bed.
                (*The White Devil,* 4, ii, 98–128)

Here Vittoria's speech is delivered privately, in her place of imprisonment. We have not seen her since she left the stage in Act 3, Scene ii,
under guard. Before this extract begins, we see Flamineo's and
Bracciano's arrival at the house of convertites, their discussion with

the matron about their continued ability to evade the prohibition on visiting Vittoria, and Bracciano's interception of, and belief in, the false love letter Francisco has written to Vittoria. Although Vittoria is imprisoned she is in relatively comfortable surroundings, her friends able to visit. The scenic structure imprisons her symbolically, she is surrounded by and juxtaposed with the plots and counter-narratives of men whom we are led to distrust.

The extract opens with Bracciano ranting against her, and harking nostalgically, remembering his murdered ex-wife. He adopts the attacking metaphor which others formerly applied to Vittoria: of seditious and lustful magic and witchcraft, linking her supposed magical powers with sexual incontinence (ll. 100–1). His climactic accusation disloyally echoes Monticelso's summative proof of her guilt at her trial (3, ii, 247–8): 'For all the world speaks ill of thee' (l. 102). We already know that his suspicion is groundless and his citation of rumour and public notoriety as proof further alienates us from him. Scenes and dialogues are structured to build sympathy for Vittoria and to enable us to see her situation as one created and perpetuated by a masculine world of authority, reputation, and inherent distrust of women. Bracciano's rant contrasts with Vittoria's quiet and resigned response, which rhythmically completes the line in a falling three-syllabic sentence: 'No matter' (l. 102). Her rhetoric, delivery and quietness here make a positive contrast with Bracciano's intemperance: we feel her response is genuine, reinforced by her claim that she'll now live in a manner to 'make all that world recant' (l. 103).

Vittoria tries to clarify his reference to Isabella. In a swift exchange, they each speak twice in two lines. Bracciano's half-line response to Vittoria's stated question ('You did name your duchess') is a false piety: 'Whose death God pardon' (l. 105). The content demands a pause, but Vittoria completes his line, counter-attacking with a reminder of the truth, repeating some of his terminology and running on to the next line: 'Whose death God revenge / *On thee*, most godless Duke.' Her response refutes his piety, reminding us of his guilt. Vittoria's mode of participation in this dialogue, in which she gives no space to hypocrisy, links her to the audience. She becomes the agent through whom the audience comes closest to truth.

Her subsequent speech (21 lines) is her longest in the whole play, and comes closest to a manifesto of her feelings, beliefs and character. It falls clearly into two parts. The first half (to the end of line 119) is a series of rising rhetorical questions: the rhythms, rhetorical devices and metaphors combining to reinforce our belief in, and even support for, her righteous indignation. Although each of her questions is technically a rhetorical one, given she does not ask Bracciano to answer them, effective answers are provided within the speech. Her question 'What have I gained by thee but infamy?' (l. 107) answers itself, as a good rhetorical question should. However, Vittoria emphasises her point by providing a statement expanding on the unexpressed answer, clarifying explicitly the nature of, and blame for, that infamy: 'Thou hast stained the spotless honour of my house' (l. 108). Her term 'house' resonates metaphorically through the play, indicating her place of abode, her body, and her genealogy. Throughout the play, in characterisation, dramatic structure and plot, we are asked to focus on Vittoria's sexuality and identity as intimately connected to her body, her family position, and the place where she appears (garden, court, prison, court, private chamber). Webster makes this explicit through Vittoria's conscious acknowledgement of the current status of her 'house' (l. 113).

Her lucid apportioning of blame is given a visual and pungent reinforcement through her extended simile: 'Like those which, sick o'th'palsy, and retain / Ill-scenting foxes 'bout them, are still shunned / By those of choicer nostrils' (ll. 110–12). This generates a powerful image of her exiled and outcast status, simultaneously apportioning responsibility for her fall to Bracciano's lust. The subsequent six lines contain eight rhetorical questions, echoing her rising anger, and reminding the audience of the trial scene. Her first question ('What do you call this house?', l. 113) is actually answered by the third question (ll. 114–15). The second ('Is this your palace?', implying a negative response) rhetorically reminds us of his promises to protect her, and inability or failure to do so. Her fourth and fifth questions (ll. 115–16) are different ways of asking the same question: 'Who sent me to it? / Who hath the honour to advance Vittoria . . . ?' This emphatic repetition is increased by answering with two more questions: 'Is't not you? / Is't not your high preferment?' (ll. 117–18).

Repetition of form (the questions) and content rise to this climax, which is then punctuated by a tired statement. The rhythms and punctuation slow, enhancing the meaning of her dismissal ('Go, go brag / How many ladies you have undone, like me'), and preparing us for a pause. This marks the transition from anger to resignation.

The remainder of the speech is far quieter: a quietness to which we listen with attention, having followed her reasoned and angry argument. How far is she manipulating a response from Bracciano here? Some critics argue this is a calculated act, denoting petulance and self-interest rather than real anger. Let us analyse the second half of the speech to help us to decide.

In the first half of her speech, her anger is tangible: the rising list of questions suggest righteous indignation and an unanswerable anger. This is her longest uninterrupted speech in the play: Bracciano says nothing for twenty-one lines, suggesting uncontrolled anger, not calculation. The final nine lines are slower and sadder, and the contrast with the former anger generates pathos. The rhythm creates a quieter mood: there are no more questions; all lines are run-on apart from the first in this section (l. 120); each new phrase, of the six, is unconnected to the last; and the one exclamation is accompanied by a physical action.

Her first sentence ('Fare you well, sir; let me hear no more of you', l. 120) marks a conclusion and an opening. The tone is saddened, but aristocratic and polite, shifting to the passive subjunctive in the second half. The effect is dismissive and de-personalising: her love for Bracciano has died. Her second sentence, run-on over three lines, is an extended metaphor of New Testament provenance (Mark 9: 45): 'I had a limb corrupted to an ulcer, / But I have cut it off; and now I'll go / Weeping to heaven on crutches' (ll. 121–3). The tone is sadly wondering: how could this have happened? The New Testament metaphor for salvation further suggests her repentant reformation. Her third point ('For your gifts, / I will return them all', ll. 123–4) moves from the spiritual to the material, continuing graphically to demonstrate a complete rejection of Bracciano from her life. The salvation imagery is reinforced by her fourth point: 'and I do wish / That I could make you full executor / To all my sins' (ll. 124–6). Her anguished exaggeration is here combined with a kind of black humour purveying a searing honesty: her wish to blame all her sins on him is self-consciously ironised. It demonstrates a lucid and attractive self-knowledge. These four points, although connected through her personal responses to this crisis, lack the kind of coherent rational and logical links we usually observe in her speech patterns.

The fifth point marks another break in the rhythm of this speech: 'O that I could toss myself / Into a grave as quickly!' (ll. 126–7). The exclamatory construction ('O . . . ') suggests an exaggerated or extreme emotion or action. The stage direction ('*She throws herself upon a bed*'), which editorially is placed after line 128, should accompany this exclamation. Action, intention and words then merge: and this combination generates a sense of verisimilitude. It does not look calculated. Her final phrase on top of this ('For all thou art worth / I'll not shed one tear more; I'll burst first') is delivered from the bed. The image she uses here is apt and realistic: despite deeply felt internal emotion, pride and anger forbid her tears, generating our sympathy, because she refuses to humiliate herself to a man whom we have seen behaving both faithlessly and hypocritically.

In summary, then, Vittoria's two long speeches illustrate a strength and nobility of character which is actually enhanced by her own knowledge of her past wrong-doing. The sins she has committed in the first Act effectively cause her downfall. We have seen that her character is complex: not simply good or evil, innocent or guilty, naive or calculated. It is impossible to make black-and-white judgements about her. She comes across as intelligently self-conscious. Webster gives her a rhetoric which is calculated, but also the language to defend that calculation as necessary. He always asks us to see her language and action within a wider context: that of the necessities of an individual's situation. This contextualisation is an essential part of Webster's typical characterisation. Let us now turn to his other tragic heroine.

*   *   *

[Act 1, Scene i]
Duchess.   Now she pays it.   440

The misery of us that are born great –
We are forced to woo, because none dare woo us;
And as a tyrant doubles with his words,
And fearfully equivocates, so we
Are forced to express our violent passions   445
In riddles and in dreams, and leave the path
Of simple virtue, which was never made
To seem the thing it is not. Go, go brag
You have left me heartless – mine is in your bosom,
I hope 'twill multiply love there. You do tremble: 450
Make not your heart so dead a piece of flesh,
To fear more than to love me. Sir, be confident.
What is't distracts you? This is flesh and blood, sir;
'Tis not the figure cut in alabaster
Kneels at my husband's tomb. Awake, awake, man!   455
I do here put off all vain ceremony,
And only do appear to you a young widow
That claims you for her husband and, like a widow,
I use but half a blush in't.
                                   (*The Duchess of Malfi*, 1, i, 440–59)

The Duchess and Antonio are alone, Cariola hidden behind a curtain. This speech comes towards the end of their debate about their relationship, which acts as the precursory courtship to the marriage vows in Cariola's presence. The Duchess has transferred her ring to Antonio's finger and we have observed her active wooing of Antonio. Her opening 'Now' is Fortune's reward for Antonio's former virtuous service.

The intimate tone and setting contrast with the public state occasion in the first part of the Act. Her lines are flowing, using rational argument combined with endearments and invocations to dissuade Antonio's objections. These twenty lines reveal much about the Duchess's character. Overall the speech falls into two halves after the opening half-line: the first, long sentence (ll. 441–8) is expository; and the subsequent seven shorter sentences (ll. 448–59) form the second half, which is intimately persuasive. The tone and rhythms of each half differ, although both use plain language. The first half flows more elegantly, playing out the logic of her argument. Its rhetoric belongs to her public world. The second half is more playful, abrupt and humorous: suitable to the private sanctuary of her marriage to Antonio. The rhythm of the first sentence is very regular for Webster: each line is a regular pentameter, except for line 442, which has 11 beats, the final foot a falling anapestic.

Both content and rhetorical regularity establish the public focus of this part of the speech. Although ostensibly addressed only to Antonio, these words also defend the Duchess's actions to us. The long sentence grammatically links the three main points she makes. Great women are forced to actively court men; the language and actions of their courtship are necessarily equivocal because their political position makes such courtship contentious; and consequently such women abandon a transparent virtue. The Duchess clarifies her paradoxical status: trapped between the demands of her political position and her own personal desires, she is forced into conduct perceived as deceitful. The metaphor she uses in this section is revealingly ironic in both its vehicle and tenor. The vehicle is the rhetoric of tyranny: 'as a tyrant doubles with his words, / And fearfully equivocates' (ll. 443–4), positing an unconscious link between political chicanery and her own actions and language. The tenor suggests that violent passion can only be represented through dreams and riddles (ll .444–6): and this evokes the world and language in particular of Bosola and Ferdinand, who continually use rhetorical indirection to represent violence and desire. Elsewhere in the play we tend to see the Duchess as a character uninvolved in such a turbulent, deceptive and two-faced world. Here she honestly tells us that she cannot avoid that world. Such corruscating self-knowledge is admirable. She knows how she will be perceived: but she chooses nevertheless to fulfil her own private desires. She implicitly acknowledges that a confrontation with the political world is inevitable and that in her view she has left 'the path / Of simple virtue' (ll. 446–7). She never voices naïve confidence about the potential outcomes of her decision. This sentence's length and complex content, particularly its last line and a half, suggest a slowish and contemplative delivery. There is a natural pause at the end of the sentence, as she shifts into a lighter mood.

The second half of the speech, in a mere eleven lines, contains seven sentences, each shifting the subject matter. The rhythms are much more irregular, although the lines range between 10 and 12 beats, generating a sense of greater intimacy and urgency. The different grammatical and rhythmical structure contrasts with the first half. Such short sentences in combination with the setting and the actor's delivery help create a happy sense of intimacy and of the freedom to express the first thought that comes into the mind. The pauses are irregular: it is clear there is a pause after each sentence, and these fall at various points, both in and at the end of lines. The longest sentence comes last in the speech, as she comes to a rhetorical and argumentative climax. Let us look at each sentence in turn.

The first sentence, 'Go, go brag / You have left me heartless – mine is in your bosom, / I hope 'twill multiply love there' (ll. 448–50) echoes the words of Vittoria in *The White Devil* (4, ii, 118–20) which we have just looked at. The words betray the women's consciousness of a masculine world in which boasting about sexual conquest validates male status and power. However, the tone and situation of both women are different. Vittoria delivered her words in near despair, at a later stage in the drama. The Duchess delivers her words flirtatiously: she is courting. There are several changes of pace within the sentence. First, that invited by the slow repetition and monosyllables of 'Go, go brag' followed by the swifter run-on line; and secondly, that indicated by this edition's hyphen ('You have left me heartless', l. 449). The Duchess probably touches Antonio's chest here: indicating the transfer of her heart to his body, intimated by the subsequent half-line ('You do tremble'). Physical contact is an essential part of her persuasion of Antonio.

Her second sentence flows naturally from her first, beginning with this observation of the trembling she feels in his body. The observation then becomes the exemplum from which she continues to argue against caution and for commitment: 'Make *not* your heart so dead a piece of flesh, / To fear more than to love me' (ll. 451–2). Her argument over-rides the regularity of a line: the sentence ending after the seventh beat. The caesura, falling at the end of the sentence, lengthens what is already a 12-beat line. Emotion and intimacy over-ride poetic necessity. This is further enhanced by the third sen-

tence, of only three words: 'Sir, be confident' (l. 452). The apparent
abruptness is again belied by dramatic situation and delivery. She
entreats him, urging him to believe in both himself and her arguments. There must be a further short pause at the end of the line,
perhaps she holds his shoulders and peers into his face as she urges
her encouragement. The subsequent, fourth, sentence is also short,
and this time the content and delivery speed her argument along,
because the unanswered question ('What is't distracts you?', l. 453)
forces the next sentence to follow immediately. The fifth sentence, a
response to her own question, uses both physical and metaphorical
ploys to bring him to a decision: 'This is flesh and blood, sir; / 'Tis
not the figure cut in alabaster / Kneels at my husband's tomb.' This
suggests she holds his hand to her breast ('this'), and then uses the
lifeless image of a funeral ornament as a contrasting, negative
example. This image later recurs in the wax-work monuments in
Act 4. Here, however, the image is positive. We take it at face
value, indicating her genuine desire to put aside grief and reawaken
sexuality.

The sixth sentence is urgent ('Awake, awake, man!'). It is the final
and climactic turning point of her speech, leading straight into her
final and longest sentence, her plainest declaration of sexual intent,
although framed through a persona: 'I do here put off all vain ceremony, / And only do *appear to you* a young widow / That claims you
for her husband and, like a widow, / I use but half a blush in't'
(ll. 456–9). The first part of the sentence ('I do *here*') suggests
further physical action. Perhaps she takes off a ceremonial headdress,
or partly kneels to him, or draws him to her. She claims a purely
private identity (that of a widow looking for a husband), in con-
tradistinction to the 'vain ceremony' of her public life and duties.
This private self can then make a private sexual joke. Her widow's
'half-blush' makes explicit her previous sexual experience, intimating
that she need only be half-embarrassed to claim him because as a
widow she need not display a virgin's sexual ignorance and modesty.

There are several additional aspects of this speech which build
characterisation. The first is that Antonio does not speak at all: the
Duchess dominates their exchange and their relationship. She
defends this on the grounds of her higher status. Antonio never

actively decides to transgress his social or political status: her transgression is doubly of gender and status. As a woman, she should not be wooing; and as a head of state, were she to woo, she should woo one of her own class. The second point is that she increasingly uses more direct language. Beginning with the indirection of analogy, moving on to a jokey tone, and then to negative exemplum (which tell us what she is not, or does not feel, rather than what she is or does feel), she only finally speaks directly in the final sentence. Her doubled use of the more formal and public 'sir' in the earlier part of the speech, followed by the later 'man!', also shows her shift towards a more expressive intimacy. This gradual rhetorical movement towards elucidation and intimacy echoes and suggests that female desire must be spoken by women indirectly. She is self-conscious about any perceived immodesty if she does speak directly. The fears which she expressed in the first sentence are thus seen to inform the mode and content of this whole speech, and aid our sense of a complex woman. She shows an acute awareness of the way in which public women were in a double bind: despite their political power, public sexualised behaviour would always be judged as immodest, because feminine sexuality belonged to the domestic realm. The Duchess's speech is both a summary of her situation and a dramatic scene in which she tries to escape from that position. It is consequently moving and engaging. But it remains overshadowed by tragic potential implicit in the conflicts between private desire and public duties to which the Duchess herself gives such eloquent voice.

Let us now move on to the next extract.

[Act 3, Scene v]

Bosola.   Fie, Madam,
      Forget this low, base fellow.
Duchess.   Were I a man
      I'd beat that counterfeit face into thy other.
Bosola.   One of no birth –
Duchess.   Say that he was born mean;
      Man is most happy when's own actions   120

	Be arguments and examples of his virtue.	
Bosola.	A barren, beggarly virtue.	
Duchess.	I prithee, who is greatest, can you tell?	

Sad tales befit my woe; I'll tell you one.
A salmon, as she swam unto the sea,   125
Met with a dogfish, who encounters her
With this rough language: 'why art thou so bold
To mix thyself with our high state of floods,
Being no eminent courtier, but one
That for the calmest and fresh time o'th'year   130
Dost live in shallow rivers, rank'st thyself
With silly melts and shrimps? And darest thou
Pass by our dog-ship, without reverence?'
'O,' quoth the salmon, 'sister, be at peace;
Thank Jupiter we have both passed the net!   135
Our value never can be truly known
Till in the fisher's basket we be shown;
I'th'market then my price may be the higher
Even when I am nearest to the cook and fire.'
So, to great men, the moral may be stretched: 140
Men oft are valued high when th'are most wretch'd.
But come; whither you please. I am armed 'gainst
   misery,
Bent to all sways of the oppressor's will.
There's no deep valley but near some great hill.   *Exeunt.*
(*The Duchess of Malfi*, 3, v, 116–44)

This extract comes at the end of the third Act, and marks both the end of the first half of the play, and of her freedom, and the beginning of her imprisonment and thus the beginning of the end. The scene opens with the Duchess, Antonio, their children and Cariola discovering that the Cardinal has banished them from Ancona. Bosola arrives with a letter of politic friendship from Ferdinand, begging Antonio's 'head' in a matter of business. After he departs, the Duchess suggests they split up and that Antonio take their eldest son to Milan. Their poignant parting is immediately followed by the arrival of Bosola, masked and with armed men. His appearance is threatening and frightening and he tells her she will never see her husband again. When he asks, 'These are your children?' (l. 114), both the audience and the Duchess fear his potential violence. Visually and dramatically the Duchess is represented as vulnerable, frightened, and victimised. This is where this extract opens.

Contextually, then, her words resonate as extraordinarily brave and her character as both self-possessed and resilient. In the first speech we analysed it was possible to perceive flaws in her decisions, to which she herself drew attention. Here, without Antonio, she plays the role of the captured woman of state: she does not stoop to beg for either her children or her life. Her integrity begins to persuade Bosola of her nobility. She is paradoxically dominant here: through volume of words; through visual positioning; through Bosola's masking; and through her arguments. Bosola speaks only two and a half lines to her twenty-five. He speaks on three occasions: the first is countered with a threat by the Duchess, the second is interrupted and dismissed. The third is a grudging and sneering comment, which she turns to develop an argument about inherent nobility. Bosola's comments and presence are thus completely turned around in this extract: the content denied, and the threat transposed by the Duchess's lack of fear.

How is this achieved? First, as we have argued, by her linguistic and rhetorical dominance of his words: she does not allow him to complete a sentence. Secondly, and perhaps paradoxically, Bosola's power is lessened by the fact that he is masked, and she is in her princely garb. Although this contrast initially engenders fear, her response to him and to the silent armed men around her allows her physical presence to dominate visually. She is likely to be in sumptuous clothes: they are likely to be uniformly black and masked. Her lack of physical power merely underlines her symbolic political power, which is being abused by her brothers and their agent. Thirdly, the silent presence of the children and Cariola is a powerful visual, but unspoken, reminder of what she is defending. We see a mother defending her own life and that of her family. This secures the audience's sympathies: there are no ambiguous loyalties in this scene. Fourthly, the content of her speeches turns around Bosola's threats. The Duchess's argumentative skills are supreme: indeed, they appear to silence Bosola, to the extent that she closes the act, both linguistically and physically. Although returned to her palace under guard at the end, the rhetorical and dramatic victory lies with her. Let us look closely at both the content and mode of her three speeches.

Her first words are a displaced threat: 'Were I a man / I'd beat that counterfeit face into thy other' (ll. 117–18), but also the realisation of a nightmare world in which someone known to us is transformed into a masked, fearful and threatening figure. Webster manipulates the audience's fears as much as those of the Duchess. The Duchess's words, in direct response to a social slur on her husband, are an offensive defence, and a recognition of her gendered powerlessness. Physical fighting belongs to the realm of masculinity. So ostensibly her threat is completely self-defeating: a simultaneous acknowledgement of her inability to fight back physically. However, her continued argument with Bosola illustrates where her ability lies: in her rhetoric and power of argument. Thus her second speech immediately counters his argument, and this is reinforced by the fact that she interrupts him, refusing him the power of fully articulating his argument that men of low birth are not worthy of her (l. 119). Both the structure and content of her argument are hortatory: '*Say* that he was born mean', as she moves on to state her radical argument, 'Man is most happy when's own actions / Be arguments and examples of his virtue' (ll. 120–1). She explicitly negates the status-led arguments of her brothers about her marriage: virtue and virtuous action, not birth, determine happiness and eventual status. She posits an argument for a natural or earned nobility, as opposed to one of birth. Bosola's reply, a resentful mutter ('A barren, beggarly virtue', l. 122), provides the intellectual starting point for the rest of her argument. His view, a purely economic one, is that virtue is worthless if it produces no status or wealth. The Duchess's response, through her rhetorical question, 'I prithee, who is greatest, can you tell?' (l. 123), transposes the debate from the political and economic realm to the philosophical and spiritual. Her question hangs in the air a moment: a precise iambic pentameter, echoing for the audience and Bosola, who remains silent: who *can* tell?

Having engaged the attention of the audience both on stage and in the auditorium, the Duchess assumes the rhetoric of a character with plenty of time, 'Sad tales befit my woe; I'll tell you one.' She signals a lack of fear and a self-control through her appropriation of stage space and time here: anyone with time to tell a story in this situation, is someone signalling her disdain for and rejection of her enemies' tactics. Her lengthy digression (ll. 124–41), of eighteen lines, is delivered in the conventional rhetoric of a parabolic fairy-tale. It includes a narrator's introduction, direct quotations, and a moralised authorial couplet at the end. The self-enclosed narrative is then supplemented by three lines, including a further couplet to close the act.

The eighteen-line parable has an unusually regular rhythm: every single line is a regular iambic pentameter, except for the last line of the salmon's speech, engendering a sense of linguistic control. The lines of the narrative are mostly run-on, creating a naturally flowing story. The Duchess gives verbal characteristics to both fish. She gives the dogfish a parodic haughty tone of pride (using phrases such as 'our dog-ship', l. 133), which she delivers with the pomposity his character seems to demand. This parodic tonal delivery alerts the audience to the fact that she is using this character to mock analogous pompous courtiers who advocate a closed noble society. The salmon, by contrast, is gentle, open, friendly and philosophical: 'sister, be at peace; / Thank Jupiter we have both passed the net!' (l. 134). She articulates a more egalitarian set of beliefs. The subsequent six lines are all rhyming couplets, and this changes the delivery from that of a flowing narrative to one reflecting a slower proverbial knowledge. Each couplet acts as a self-professed truism. The first couplet, 'Our value never can be truly known / Till in the fisher's basket we be shown' (ll. 136–7), ostensibly uses Bosola's language of the economic market-place, only to refute his conclusions: because she has transposed the measurement of value to a time after death. The spiritual implications of this transition are explicit in the Christian overtones of the fisher's basket: Christ is frequently figured in Gospel parables as a fisherman. The second couplet rejects worldly evaluation, continuing the economic metaphor, and reiterates the egalitarian and spiritual senses already invoked: 'I'th'market then my price may be the higher / Even when I am nearest to the cook and fire' (ll. 138–9). She suggests that the salmon has a greater final worldly value; but that such values, only evident at the moment of death, are also ultimately irrelevant in the face of death. The final line spoken by the salmon is a 12-beat line, allowing the speaker to linger emphatically on the sense of the words, an emphasis reiterated by the rhyme. This third couplet makes explicit the parabolic and moralised intention of her tale: 'So, to great men, the moral may be stretched: / *Men oft are valued high when th'are most wretch'd.*' Here the Duchess states her belief in transcendent moral and spiritual values: her interior strength overcomes mortal adversity.

The final three lines of the Act mark a shift in her delivery. The first line is a 12-beat line, and self-consciously signals a change in pace, physical movement and determination: 'But come; whither you please. I am armed 'gainst misery'. The first words of the line show that she is in control of this change of direction: telling them to lead her off. The second half of the line bravely asserts that their actions cannot harm her (she is *armed* against misery), displaying Christian and spiritual overtones. The final couplet is not fully self-contained, but runs on from this previous line: 'Bent to all sways of the oppressor's will. / *There's no deep valley but near some great hill*' (ll. 143–4). Here she explicitly articulates a political critique of her brothers ('sways of the oppressor's will'), combined with a belief that present injustice will be resolved in some way. Whether such a reso-lution will be a worldly one or a spiritual one is unclear: her metaphor may be taken either way, and remains suitably ambiguous to maintain dramatic tension.

In summary, the Duchess illustrates a noble strength of character, a refusal to submit to arbitrary power, an ability to articulate rea-soned and principled arguments under pressure, a maternal defence of her children, an insouciance about potential violence against her body, and a deprecating humour. All these characteristics present her not as a victim, or simple martyr to her brothers' various jealousies, but as a powerful woman working with the only weapons left at her disposal: a linguistic aptitude, personal strength, and some kind of spiritual belief. The audience (and later Bosola) perceive that these weapons are ultimately more successful than those of violence, because they convince us (and him) that she was right. Webster thence uses the character of the Duchess to help convince the audience that closed economic and social societies are both dangerous and inequitable.

Conclusions

1. The tragic heroine's character is constructed through a combination of external and internal influences. Her emotions, responses and arguments are placed within the wider, overall narrative context. This context is dramatically emphasised by scenic juxtapositions, internal scenic contrasts, and the heroines' lack of space or time to deliver a monologue. The staging of their own personal crises, of belief, desire and action, coincide with key scenes in the plays' structure. This centres the heroines dramatically, drawing our attention to them: but it also symbolically traps them within the dramatic structure, which acts as a metaphor for their social entrapment. These heroines are literally physically and linguistically circumscribed by environment. Nevertheless, within this environment their dialogue and action demonstrate how they both deal with, and develop through, adversity. Strength of character, individualism and spiritual belief all emerge through conflict.

2. The heroines remain rational, a rationality demonstrated through their purposive control of rhetoric, but they also respond convincingly to changing situations.

3. Since character is established through dialogue and context, rather than through monologues, characterisation is essentially dramatic rather than poetic. This gives Webster's characterisation a dynamic, responsive and individual flavour. Language, thought and feeling are integrated with dramatic action, and this integration creates believable characters. Their speeches are not static, but develop with the dialogue and action of the narrative on stage.

4. Despite the centrality of female protagonists, female dominance is always posited as ambiguously transgressive. Both Vittoria and the Duchess are admirable because of their strength of will: but

they also come to political grief because of it. Their tragic fall is partly caused by their transgression of ideological gender behavioural norms. Nevertheless, Webster's judicious combination of compelling characterisation with careful dramatic structuring ensures that we see tragedy as a collision between corrupt political conservatism and individual freedom. Furthermore, political corruption is clearly linked to masculinity, and individual freedom and justice to femininity. The latter is finally defeated: but the tragic heroine's fall explicitly critiques the masculine political world. Tragedy lies in this structural conflict and our own perception that the tragic heroines died undeservedly. Theories of tragedy should not focus only on the flaws of individual characters, but on fundamental ideological and political conflicts.

5. Both tragic heroines articulate ideas, feelings and beliefs that the audience has already been asked to think about, through immediately preceding scenes or parts of scenes. In this way Webster prepares us to agree with his heroines' points of view about oppressive brothers and gradually alters our own views on tragedy and their individual predicaments. Webster is continually aware of his audience and asks for a combined emotional and intellectual response from us.

6. The characters illustrate a remarkable overall self-possession and internal confidence: they perceive chaos and disorder to be in the political and judicial world, rather than within themselves. They retain self-knowledge (Vittoria and the Duchess display a lucid awareness of their own faults) but place the greatest blame for their fall on the corrupt and disordered world around them.

7. The heroines engage in role-playing and are conscious of the restrictive demands placed upon individuals by status and situation. Role-playing is not wholly a negative characteristic.

Methods of Analysis

This chapter has further developed the ways of analysing speech, action and plot of the preceding chapters, linking rhythm, metre, rhyme and metaphor in analysing the rhetorical movements of a particular speech or dialogue. You should look in detail at the following areas in any consideration of character:

1. Examine the way an individual speech shifts in its rhythms and meaning as a way of indicating mood and emotion. Look at the metaphors used within this structural framework. Is the character in control of their language or vice-versa?
2. Always contextualise the speech: to whom and to what is it a response? Is it a rational or irrational response? Where on the stage is it spoken and to whom? How are the audience positioned by the speech and the character? Does our view change?
3. How does this particular speech or dialogue develop or change our ideas of a character? How does any change integrate with the rest of the play's action? Is the speech linked to other speeches in the play, either by the same character or by others? What is the effect and importance of such connections?
4. Look at the reasoning behind a character's response and ideas: do we feel it is justified? Is their 'world-view' one we are asked to share, or are we asked to be sceptical?

Suggested Work

In analysing two extracts for each heroine we have only scratched the surface of a comprehensive account of their characters. You need to do some further work, to broaden and deepen this account. The best way is to identify other key speeches and moments in the play where they respond to a crisis or new event.

The White Devil
1. Look at 1, ii, 196–302. This is quite a long extract, where Vittoria speaks with her husband, her lover and her mother. The transitions in character involved in managing the three dialogues is instructive. Why does Webster juxtapose the three dialogues in a mere 100 lines? What view do we develop of Vittoria's character? What happens immediately before and after this extract,

and how does this affect our interpretation of her character? Her character is often described to us by others and differs from that which she herself presents. Why is this?

2. We have already looked at Vittoria's final speech in Chapter 2. You should look back over what we said then and examine the rest of that scene (5, vi, 1–247). What view do we develop of Vittoria? Does she change during the scene's action? Do we believe she is redeemed? How and where does she demonstrate self-knowledge? What is the effect of other characters' presence and actions on our understanding and judgement of Vittoria?

3. How many scenes does Vittoria appear in? Despite her dominance of and connection to the action, she appears infrequently. Discuss the significance of this.

4. Look at the other female characters in the play: Isabella, Cornelia and Zanche. How do they contrast or complement Vittoria? How does our understanding of them aid our perception of Vittoria? In what ways do the answers to these questions deepen our understanding of the symbolic role femininity plays in the drama?

The Duchess of Malfi

1. Comment on the initial appearance of the Duchess on stage (1, i, 147–351). Look at where and how the way she speaks changes. Why does it? What does it tell us?

2. Why is she always called 'the Duchess'? What is the effect of her having no personalised name?

3. Look at her death scene (4, ii), which demonstrates her nobility and stoicism, most famously in her phrase, 'I am Duchess of Malfi still' (4, ii, 141). What else does it tell us? How does Bosola develop our understanding of the Duchess's character? Comment on her views on her forthcoming death, and the relationship between what she says and how she actually confronts death.

4. How many scenes does the Duchess appear in? Comment on her character as it develops. Is her self-perception integrated with the action and other crisis points of the play? To what extent does she develop a symbolic spiritual resonance?

5. Look at the characterisation of the other women in the play (Julia and Cariola), and their function as foils to the Duchess.

5

Heroes and Villains

The male protagonists in Webster's tragedies are nearly all villains or malcontents. Antonio is one exception, but he never dominates the action nor the imagination of an audience as do Bosola or Ferdinand, and he lacks a hero's independence. No single male character has the central dramatic status of his heroines, nor the interior monologues of Shakespeare's tragic heroes. What is the function of Webster's male heroes? Are they flawed tragic individuals or participants in a world that is more flawed than they? Why is his focus on tragic heroines rather than heroes? You need to keep in mind what we have decided in Chapter 4, and place any conclusions you make here in that context.

We shall look at two extracts from each tragedy, and at a different character in each extract. You will find that, as with the heroines, the male protagonists make few direct addresses to the audience. I have included four different kinds of examples of characterisation here: a nominal dialogue where one speaker acts merely as a prompt; a soliloquy; a monologue with other characters present on stage; and a genuine dialogue.

*   *   *

In this scene Flamineo has arranged Vittoria's assignation with Bracciano, conniving her husband's absence. Here Flamineo shamelessly defends his actions.

[Act 1, Scene ii]

Cornelia.	What? Because we are poor, 315

Shall we be vicious?

Flamineo.   Pray, what means have you
To keep me from the galleys, or the gallows?
My father proved himself a gentleman,
Sold all's land, and like a fortunate fellow
Died ere the money was spent. You brought
     me up   320
At Padua, I confess, where I protest,
For want of means – the university judge me –
I have been fain to heel my tutor's stockings
At least seven years; conspiring with a beard
Made me a graduate; then to this duke's service.   325
I visited the court, whence I returned,
More courteous, more lecherous by far,
But not a suit the richer. And shall I,
Having a path so open and so free
To my preferment, still retain your milk   330
In my pale forehead? No, this face of mine
I'll arm and fortify with lusty wine
'Gainst shame and blushing.

Cornelia.   O that I ne'er had borne thee,

Flamineo.   So would I.
I would the common'st courtesan in Rome   335
Had been my mother rather than thyself.
Nature is very pitiful to whores
To give them but few children, yet those children
Plurality of fathers; they are sure
They shall not want. Go, go,   340
Complain unto my great lord cardinal;
Yet may be he will justify the act.
Lycurgus wond'red much men would provide
Good stallions for their mares, and yet would suffer
Their fair wives to be barren.   345

Cornelia.   Misery of miseries!   *Exit Cornelia.*

Flamineo.   The duchess come to court! I like not that.

We are engaged to mischief and must on.
As rivers to find out the ocean
Flow with crook bendings beneath forced banks,   350
Or as we see, to aspire some mountain's top,
The way ascends not straight, but imitates
The subtle foldings of a winter's snake,
So who knows policy and her true aspect,
Shall find her ways winding and indirect.   355
(The White Devil, 1, ii, 315–55)

Cornelia's words act as dramatic prompts or as short despairing moralised commentaries on Flamineo's speech. She functions as a marker through whom the audience judge Flamineo, meanwhile giving Flamineo full rein to delineate and demonstrate his personality. Our judgement is encouraged by the deliberate dramatic contrast set up between a mother and a son, where the son rejects maternal teaching for a self-interested acquisitive ideology. What does Flamineo's language and speech tell us about his character?

First, he explicitly rejects both what his mother says and her right to say anything to him. His attitude to her is a continual double rejection: he refutes not only her ideas, but her very relationship to him. The philosophy he propounds is self-consciously in contra-distinction to hers. Her disbelieving and moralised rhetorical question, 'What? Because we are poor, / Shall we be vicious?' (ll. 115–16), is not directly answered by Flamineo. His rejection comes in the form of indirect counter-positions (the first speech), intensification of her curses (ll. 334–9), and oppositional imagery which constructs femininity and maternity as threatening and masculinity as militaristic (ll. 330–3). Flamineo is a man who rejects natural social bonds: we clearly see him abusing his filial duties, both in the content and manner of his speech and in the near-linguistic violence to his mother. Such 'unnatural' behaviour and views alert the audience to Flamineo's status as a villain.

Secondly, as we have noted, he typically answers indirectly, thus effecting two ends at once. His indirection displaces and appears to ignore her moralised agenda, establishing him as an ungrateful and unloving son. Additionally, he explicitly negates the values and virtues she represents by setting up an alternative amoral world-view. In response to her moral outrage (subtextually based upon conventional Christian morality) he narrates his alternative: economic humiliation at university and courtly service have taught him a different philosophy. He displaces her questions onto direct insults about her poverty and chastity: poverty means lack of advancement; if his mother were a whore she would have earned greater political opportunities for her son. His advocacy of a philosophy of female sexual excess as the way to his own political advancement is another indirect way of defending his pandering of Vittoria. The play's link between political advancement and the control, manipulation and sale of female sexuality is clear, and is echoed in the gleeful assertions about his courtly education ('More courteous, more lecherous by far', l. 327). His positive rejection of three traditional Christian virtues (poverty, chastity and obedience), albeit indirectly achieved, explicitly marks him out as a transgressive vice figure.

Thirdly, he focuses on worldly issues: the perceived failures of patrimony, economics and patronage, justifying his parasitism. His argument is three-fold: his parents did not provide for him; his education had to be self-financed in what he feels was a humiliating way (darning his tutor's socks); and political service at court brought him no advancement or wealth. Flamineo articulates the philosophy of the Jacobean stage malcontent, such as that in Marston's play *The Malcontent*. Such a character complains of lack of familial and political advancement and their social and political discontent becomes both a focus and a dramatic means through which disorder erupts. However, he goes further than negating the old allegiances of family and privilege: 'Having a path so open and so free / To my preferment' (ll. 329–30), and posits a world of unadulterated and amoral competition. His solipsistic libertinism, which is both political and sexual, linked with his malcontent dramatic status, establishes his character as completely amoral and completely selfish: the polar opposite to his mother. The audience is asked to judge him as such from this scene: this early in the play he is established as a self-consciously disruptive and evil influence.

Fourthly, his character echoes the cynicism and ennui of Lodovico, whose attitudes are displayed in the play's opening, as we saw in Chapter 1. The echo is a structural one also: Lodovico opened Act 1, whilst Flamineo's words close it, negating the meaning of Lodovico's banishment and returning full-circle to the continual presence of corruption.

Fifthly, the tone and language he uses reinforce an image of a selfish, self-confident young man. The rhythms are relatively regular, but the lines are run-on: he does not allow his mother to argue back. We imagine him strutting about the stage propounding his arrogant self-taught individualism. The tonal scorn for his mother, emphasised in patronising statements and belittling and humiliating insults, alienates the audience. He dismissively cries: 'Go, go, / Complain unto my great lord cardinal; / Yet may be he will justify the act' (ll. 340–2), in the same breath as he effectively asserts his own sympathies with a culture of political and sexual scandal and gross individualism.

Sixthly, in the last speech and his last words to his mother, his rhetorical delivery changes. He moves from the literal assertion and refutation of his insulting bombardment of his mother to a more generalised and philosophical discourse characterised by detailed use of analogy and metaphor. His final words to his mother on Lycurgus, the great Roman legislator, indirectly and slyly suggest that the prince could treat courtiers' wives merely as breeders: if they do not generate, like mares, why sentimentally hold onto them? Cornelia's horrified response precipitates her departure. Her moral position has literally been driven off stage by her son's mocking reduction of women to breeding mares. The final set of metaphors are used when he is on stage alone, for nine lines at the close of the act. His language is less hectoring, although his philosophy remains the same. He never pretends to be someone whom he is not. This short soliloquy is addressed to the audience, and further reinforces his dramatic function as stage villain: both in the direct address and in the content: 'We are engaged to mischief and must on' (l. 348). He then uses three successive natural analogies (the crooked river, the winding mountain path, and the 'subtle foldings of a winter's snake', ll. 350–3) to defend his own actions. His use of natural images gives a surface plausibility to his argument: if it is natural, it must be right. However, the final analogy (of the snake) robs his argument of validity. For the snake's other connotations are of temptation and fall. His closing couplet ('So who knows policy and her true aspect, / Shall find her ways winding and indirect') is thus, though superficially valid in the world which he describes and we experience, undermined via the snake analogy. His own words finally condemn him.

The audience is led successively to judge him by all these different dramatic and rhetorical means: there are no redeeming features in his actions, his relationships, his politics, or the dramatic function of malcontented villain which he gleefully appropriates. The overall effect of his characterisation causes us to reflect on Vittoria's character in this scene. How far is she to blame, and how far is she being manipulated by her brother? Who is the greater devil? Webster raises such questions in the audience's mind: questions which, as we have seen, continue to dominate the play. Webster's characters do not tell us what their interior life is like: in this he differs from Shakesepeare. Instead, he illustrates character in action, in a particular dramatic situation, and he uses dialogue, setting, and a little monologue, to enable the audience to judge a character. This also gives actors greater freedom of interpretation in a role: an interpretation based on situation and dialogue, rather than an illustration of the words of an interior monologue.

How are the other villains of this play characterised? The following speech by Francisco is one of the longest monologues in the play.

[Act 4, Scene i]

Francisco.	To fashion my revenge more seriously,	
	Let me remember my dead sister's face;	
	Call for her picture; no, I'll close mine eyes,	100
	And in a melancholic thought I'll frame	
	Her figure 'fore me.	
	Enter Isabella's ghost.	
	Now I ha't – how strong	
	Imagination works! How she can frame	
	Things which are not! Methinks she stands afore me;	
	And by the quick idea of my mind,	105

Were my skill pregnant, I could draw her picture.
Thought, as a subtle juggler, makes us deem
Things supernatural, which have cause
Common as sickness. 'Tis my melancholy. –
How cam'st thou by thy death? – How idle am I   110
To question mine own idleness? – Did ever
Man dream awake till now? – Remove this object;
Out of my brain with't! What have I to do
With tombs, or death-beds, funerals, or tears.
That have to meditate upon revenge?   115

                                        Exit Ghost

So now 'tis ended, like an old wives' story.
Statesmen think often they see stranger sights
Than madmen. Come, to this weighty business.
My tragedy must have some idle mirth in't,
Else it will never pass. I am in love,   120
In love with Corombona and my suit
Thus halts in her to verse.   *He writes.*
I have done it rarely. O, the fate of princes!
I am so used to frequent flattery
That being alone I now flatter myself;   125
But it will serve, 'tis sealed.

                    Enter Servant
                        Bear this
To th'house of convertites, and watch your leisure
To give it to the hands of Corombona,
Or to the matron, when some followers
Of Bracciano may be by. Away. –   130

                                Exit Servant.

He that deals all by strength, his wit is shallow;
When a man's head goes through, each limb will follow.
The engine for my business, bold Count Lodowick: –
'Tis gold must such an instrument procure,
With empty fist no man doth falcons lure.   135
Bracciano, I am now fit for thy encounter.
Like the wild Irish I'll never think thee dead
Till I can play at football with your head.

Flectere si nequeo superos, Acheronta movebo.
(*The White Devil* 4, iv, 98–139)

Francisco has just demanded and received from Monticelso his 'black book', a list of all known murderers, panders, poisoners and rogues, and told the audience that he does not trust Monticelso, keeping his own revenge plot between himself and the audience. Francisco's soliloquy falls into three distinct parts, each of which represents a development and shift in his thinking. Each part is announced by a clear and firm directional proposition or change of pace, and two out of the three end in a rhyming couplet.

The first part of this soliloquy (ll. 98–118) is focused on internal feelings ('Let me remember my dead sister's face'), and on what becomes a logical extension of that, Isabella's appearance on stage as a ghost. It falls into four parts: the calling up of Isabella; Francisco's musings on the ghost's appearance; his questioning of her; and his dismissal. Webster gives Francisco's internal feelings and thoughts a visual embodiment on stage, endowing his revenge with an added intensity for the audience. We literally see his inner life embodied and debated on stage. The summoning of the ghost has a magical quality to it: the stage must be darker, the delivery of the lines slower, as we observe her sliding across the stage. The rhythm of the invocation is slower (ll. 98–101), a change of pace continuing in the second more reflective section (ll. 101–9) where we see run-on lines, exclamations, questions, and pauses. In this second part, the internal rhythms of the lines are more irregular: he makes two exclamations, both under ten syllables, run-on and ending mid-line (ll. 102–4). This is followed by two longer sentences, also of roughly equal length (ll. 104–6 and 107–9). Both the exclamations and the two sentences marvel at the phenomenon of imagination: at how clearly she is imaged, and at the power of thought to deceive us. The content of these seven lines is a diversion from his revenge: an internal philosophical musing. Francisco is conscious of the inwardness of his thoughts: appending an explanatory ''Tis my melancholy' (l. 109). This creates a pause before he shifts into inquisitorial mood, and the second part of this section. The following five lines are a set of questions, and an exclamatory command: the first to Isabella, and the rest more wryly to himself. The first three questions illustrate his grief, distraction and a generalised intelligent awareness of his current situation. The first two alternating questions (the first to the ghost, the second to himself) engender an ironised self-mockery, emphasised by the repetition of 'idle'/'idleness'. The third question is more generally rhetorical and philosophical, allowing him now to stand completely outside himself and observe the situation: 'Did ever / Man dream awake till now?' (ll. 111–12).

The emotional logic of his speech draws the audience into his mind and his situation. At one moment he is engaging intensely with the fictive image of his sister, at the next berating himself for his folly in speaking to figments of his imagination, at the next gently mocking all humans for folly. Whatever we might feel about his subsequent chosen course of action and morality, here we sympathise with his grief, distraction, and the manic self-mockery of an intelligent man pushed to the edge of existence and sanity. The final lines of this section (ll. 112–18) are marked by a change of mood and pace, indicated by the move to a peremptory ordered exclamation ('Remove this object, / Out of my brain with't'), and the final rhetorical question which rejects emotion and plumps for action. This opposition between the passivity of sorrow and the activity of revenge is both gendered and naturalised by his metaphor and analogy. His passive distraction is 'like an old wives' story' (l. 116), but excused because 'statesmen think often they see stranger sights/Than madmen' (ll. 117–18): a feminine weakness that is attendant upon the stresses of political life, but to be disregarded.

The second part of his soliloquy is introduced and marked by a commanding vocative ('Come, to this weighty business'), and an invocation of theatricality, which infuses his views and actions ('My tragedy must have some idle mirth in't, / Else it will never pass', ll. 119–20). He has twice stated that he plots 'revenge' (l. 98 and l. 115), positing his character's self-conscious status as revenger. We have discussed the significance of the revenge figure for Bosola in Chapter 2. Francisco takes on this dramatic persona quite self-consciously: this is clear in his machinations and the masques of Act 5. It is important for the audience to see this self-consciousness because it makes the plot and our sympathies less black and white. Whilst we see Francisco's actions as both duplicitous and evil, we are distanced from complete condemnation by the fact that he tells us he is a conventional character undertaking a conventional role. This has two divergent effects: it helps us to listen objectively to him, and thereby to sympathise with his losses, but it also makes us see all the characters as manipulated puppets. Francisco expresses his self-consciousness as an attractive and witty self-parody: 'O, the fate of princes! / I am so used to frequent flattery / That being alone I now flatter myself' (ll. 123–5). He sends off the false letter to further blacken Vittoria's name, ending this section on a couplet: 'He that deals all by strength, his wit is shallow; / When a man's head goes through, each limb will follow' (ll. 131–2). This self-congratulation on his rational wit and wiliness are those of a typical revenger: witty and attractive, but self-destructively arrogant. He has moved from the self-consciousness of commenting on his own actions to a statement of absolutism, which must be read as self-deception. The audience recognises the shift by the couplet, emphasising through its 'de-dum-de-dum' rhythm and rhyme the simplistic wisdom Francisco is peddling to justify revenge. His pride and arrogance, that amoral wit will win, is later echoed by Lodovico in the closing moments of Act 5. Lodovico's connection to the absent Francisco in the finale is thus both physical and intellectual: when the audience watch the finale, Lodovico's words and actions eerily echo his absent master's.

The third, and final, part of this soliloquy (ll. 133–9) is the most direct section: Francisco delineates his plot to use Lodovico and to kill Bracciano. The seven lines contain two couplets and one Latin tag: so their cumulative effect is of a surfeit of proverbial wisdom. This again distances the audience from Francisco: his platitudes suggest actions directed by proverbs and not his own decisions. Yet the individual meaning of his final couplet is genuinely disturbing: 'Like the wild Irish I'll never think thee dead / Till I can play at football with thy head' (ll. 137–8). The intensity of his venom is graphically conveyed in his doubled analogy: of himself as an Irishman, who were perceived as savages by the English, and of playing a triumphal game with Bracciano's head. The disturbing and horrific nature of this prospective revenge is underlined in the meaning of his Latin tag, 'If I cannot prevail on the Gods above, I will move the infernal regions', which explicitly acknowledges his parallel with the devil. The dramatic revenger figure is here explicitly also the Vice figure of the older morality plays, who represented the devil in human form, tempting mankind to evil. The Vice always drew explicit attention to their devilish status to clarify the audience's judgement against them. These final words, spoken by Francisco directly to the audience, have precisely this effect.

In summary, then, this long soliloquy illustrates an intimate connection between language and thought: changes of pace, rhythm and rhyme are used to convey a sense of shifting thought processes and emotions. The abrupt transitions between each part of the speech create a sense of realism: that we really are listening to a man in an emotional tangle, and that there is an emotional logic to his words. This increases both our absorption and our horror: a combination making for an effective tragic villain. The staging helps validate this: we believe in the fiction that he is speaking frankly, because for the most part he is alone on stage. The vicious truths, his invocation of hell and revenge, are spoken only to himself and to us. We share in his black world: and this both repulses and attracts. His self-knowledge extends only to the nature of the roles he plays and his own damnation: he does not place his actions within the wider framework of political and theological corruption.

However, the audience has been encouraged to position him within that framework in two ways. First he is literally and physically framed by corruption in the scene. The soliloquy begins after Monticelso has left, having displayed his manipulating character, and the subsequent scene moves on to the consequences of their deception in the house of convertites. Secondly, his own plans echo, unconsciously, the very corruptions of which he accuses Monticelso.

Thus staging, stage directions, scenic structure and the language of the soliloquy conspire to place the audience in an ambiguous position towards Francisco. We sympathise with his emotions: but we condemn the conclusions he comes to. Webster ensures that the tension between these two poles is maintained throughout the scene, and it is essential to our engagement with the play and the characters. Our perception of this tension is our means of comprehending the nature of the tragedy.

*   *   *

Let us now turn to the men in *The Duchess of Malfi.*

[Act 2, Scene i]

Old lady.   It seems you are well acquainted with my closet.

Bosola.   One would suspect it for a shop of witchcraft, to find
in it the fat of serpents, spawn of snakes, Jew's spittle, and
their young children's ordure – and all these for the face.   40
I would sooner eat a dead pigeon, taken from the soles of
the feet of one sick of the plague, than kiss one of you
fasting. Here are two of you whose sin of your youth is the
very patrimony of the physician, makes him renew his
footcloth with the spring and change his high-prized   45
courtesan with the fall of the leaf: I do wonder you do not
loathe yourselves. Observe my meditation now:

     What thing is in this outward form of man
     To be beloved? We account it ominous
     If nature do produce a colt, or lamb,   50
     A fawn, or goat, in any limb resembling
     A man, and fly from 't as a prodigy.
     Man stands amazed to see his deformity
     In any other creature but himself.
     But in our own flesh, though we bear diseases   55
     Which have their true names only ta'en from beasts,
     As the most ulcerous wolf and swinish measle,
     Though we are eaten up of lice and worms,
     And though continually we bear about us
     A rotten and dead body, we delight   60
     To hide it in rich tissue. All our fear –
     Nay, all our terror – is lest our physician
     Should put us in the ground, to be made sweet. –
Your wife's gone to Rome; you two couple, and get you
To the wells at Lucca, to recover your aches.   65
                 Exit Castruchio and Old Lady.
I have other work on foot. I observe our Duchess

Is sick o'days, she pukes, her stomach seethes,
(*The Duchess of Malfi*, 2, vi, 37–67)

This scene begins with Bosola chatting to Castruchio about inconsequentials: the kind of informal chat that precedes the entrance of more important characters: echoing the informal opening of Act 1. Bosola's marginal social status is replicated in his liminal stage and narrative position. He speaks most directly, either to his equals or to the audience, at the beginnings and ends of scenes before or after characters with higher status appear. Yet this marginality belies his role in the play: as the Duchess's Provisor of Horse, as the brothers' spy, and later as Revenger figure, his actions become increasingly central to the crises and resolution of the play. Nevertheless, his social marginality remains. The mismatch between his narrative centrality and social acceptance displays fame, reward and status as dependent on birth and not on action or character. The coincidence of dramatic structure with Bosola's own critique of the dominance of social status illustrates that his interpretations and character are essential to our understanding of the play. His views often coincide with our perceptions: partly because he steps aside from the action and comments upon it; partly because Webster structures the play to encourage this; and partly since Bosola undergoes a kind of epiphany generated by the Duchess's heroic courage. Let us return now to this speech.

This is not technically a soliloquy: he addresses his insults to the old lady and, at the end of the speech, to Castruchio, and they are present on stage, listening to his 'meditation' (l. 47) until line 65. Nevertheless, the speech has many of the modal characteristics of a soliloquy. Bosola speaks uninterrupted, he self-consciously sets himself up as though he is speaking a soliloquy to the old lady ('Observe my meditation now'), and simultaneously moves into verse-speaking, and on their exit he directly addresses the audience. The content is that of a conventional soliloquy: it is philosophical, self-reflexive and revelatory, and both directly and indirectly addressed to the audience. His self-conscious theatricality consistently places him conceptually and physically midway between the action on the stage and the audience's interpretation and judgement.

This speech falls into three parts: his misogynist address to the old lady; his 'meditation' on mortality; and his address to the audience.

During this speech the audience are waiting to see what has happened between the Duchess and Antonio: tension and anticipation are paradoxically released and raised when Bosola hints at her pregnancy. His desire for explicit knowledge coincides with ours. Our sympathies were clearly with the Duchess and Antonio at the end of Act 1: Webster deliberately, then, constructs a dramatic impatience with the characters on stage here. We want the action to move on from them. What then is the function of their appearance?

The first is to establish an opposition between the private spaces and experiences of female sexuality and childbirth and the public places and postures of masculinity. Bosola's misogyny is generalised, but directed personally at the old lady: attacking her hypothecated use of cosmetics as equivalent to witchcraft. He creates an exaggerated fantasy, imagining her make-up as excreta and body fluids (ll. 39–40). His physical disgust is expressed indirectly through this displaced fantasy, and then directly through his imagining the stench of her breath (ll. 41–3). The images with which he insults her all invoke smelly body orifices (spitting, spawning, sweating fat, ordure, bad breath). The direct attack on women as physically repellent, which then slides into an attack on sexuality as sinful (ll. 44–7) echoes the views of the Duchess's brothers. Bosola's views and his employment by the brothers remind us of their agenda to control their sister's sexuality. The expression of such extreme misogyny indirectly engenders our sympathies for the Duchess. Bosola's overt misogyny ensures that the audience both await the discovery with greater trepidation, and are given the means whereby to criticise this kind of jealous, invasive and misogynist masculinity. The visual difference between an old lady and the strutting, sly Bosola here reinforces our sympathies with women and against the brothers' invasive actions. In the next scene we learn that the old lady is the Duchess's midwife. She becomes the symbolic bearer of a secret feminine knowledge in opposition to the men's desire to possess and survey such secrets. Bosola's language and character are a dramatic opposition to natural female sexuality. More intimately, his misogyny aids his general air of misanthropy and his self-construction as a malcontent-type figure.

The second part of the speech echoes this presentation of him as a malcontent. The sentence immediately following his request that they observe his meditation is framed as a philosophical problem: 'What thing is in this outward form of man / To be beloved?' (ll. 47–8). The nature of this question and its content indicate the malcontent's stance and outlook: misanthropic, apt to generalise philosophically, a commentator upon the dramatic action from a sceptical viewpoint. The overall meaning is in the Christian *contemptum mundi* (contempt for worldly things) tradition. This language lends credibility to his status of objective observer, which is reinforced by the solemnity of the turn to metrical regularity, and the academic question. His objective status is reinforced by his example of man's folly. He uses analogical arguments to point out that human perception of the world is completely subjective. In nature men are amazed at the appearance of human traits in animals. By contrast, the appearance of animal diseases in man is shamefully hidden. In other words, humans always judge the world from their own narrow human perspective, not a relativist one, and condemn aberration. This radical idea echoes throughout the play in several ways. First, it reiterates the theme of outer deceit and inner reality. Secondly, it suggests implicitly that humans are only animals underneath their fine tissues of clothing: an idea that resonates later in both the sexual desire of the Duchess and the descent of Ferdinand into the disease of lycanthropia. Thirdly, it imagines a world where worldly status is irrelevant and meaningless. Bosola's words are therefore philosophically, biologically and socially radical. The philosophy and language come from a Christian tradition of expounding on the vanity of the world, but Bosola's message is not explicitly Christian.

His words echo on stage, an echo literally created by the repetition of 'though' to make each additive point. His climactic point is made through that repetition: 'Though we are eaten up of lice and worms, / And though we continually bear about us / A rotten and dead body, we delight / To hide it in rich tissue' (ll. 58–61). Bosola exposes this hypocrisy as 'terror' of mortality. His ability to see through social and political behaviour to an inner 'truth' is both an essential part of the conventional malcontent and possibly his central characteristic. It is why, even though we may not like him or trust him, we tend to believe him. He speaks what we also see happening in Malfi.

The metaphors he uses throughout this speech consistently create a world-view sceptical of appearances. The vehicles of his metaphors here (witchcraft, animals, disease, deformity, and clothing) all occur elsewhere in the play, both as metaphors and literally within the plot, and suggest a chaotic and unredeeming world. Bosola's vision of a purposeless world explains his sense of rootlessness and anger, and acts as a critique of the status-bound world inhabited by the brothers. His critique indirectly aids our sympathy for the Duchess, who is oppressed by the hypocrisy of that world. She and Bosola are linked as social and gender victims of the privileged and closed world of degenerate aristocratic masculinity. However, they also act as dramatic contrasts in the divergent ways in which they each choose to counteract that world. The Duchess does so through fulfilling her own desire and finding a private escape. Bosola does so by taking on the unsatisfying role of malcontent: he comments on corruption, but ends by being a part of it. Nevertheless, Bosola's perceptive and powerful articulation of the disjunction of this world is precisely our perception too.

The final part of his speech is addressed directly to the audience and propels the narrative of the play forward. It is the first time we realise some time has passed since the end of Act 1. Bosola moves back to his role as spy–villain, clarifying again his alliance with her brothers against the Duchess.

Overall, then, this speech is interesting in shifting the audience's point of view three times: first we sympathise with the old lady and condemn Bosola's misogyny; then we move to agree with his attack on hypocrisy; and finally we move back to seeing him as the plotting villain. Why does Webster force us to change our point of view? Partly, because he wants a thinking and responsive audience; and partly because it helps construct a more complex character; but it is also because he wants us to see characters embedded in a political context. Bosola is never completely condemned by the play, nor the Duchess completely approved. Changing our point of view within and between speeches and scenes helps us to see character and action as dependent upon context, and moral judgement as complex. It also aids dramatic tension: we are always aware of Bosola's ambiguous allegiance to the brothers, but can only hope he changes sides before a tragic denouement. This tension and ambiguity are essential to our responses to some of the key confrontation scenes between Bosola and the Duchess. His vacillation between misogyny, philosophical objectivity and plotting, mark him as a character with whom we have a love–hate interest. Bosola functions more generally in the play as a *memento mori* character: reminding us of our own mortality through action and attitude.

*   *   *

Let us move on to the characterisation of the two brothers.

[Act 2, Scene v]

Cardinal.	Shall our blood,
	The royal blood of Aragon and Castile,
	Be thus attainted?
Ferdinand.	Apply desperate physic.
	We must not now use balsamum, but fire,
	The smarting cupping glass, for that's the mean 25
	To purge infected blood, such blood as hers.
	There is a kind of pity in mine eye;
	I'll give it to my handker; and now, 'tis here,
	I'll bequeath this to her bastard.
Cardinal.	What to do?
Ferdinand.	Why, to make soft lint for his mother's wounds, 30
	When I have hewed her to pieces.
Cardinal.	Cursed creature!
	Unequal Nature, to place women's hearts
	So far upon the left side!
Ferdinand.	Foolish men,
	That e'er will trust their honour in a bark
	Made of so slight, weak bulrush as is woman, 35
	Apt every minute to sink it!
Cardinal.	Thus ignorance, when it hath purchased honour,
	It cannot wield it.
Ferdinand.	Methinks I see her laughing –

	Excellent hyena! – Talk to me somewhat, quickly,	
	Or my imagination will carry me	40
	To see her in the shameful act of sin.	
Cardinal.	With whom?	
Ferdinand.	Happily with some strong-thighed bargeman,	
	Or one o'th'woodyard, that can quoit the sledge	
	Or toss the bar, or else some lovely squire	
	That carries coals up to her privy lodgings.	45
Cardinal.	You fly beyond your reason.	
Ferdinand.	Go to, mistress!	
	'Tis not your whore's milk that shall quench my wildfire,	
	But your whore's blood.	
Cardinal.	How idly shows this rage, which carries you,	
	As men conveyed by witches through the air,	50
	On violent whirlwinds! This intemperate noise	
	Fitly resembles deaf men's shrill discourse,	
	Who talk aloud, thinking all other men	
	To have their imperfection.	
Ferdinand.	Have not you	
	My palsy?	
Cardinal.	Yes – I can be angry	55
	Without this rupture. There is not in nature	
	A thing that makes man so deformed, so beastly,	
	As doth intemperate anger. Chide yourself:	
	You have divers men who never yet expressed	
	Their strong desire of rest but by unrest,	60
	By vexing of themselves. Come, put yourself	
	In tune.	
Ferdinand.	So. I will only study to seem	
	The thing I am not. – I could kill her now,	
	In you, or in myself, for I do think	
	It is some sin in us heaven doth revenge	65
	By her.	
Cardinal.	Are you stark mad?	
Ferdinand.	I would have their bodies	

> Burnt in a coal-pit, with the ventage stopped,
> That their cursed smoke might not ascend to heaven;
> Or dip the sheets they lie in in pitch or sulphur,
> Wrap them in't, and then light them like a
>   match;   70
> Or else to boil their bastard to a cullis,
> And give't his lecherous father, to renew
> The sin of his back.

Cardinal.   I'll leave you.
Ferdinand.   Nay, I have done.
> I am confident, had I been damned in hell
> And should have heard of this, it would have put me   75
> Into a cold sweat. – In, in; I'll go sleep. –
> Till I know who leaps my sister, I'll not stir:
> That known, I'll find scorpions to string my whips,
> And fix her in a general eclipse.   *Exeunt.*
>   (*The Duchess of Malfi*, 2, v, 21–79)

Ferdinand comes onto the stage at the beginning of this scene, reading a letter from Bosola informing him of his sister's pregnancy. None of them yet know the identity of her lover. Webster uses a minimum of exchanges to begin to establish the divergence in the two brothers' characters. This is a genuine dialogue, moving forwards as they engage with each other. Because they are brothers we note their divergent responses to the same event: they express anger differently and their proposed actions are different. The doubling of characters enables Webster to show the audience different points of view and encourage us to judge comparatively. It also helps us to think of them as believable and realistic characters. The scene as a whole is very short (a mere 79 lines), aiding our sense of quick-moving events precipitated by the discovery, and of intensity of emotion and response. The Cardinal speaks about twenty-two lines to Ferdinand's forty: the latter's doubled volume representing his uncontrolled emotions.

The Cardinal's response to the news remains constant all the way through this scene, creating the impression of a cold, calculating anger. This characterisation is validated by his actions later in the play: his punishment of his sister is political, his brother's, emotional. His first response to the news is about how the news affects his own political and social status (the royal blood is tainted). His third response displays a generalised patriarchal misogyny: in which women are condemned as both cursed (from Eve's inheritance) and physiologically inferior (their heart is further to the left). The mode and content of his curse pre-suppose a personal superiority. He can look down and condemn her: he is not emotionally involved. Five of his responses are objectively enquiring, short questions or statements to or on Ferdinand's raving: 'What to do?' (l. 29); 'With whom?' (l. 42); 'You fly beyond your reason' (l. 46); 'Are you stark mad?' (l. 66); and 'I'll leave you' (l. 73). The terse questions and statements reflect his unemotional reaction as well as his amazement at Ferdinand's excess. When the Cardinal speaks at any greater length he does so in very regular iambic pentameters, conveying the impression that his anger and emotions are under control. The content of everything else he says is confidently rational: but all are commentaries on Ferdinand's response, we do not really gauge a sense of his interior or emotional response to the Duchess's actions, other than concern for his loss of honour. Hence his comment at lines 37–8, beginning with a logical 'Thus', sounds like a proverbial pat piece of wisdom. Similarly, his 'How idly shows this rage' (ll. 49ff) objectifies and slows down Ferdinand's ranting.

He rebukes Ferdinand for his violent loss of reason and assumption that everyone feels in the same way, 'This intemperate noise / Fitly resembles deaf men's shrill discourse/ Who talk aloud, thinking all other men / To have their imperfection' (ll. 51–4). He uses the judgement 'intemperate' twice (again at line 58), opposing this to his self-description as 'angry' without 'this rupture', positing a colder, planned out, balanced anger. He argues that Ferdinand's extremity is dangerous: 'You have divers men who never yet expressed / Their strong desire of rest but by unrest, / By vexing of themselves. Come, put yourself / In tune' (ll. 59–62). His loving care for his brother's emotional balance here is unique in the play, and it is only momentary. The Cardinal is a supremely rational, cold and controlled man: he displays no feelings of affection for his sister, and only some for his brother. We do not get a feel for an interior life. His professed rationality both makes Ferdinand seem more unbalanced, and uses the language of balance and harmony to signify mental stability.

Ferdinand has three types of response here: violent threats; rationally articulated imaginings about the lovers; and direct addresses to the Duchess as though she is present. Despite the Cardinal's urgings to a cooler response, his threats become progressively more violent. In one line he veers from an acceptance of the Cardinal's advice (ll. 61–2) straight back to a threat: 'I could kill her now' (l. 62): so linguistically we see him unable to eschew his 'palsy' (l. 55). His threatened violence is mostly expressed through metaphor and analogy. Despite the fact that metaphor is an indirect expression (denoting something by something that it is *not*), the surprising overall effect of these metaphors is of a more frightening, pervasive violence. He uses no metaphors between lines 48 and 78, and we shall return to his more literal statements in a minute. His first metaphor is the purgation of infected blood with cupping glasses, by fire (ll. 24–6). This is an explicitly sadistic misogynist reference: cupping glasses were used to purge blood from women's breasts. His second is a metonymic reference to killing Antonio's mother, through the conversion of his handkerchief to lint (ll. 30–1). The third is of woman as a frail, sinking boat (ll. 34–6); the fourth, his address to the Duchess as 'hyena' (l. 39); and the fifth, his description of his anger as 'wildfire' (l. 47). The sixth is in the final couplet: 'That known, / I'll find scorpions to string my whips, / And fix her in a general *eclipse*' (ll. 78–9): echoing forth the arrival of complete and utter darkness. In all cases except the fourth and fifth, he uses metaphors as part of his threatening violence and misogyny. They all share a common frame of reference: a world in which natural forces have become violently out of control. Thus vehicle, tenor and intent merge. Ferdinand's perception of the world mirrors his own internal turmoil. Webster suggests these perceptions are a displacement of his inner emotions.

Ferdinand's more literally expressed violence, after he agrees to 'study to seem / the thing I am not' (ll. 62–3), nevertheless retains the quality of metaphor. He imagines situations of torture and violence and eagerly describes very detailed punishments for the audience to envisage. They include burning the lovers in a coal pit, dipping sheets in sulphur and pitch to burn them in, boiling their child in a broth, stinging them with a whip made of scorpions, and imagining himself damned in hell, put into a cold sweat by the news. This literalisation of popular images of hell and damnation imagines a disordered and abusive world. Ferdinand places himself in the role of devil as punishment-giver.

His second type of response, rationally articulated imaginings about the lovers, form the fewest lines here (ll. 40–5): the rhetoric is lucid, the lines run-on and very regular. But paradoxically, the linguistic regularity sandwiched by emotional irrationality makes his imaginings both frightening and insane. This is intensified by the almost manic detail he allocates to these images: the strong-thighed bargeman, the carrying of coals. The images he conjures here share two semantic fields. Their intense physicality suggests Ferdinand is madly jealous, obsessive about his sister's sexual actions. Secondly, the men he imagines are all labourers, denoting his fears about his sister's marriage, inheritance and status. The closed aristocratic society advocated by the brothers is thence demonstrated by the linking of these two semantic fields to be both incestuous (in the wider sense of the word) and obsessively status-led. His imaginings echo the Cardinal's more measured statements.

Ferdinand's third type of response is manic delusions: addressing his sister directly as though she is present. In doing so he uses two of the metaphors we referred to above, one to characterise *her* (as a hyena), the other *himself* (as wildfire). When he conjures her up, 'Methinks I see her laughing – / Excellent hyena! – Talk to me somewhat, quickly, / Or my imagination will carry me / To see her in the shameful act of sin' (ll. 38–41), the rhythms and beat of the line become very irregular, ranging between 10 and 13 beats in the first speech, and 11 and 4 in the second ('Go to, mistress . . .', ll. 46–8). The last line, of 4 beats, ensures a pause in his delivery, and, followed by the Cardinal's 'How idly shows this rage' (l. 49), suggests that Ferdinand may be gasping from anger and distress in this pause. His excessive emotionalism is clear through his earlier reference to his weeping (ll. 27–8) as well as the 'wildfire' analogy: and this pause suggests he actually requires a break to recover physically.

Finally, there are three other features of his self-presentation that deserve commentary. The first is the unnatural detail he gives to his imaginings and metaphors: not only does he imagine a bargeman, but a strong-thighed one; not only does he imagine the lovers burning, but he envisages it in a pit without vents so their smoke cannot ascend to heaven. These kinds of details render his madness credible: the delineation of a visualisable alternative world partly defines our idea of madness. Webster thus succeeds in drawing us into an understanding and visualisation of Ferdinand as believably unhinged.

The second feature of his delivery is the number of times he refers to himself, both through the use of the first person pronoun, and through his description of actions he proposes. He uses 'I' or 'my' or 'mine' 24 times and 'us' twice, in about thirty lines. This self-referentiality is unusual in Webster's dialogues, and further displays Ferdinand as both obsessively introspective and selfish. Along with the Cardinal, then, Ferdinand is only concerned about the Duchess in so far as it concerns himself. However, the Cardinal is mostly worried about blood-taint. Ferdinand's motives are less explicitly articulated, but clearly invoke a jealous ownership over his sister's sexuality. Thirdly, the rhythms and delivery of Ferdinand's lines are both very varied and expressive, ranging from regular pentameters to the 4-beat line. In his last three speeches, the mania of what he says spills into the delivery: although the Cardinal interrupts him twice, these are short mid-line interventions, and Ferdinand completes the line (lines 66 and 73). Delivery and dialogue concur to render a realistically increasing mania.

Characterisation thus clarifies the audience's perceptions of Webster's criticism of a closed masculine world: the brothers' divergent responses to the same event are seen as equally extreme to the audience, both dangerous and selfish, a perception engendered by the suppressed, terse violence in this scene and those surrounding it.

Conclusions

1. Male protagonists often express a self-consciousness about their dramatic functions: either as Vice, Revenger or malcontent

figures, or a combination of all three. Their characteristics are both conventional and unconventional in Webster's plays. The Vice and Revenger are conventional in being the agents of chaos and disruption, in their self-conscious links to the devil; the malcontents in their political critiques; and both, in their liminal staging position that allows them to speak directly to the audience. They are unconventional in their occasionally doubled function: Bosola begins as a malcontent and becomes a revenger.

2. The ethically ambiguous male protagonists alone address the audience directly: the heroines do not. This generates a morally ambiguous drama, demanding a self-reflexive audience. Are we closer to Bosola than to the Duchess?

3. Webster characteristically uses doubled and contrasting male characters: Flamineo and Bracciano; Francisco and Monticelso in *The White Devil*; and Bosola and Antonio; the Cardinal and Ferdinand in *The Duchess of Malfi*. The latter pair is ultimately more corrupt than the former, who become victims of the other's abuse of power. Additionally, within each pair, the characters face similar trials but respond differently. Antonio's lower status and distaste for courtly life have moulded an honest and self-effacing servant: in contrast, Bosola's similar status turns him into a Vice figure. We have seen how both the Cardinal and Ferdinand, and Francisco and Monticelso are contrasted in these extracts. Doubling creates several ends: it enables the audience to judge the Vice characters comparatively; it places all characters within a broader moral and political context; and it encourages us to see the colder, hands-off characters as the most politically dangerous.

4. Webster shows brothers manipulating their sisters' sexual behaviour and marriages (Flamineo manipulates Vittoria, and Ferdinand and the Cardinal attempt to control the Duchess). He displays the brothers' controlling function through visual staging mechanisms, narrative structure, plot and characterisation. This emphatic dramatisation asks the audience to criticise the brothers' actions.

5. Self-knowledge in the villains is often partial: for example, in both Francisco and Ferdinand. However, self-knowledge comes to Bosola, and to some extent to Flamineo (as we saw in Chapter

2), in whom it produces a partial redemption in the eyes of the audience.

6. Webster concentrates his dramatic energies on multiple villains, not individual heroes.

7. Imagery, rhythm, pace, stage position and verbal content all fuse to construct and illustrate both internal characteristics and a character's external place in the world.

8. Extremity of emotional response is indicated by the break-up of regular rhythms and structures, by the use of characters' over-active imaginations, and by an emphatic and extreme egoism. Both Francisco and Ferdinand, two brothers intent upon revenging a sister's honour, go mad in similar ways: imagination makes other worlds visible to them, and renders their view of the world around them completely solipsistic.

Methods of Analysis

1. This chapter has followed the methodology of the previous chapters, most particularly Chapter 4, on characterisation.

2. In addition, we have begun to consider how Webster uses character pairs, and contrasting and divergent responses to the same or similar situations, in order to deepen characterisation and demand judgement between characters.

3. We have noted the self-conscious nature of Webster's characterisation: both its theatricality and the way a sense of realism is built up from a set of mechanical building blocks (such as rhythm, pairing, stage placing, self-reference, imagery, action and so on).

4. We have made judgements about Webster's dramatic intentions (for example the power of brothers and political systems against women): but in doing so we have focussed on internal dramatic evidence, rather than imposing contemporary judgements on a Jacobean text.

Suggested Work

We noted in our Conclusion (point 3) that Webster doubles his male villains to complicate plot and characterisation. Here we need to do two things: broaden and deepen our analysis of the characters we have looked at, and extend that analysis to those we did not have space for: Monticelso, Bracciano and Antonio.

The White Devil
1. Look at Flamineo's speech in 5, iv, 114–53 ('I have a strange thing in me, to th'which / I cannot give a name, without it be / Compassion'). To what extent is this moment epiphanic for the character's tragic self-awareness?
2. Bracciano is sometimes described as the 'hero' of the play: he appears in many scenes, and his immediate actions and desires bring about Vittoria's fall. Analyse the different ways in which he is characterised in Act 1, Scene ii and Act 2, Scene i. What is the effect of the differences between and juxtaposition of these two scenes? What do you think of the relationship between Flamineo and Bracciano? Have a look at Act 4, Scene ii, in order to deepen your response to this question. Look at his wedding and then his death in Act 5, Scene iii. In what ways and why does Webster represent him as heroic? What is the effect of this?
3. Look at all the scenes in which Monticelso appears (Act 2, Scene i; Act 3, Scenes i and ii; Act 4, Scenes i and iii): how does Webster characterise him? What dramatic means does he use to encourage us to judge him and what do you think that judgement is?
4. Finally look also at Giovanni: he appears in 2, i, 95–146 and then is on stage during the fight in Act 5, Scene iii, and again at the close of the play. Does his earlier characterisation enable us to believe in his ability to restore order?

The Duchess of Malfi
Look at the character of Antonio, building on our observations in Chapters 1 and 4. How far is he overshadowed by both the Duchess and Bosola? Does he establish a moral yardstick in the play? To what

extent is he merely a foil for the Duchess's forcefulness, Bosola's mal-contentedness and the brothers' jealousy? Is a 'good man' a contradiction in terms for Webster? Look at Act 5, Scenes iii and iv: the graveyard echo scene, and then Antonio's accidental murder. Does our view of him change here? Does he become a tragic hero, or simply an accidental casualty of war?

6

Society and Politics

Webster repeatedly draws attention to political situations and to the way in which all individuals are embedded in their social and political milieu. We have also seen that he dramatises political and legal conflict and corruption, often focusing on debates about, and struggles for, female sexuality. In the first two chapters we discussed how he created a corrupt and divided society through staging and content, raising questions about the correct ethical path within a political world and about the relationship between individualism and the state. We saw in Chapter 2 how the plays' closing moments both resolve some of these issues and posit open-ended questions about the endemic nature of self-interest and political corruption. In this chapter we shall look explicitly at the society and politics of his dramatic worlds within two extracts, analysing how social structure and political conduct are intimately connected; how characterisation is a key way in which Webster engages our own political views; and the function of gender within the political crises.

Let us turn first to the extract from *The White Devil*.

*   *   *

Act 2 opens very formally with the entrance of the Cardinal's court, but the first conversation is a private one between Francisco and his sister Isabella, and some jesting with Giovanni. Mother and son are asked to depart before the main political business commences. From its opening, the scene thence sets up a contrasting visual and conceptual image between public and private: they are separate but inti-

mately connected. On the arrival of Bracciano, Monticelso commands all the courtiers to 'void the chamber' (l. 19).

[Act 2, Scene i]

Monticelso.	It is a wonder to your noble friends
	That you that have as 'twere entered the world
	With a free sceptre in your able hand,
	And have to th'use of nature well applied
	High gifts of learning, should in your prime age 30
	Neglect your awful throne for the soft down
	Of an insatiate bed. O my lord,
	The drunkard after all his lavish cups
	Is dry, and then is sober; so at length,
	When you awake from this lascivious dream, 35
	Repentance then will follow, like the sting
	Placed in the adder's tail. Wretched are princes
	When fortune blasteth but a pretty flower
	Of their unwieldy crowns, or ravisheth
	But one pearl from their sceptre; but alas! 40
	When they to wilful shipwreck loose good fame,
	All princely titles perish with their name.
Bracciano.	You have said my lord, –
Monticelso.	Enough to give you taste
	How far I am from flattering your greatness?
Bracciano.	Now you that are his second, what say you? 45
	Do not like young hawks fetch a course about;
	Your game flies fair and for you.
Francisco.	Do not fear it.
	I'll answer you in your own hawking phrase:
	Some eagles that should gaze upon the sun
	Seldom soar high, but take their lustful ease, 50
	Since they from dunghill birds their prey can seize.
	You know Vittoria,
Bracciano.	Yes.
Francisco.	You shift your shirt there
	When you retire from tennis.
Bracciano.	Happily.

Francisco.	Her husband is lord of a poor fortune,
	Yet she wears cloth of tissue,
Bracciano.	What of this? 55
	Will you urge that, my good lord cardinal,
	As part of her confession at next shrift,
	And know from whence it sails?
Francisco.	She is your strumpet,
Bracciano.	Uncivil sir, there's hemlock in thy breath
	And that black slander. Were she a whore of mine, 60
	All thy loud cannons and thy borrowed Switzers,
	Thy galleys, nor thy sworn confederates,
	Durst not supplant her.
Francisco.	Let's not talk on thunder.
	Thou hast a wife, our sister; would I had given
	Both her white hands to death, bound and locked
	fast 65
	In her last winding-sheet, when I gave thee
	But one.
Bracciano.	Thou hadst given a soul to God then.
Francisco.	True.
	Thy ghostly father, with all's absolution,
	Shall ne'er do so by thee.
Bracciano.	Spit thy poison, –
Francisco.	I shall not need; lust carries her sharp whip 70
	At her own girdle. Look to't, for our anger
	Is making thunderbolts.
Bracciano.	Thunder? In faith,
	They are but crackers.
Francisco.	We'll end this with the cannon.
Bracciano.	Thou'lt get nought by it but iron in thy wounds
	And gunpowder in thy nostrils.
Francisco.	Better that 75
	Than change perfumes for plasters, –
Bracciano.	Pity on thee.
	'Twere good you'd show your slaves or men
	condemned

	Your new-ploughed forehead. Defiance! And I'll meet thee	
	Even in a thicket of thy ablest men.	
Monticelso.	My lords, you shall not word it any further	80
	Without a milder limit.	
Francisco.	Willingly.	
Bracciano.	Have you proclaimed a triumph that you bait	
	A lion thus?	
Monticelso.	My lord.	
Bracciano.	I am tame, I am tame, sir.	
Francisco.	We send unto the duke for conference	
	'Bout levies 'gainst the pirates; my lord duke	85
	Is not at home. We come ourself in person;	
	Still my lord duke is busied; but we fear	
	When Tiber to each prowling passenger	
	Discovers flocks of wild ducks, then my lord –	
	'Bout moulting time I mean – we shall be certain	90
	To find you sure enough and speak with you.	
Bracciano.	Ha?	
Francisco.	A mere tale of a tub; my words are idle, -	
	But to express the sonnet by natural reason,	
	Enter GIOVANNI.	
	When stags grow melancholic you'll find the season –	
Monticelso.	No more, my lord. Here comes a champion	95
	Shall end the difference between you both,	
	Your son the prince Giovanni.	

(The White Devil, 2, i, 26–97)

This extract is framed by Giovanni's exit and entrance, the child of Isabella's and Bracciano's marriage. His symbolic and exemplary function within the drama is delineated explicitly by Monticelso. The child should bring peace between Francisco and Bracciano and ensure future good political succession. He acts as both a peace-offering and pledge between fighting men: a symbolic and actual conjoining of their blood through Isabella. She herself, however, is merely a vessel of the pledge, and does not reappear in public in this part of the scene. Giovanni is central to the whole play: but he appears only in this scene and Act 5. But, as we saw in Chapter 2, his appearance at the end of the play reminds the audience of the *possibility* of innocence and integrity. The plays show that political inheritance depends upon controlling women, but display this system as the product of patriarchal structures and power-play. This extract is a key moment in making such an interpretation dramatically visible. Let us look at how this is achieved.

The juxtaposition between Isabella and Giovanni's brief opening presence, and Bracciano's confrontation with her brother and Monticelso, acts as a visual critique of Bracciano's personal betrayal. In this scene we sympathise with Francisco, a brother defending his family, against Bracciano. The juxtaposition displays the physical separation between the domestic world of wives and children and the public world of political negotiation, status and judgement. Simultaneously, the plot displays the narrative link between these separate spheres. Women and children belong away from public view, but marriage and legal inheritance via primogeniture is the social and political cement. Giovanni is the visual and blood link between these two worlds. But his legal and political importance is always represented simultaneously with his childishness, and this has four important effects on the meaning of the play as a whole.

First, it posits the possibility that his function as a future effective leader may be jeopardised by his naivety: an interpretation we have discussed in Chapter 2. Secondly, and equally importantly, it displays the intimate link between the production of children as legal heirs and peaceful political succession. This links orderly sexual behaviour and orderly political states: lust outside marriage disturbs familial and political alliances and destabilises legal political succession. Thirdly, his childishness generates a pathos for the audience about the destruction of innocence: the adults in the play are all corrupt, acting only from self-interest, and effectively destroying our faith in justice and truth. And fourthly, his childishness links him explicitly to the private domestic world of Isabella and femininity. By seeing him as subject to the dominant forces of political power and patronage, the audience are reminded that both women and children are trapped and constructed by a world of masculine power politics.

Internal scenic structure, the physical organisation of actors' exits and entrances on stage, and exemplary symbolism, thus replicate social and political structures and do so in such a way as to construct an audience that is both critical and sceptical of those social and political structures.

So far, we have only talked about how the framing of this extract constructs a vital, symbolic and dramatic image of Webster's fictional politics. Let us now turn to its content and look at the way in which the words and *internal* structure of our chosen extract reinforce our critical impression.

First, the overall content of this extract is paradoxically both private and public: Monticelso has asked all but Bracciano and Francisco to leave his presence. However, as a senior churchman and politician, within his own presence chamber, he calls Bracciano to public account. The function of such accounting is exactly parallel to that of Vittoria's trial in Act 3, Scene ii. However, the contrast with that scene is centrally pertinent to an understanding of how Webster makes us see the issues and characters of the play. Bracciano's 'trial' is public in the sense that it happens before a judge in a public place: however, the judge has cleared the public space of all observers, thence rendering it effectively private. This settling of accounts is visibly a private arrangement between public men with the power to reach a settlement of a public issue through by-passing public and legal means. By contrast, Vittoria's trial is public and she is punished through an abuse of legal process.

Secondly, the central part of this tri-partite extract, in rhythm and content, replicates and threatens military combat between Bracciano and Francisco. The threat of military action between two states (Padua and Florence) hangs over the play, and the audience should be conscious of its threat as both real and dangerous. Monticelso's actions throughout the play are aimed at preventing war. Isabella's later insistence that her divorce from Bracciano be publicly perceived as her choice is equally motivated by her desire to prevent military conflict between her brother and her husband, and to ensure her son's safe and future ascent to the dukedom. Monticelso's decision to try Bracciano in this private way, and later to use Vittoria's public trial as decoy and her as a scapegoat for Bracciano's actions and lust, is part of his political attempt to prevent war. We clearly see Monticelso's decision to pursue his role as arbiter in this way as both necessary for the political status quo and a corrupt part of that status quo.

Thirdly, the internal scenic structure invites the audience's critical view. The extract falls into three parts: Monticelso's formal charge (ll. 26–45); the reciprocal and escalating accusations by Bracciano and Francisco (ll. 45–80); and Monticelso's attempt to bring about a resolution (ll. 80–107). Monticelso plays the part of adjudicator structurally as well as by what he says, framing the insults between the two other men. He does not speak at all in the central part, and on either side his speech is measured, even pompous, and uses judicial and exemplary rhetoric. He is consequently seen as a moderator, trying to reach a solution to an intractable political situation. He clarifies the situation, making us see it not as a private matter between Isabella, Bracciano and Vittoria, but as a threat to political stability. The formal delivery of his initial charge against Bracciano (ll. 26–42), combined with its serious content, establish this. The third section of the debate portrays Monticelso in control of two battling men: in the first lines (81–3) he pulls them to heel; and in his final account of Giovanni's status and function he reminds them of their political alliance and roles.

Fourthly, the extract displays a set of conceptual oppositions, which have political implications: public versus private; social and political bonds versus individualism; honourable masculinity versus lust; political stability versus sexuality; outer versus inner. In each case, the first term of the opposition is an ideal corrupted by the second term, generating a sense of a world in which gross individualism (often symbolised by lust) destroys all social and political bonds and obligations. The oppositions are established through both staging contrasts and words. One staging contrast is that between Giovanni and Isabella on the one hand, and the men on the other. The contrast represents the ideal division, but connection, between private and public and, because the public image is a false one, the opposition between social bonds and individualism. Their physical presence invokes the absent Vittoria, reminding us of the conflict between honourable masculinity and lust, and between political stability and unregulated sexuality. The staging contrasts between Monticelso and the two opponents, through the framing we have already discussed, invokes the opposition between the public state and individualism, and between public and private impulses. Physical and visual reminders of thematic oppositions are made explicit in Monticelso's words and in Bracciano's and Francisco's argument. Monticelso's opening sentence opposes Bracciano's noble advantages, political position and consequent public duties, to his current actions. The opposition is enhanced by its rhetorical structure, run-on lines building to a climax combining moral attack with descriptive literalism in the succinct summative line and a half of the final accusation: 'Neglect your awful throne for the soft down / Of an insatiate bed' (ll. 31–2). The repetitive sibilants invoke serpent-like sounds, reminding us of the original Fall.

Monticelso uses the opposition to impress upon Bracciano the ethical gravity and political danger of his conduct. His insistence on the ethical dimension of the oppositions is emphasised in an escalating set of double analogies, introduced by the pleading, 'O my lord' (l. 32). The first set invokes a comparison between lust and drunkenness to indicate both sensory disturbance and morning-after sobriety, enforced by an illustrative moralised simile of sensory transgression ('like the sting / Placed in the adder's tail', ll. 36–7). The second set of analogies uses jewel imagery to metonymically posit an image of a whole kingdom blasted by the loss of one integral part of it. He explains this through further metaphor: that of wilful shipwreck. The cumulative images suggest two things: a world blown from its natural courses and missing integral parts. Monticelso's imagery reinforces his criticism of Bracciano, the opposition between himself and Bracciano, and the framed staging of this scene.

Fifthly, the characterisation of the relationship between Francisco and Bracciano engenders an audience critical of both men. Bracciano and Francisco trade threats and insults: Bracciano begins by taunting Francisco for not speaking and for being inferior to Monticelso ('you that are his second', l. 45). He acknowledges Monticelso's political power but draws attention to the privacy of this meeting by suggesting they are involved in a private duel (seconds were the support men in a duel). In doing so, he mocks their public impotence. Bracciano's assessment of their impotence is accurate, and later triggers Francisco's private and tragic revenge. Bracciano's dominance in the private trial and his assessment of what he can get away with, mark his character as a successfully ruthless politician. In public he acts with impunity, remaining untouched by the law and the effects of gossip: a marked contrast to Vittoria.

Characterisation and character contrasts thus establish three political 'types'. The religious leader, whose legitimate and ethical power prove unable to contain individuals; one arrogant ducal courtier who is able to manipulate and abuse legal and ethical restraints; and the wronged ducal courtier who can pursue vengeance with impunity. Webster displays no positive model of a politician. By the end of the play we understand that these three types are inter-dependent: Monticelso only contains Bracciano by proxy, through the politically weaker Vittoria, and then only by abusing ethical and legal norms. He feeds Francisco lines about revenge, and provides him with the names of potential murderers. Monticelso thus becomes as corrupt as those whose corruption he attempts to tame.

Sixthly, the metaphors used by the two opponents, and the way they use them, invoking the world of sport and war, render us critical of masculine competitive politics. This critical stance is also invoked through the dramatic double frame of Monticelso and Giovanni. The two opponents marshal their metaphors in significantly different ways. Hawking was a competitive aristocratic blood sport, and here it evokes a world of intense competition, of physical impulses, and of death. Bracciano uses the duelling and hawking metaphors actively to denigrate and mock Francisco as an inferior: Francisco tries to use them responsively to reverse the insult and as a substitute for direct attack. Francisco's verbal indirection is mocked by Bracciano, who remains physically and intellectually in control of the debate throughout, taunting Francisco to make his accusations directly (ll. 52–9). Bracciano takes the lead in shifting their argument to taunts of military action (ll. 59–63), having first forced Francisco to make an explicit accusation about Vittoria (l. 58). Francisco promises damnation (ll. 68–70) from lust: but Bracciano continues to laugh at his threatened anger through metaphoric diminution ('Thunder? In faith, / They are but crackers', ll. 72–3); and taunts about military defeat (ll. 73–5).

Bracciano indirectly but explicitly insults Francisco's masculine prowess through mockery and diminution: at hawking, in emotional response and in battle. Francisco's response acknowledges that it is masculine honour (in battle, politics and sex) that is at stake in their argument: 'Better that / Than change perfumes for plasters' (ll. 75–6), castigating Bracciano's descent into the feminine pursuits of love, metonymically indicated by reference to perfumes. This echoes the implicit opposition between masculine honour and feminine sexuality. It is this insult which angers Bracciano most, evoking from him a promise of personal combat (ll. 78–9). The whole argument continues over thirty-five lines: and until the final line of the section (l. 79) none of their speeches end at the end of a line. This creates a genuine sense of a thrust-and-parry argument, where neither man will let the other have the final say. Bracciano's last angry threat is the one exception. It is Monticelso and not Francisco who responds, suggesting that Bracciano's defiance and rhetorical skills have temporarily defeated him. Francisco's metaphors continue to wander indirectly, in the sly references to wild ducks, moulting, and melancholic stags to signal prostitution, venereal disease, and male lust (ll. 88–94), which has Bracciano gaping ('Ha?') with incomprehension. Francisco's metaphoric vehicles obscure his meaning: but the vehicles help generate an image of an animalistic and lustful world to the audience. They thus function doubly. At one level, they illustrate Francisco's political inability to defend his sister and shame Bracciano. At another level, they confirm our sense of a fallen, sick, world in which animalism cannot be contained by political, legal and civic structures, and is expressed through sterile, aristocratic, masculine combat and competition.

By contrast, where Bracciano invokes animalistic imagery he does so with more self-control and clear intent. We have already discussed his use of hawking imagery. His self-description as a lion (l. 83), and his mocking self-reference: 'I am tame, I am tame, sir' (l. 83) posit a noble, but dangerously violent identity. His control over these images, and his choice of the noble lion, combine an acknowledgement of animalistic impulses with a confident belief in his own physical superiority. Bracciano's language acknowledges a fiercely competitive, brutal, hierarchical, animalistic world. However, the audience sees this triumphal arrogance as martial posturing. Contextualised by the scenic framing, his language becomes an additional critique of dangerous masculinity.

In summary, then, this extract uses staging, structure, characterisation, metaphor and line arrangements to posit a complex model of a political world. It represents both political processes, political action, and political types. In addition, the scene encourages the audience to come to their own political judgements. The world is intensely patriarchal, competitive and hierarchical, concerned above all with aristocratic masculine honour, using proxy markers to signify that honour, such as military and sporting prowess, chastity of wives, control of lust, and the legitimacy of male heirs. However, this ideal political patriarchal world is portrayed as being fragile and vulnerable: dependent on a female chastity and masculine self-control which the play's images, metaphors and narrative suggest are impossible. Animalistic lust, extreme individualism, self-interest, and greed dominate the main characters' motivations, and exceed the attempts by law and the Church to control and contain them. The supposedly civilised, patriarchal aristocracy is displayed as a barely-controlled violent, combative, obsessive and lustful political system, in which women and children become pawns. Women are double victims. In the ideal patriarchal system they are displayed as proxies of masculine honour, and vessels of masculine legitimate power. In the real political world Webster displays, they become actual sacrificial victims to that power: Isabella is divorced and shamed in order to ensure the legitimacy and honour of her son; Vittoria is shamed and then murdered for Bracciano's lust.

*   *   *

Let us now turn to *The Duchess of Malfi*.

[Act 1, Scene i]
Cardinal.   Be sure you entertain that Bosola
                For your intelligence. I would not be seen in't;   225

	And therefore many times I have slighted him	
	When he did court our furtherance, as this	
	morning.	
Ferdinand.	Antonio, the great master of her household,	
	Had been far fitter.	
Cardinal.	You are deceived in him,	

              Enter BOSOLA

	His nature is too honest for such business.	230
	He comes; I'll leave you.	
Bosola.	I was lured to you.	
Ferdinand.	My brother here, the Cardinal, could never	
	Abide you.	
Bosola.	Never since he was in my debt.	
Ferdinand.	Maybe some oblique character in your face	
	Made him suspect you.	
Bosola.	Doth he study physiognomy?	235
	There's no more credit to be given to th'face	
	Than to a sick man's urine, which some call	
	The physician's whore, because she cozens him.	
	He did suspect me wrongfully.	
Ferdinand.	For that	
	You must give great men leave to take their times:	240
	Distrust doth cause us seldom be deceived.	
	You see, the oft shaking of the cedar tree	
	Fastens it more at root.	
Bosola.	Yet take heed,	
	For to suspect a friend unworthily	
	Instructs him the next way to suspect you,	245
	And prompts him to deceive you.	
Ferdinand.	There's gold.	
Bosola.	So:	
	What follows? Never rained such show'rs as these	
	Without thunderbolts in the tail of them.	
	Whose throat must I cut?	
Ferdinand.	Your inclination to shed blood rides post	250
	Before my occasion to use you. I give you that	

To live i'th'court here, and observe the Duchess,
To note all the particulars of her haviour,
What suitors do solicit her for marriage
And whom she best affects. She's a young
    widow – 255
I would not have her marry again.

Bosola.   No, sir?
Ferdinand. Do not you ask the reason: but be satisfied,
I say I would not.
Bosola.   It seems you would create me
One of your familiars.
Ferdinand.   Familiar! What's that?
Bosola. Why, a very quaint invisible devil, in flesh: 260
An intelligencer.
Ferdinand.   Such a kind of thriving thing
I would wish thee; and ere long thou mayst arrive
At a higher place by't.
Bosola.   Take your devils
Which hell calls angels! These cursed gifts would
    make
You a corrupter, me an impudent traitor, 265
And should I take these they'd take me to hell.
Ferdinand. Sir, I'll take nothing from you that I have given –
There is a place that I procured for you
This morning: the provisorship o'th'horse –
Have you heard on't?
Bosola.   No.
Ferdinand.   'Tis yours – is't not
    worth thanks? 270
Bosola. I would have you curse yourself now, that your
    bounty,
Which makes men truly noble, e'er should make
Me a villain. O, that to avoid ingratitude
For the good deed you have done me, I must do
All the ill man can invent! Thus the devil 275
Candies all sins o'er; and what heaven terms vile,
That names he complimental.

Ferdinand.   Be yourself:
              Keep your old garb of melancholy; 'twill express
              You envy those that stand above your reach,
              Yet strive not to come near 'em. This will gain   280
              Access to private lodgings, where yourself
              May, like a politic dormouse –
Bosola.   As I have seen some
              Feed in a lord's dish, half asleep, not seeming
              To listen to any talk; and yet these rogues
              Have cut his throat in a dream. What's my place?   285
              The provisorship o'th'horse? Say then, my
                 corruption
              Grew out of horse dung: I am your creature
Ferdinand.   Away!
Bosola.   Let good men, for good deeds, covet good fame,
              Since place and riches oft are bribes of shame –   290
              Sometimes the devil doth preach.
                              (*The Duchess of Malfi*, 1, i, 224–91)

This extract falls in the middle of the long opening scene, in the
public arena of the Duchess's presence chamber. The whole scene
contains many private and secretive conversations: illustrating visually the complicated and private plots that occur even within public
political places. This is one such example of the articulation and
development of a private plot within a public arena. Its staging and
position within the scene literally show us how the dominant political relationships within a state can be subverted from within by supposed allies and employees. The setting is the Duchess's court, over
which she is politically sovereign. The staging shows us that, whilst
this is true in theory, in practice even in public places it is possible to
arrange private conversations which threaten public political stability. This threat is amplified by the political and blood relationship
the plotters bear to the Duchess. Despite her political sovereignty,
her brothers assume a patriarchal control over her body and sexuality, an assumption which thence extends over her political state.
Their blood relationship underlines their motivation for employing

a spy to invade another's sovereignty. This complicates and personalises the way the audience are asked to see the situation. It is clear
that intervention in another's sovereign state is unethical, an interpretation that is explicitly articulated by the pilgrims who question
the Cardinal's power to banish a sovereign in 3, iv, 24–44. However,
an audience may respond in a more divided way to the question of
the extent a family member can become involved in another family
member's life. Do the brothers have a valid personal stake and
interest in the Duchess's decisions about marriage and children? If
they do, how far can they intervene in her life and political actions?
Some cultures, at some points in their history would argue that they
do have the right, and are justified; others that they go too far;
others, that they do not have any rights of intervention. How does
the play itself ask us to read their actions and intervention? This is a
very large question, and one which is not answered by this extract,
but which you should keep in mind throughout your work in this
chapter.

   This extract is framed by the departure and re-entrance of the
Duchess. It begins as the Duchess and other courtiers have either left
the stage or moved towards the back. The Cardinal and Ferdinand
must be at the front, or side-front, of the stage. The extract ends on
the return of both Duchess and Cardinal, marking the re-com-
mencement of public business. This framing, set aside from the
public business and the sovereign's presence, thence underlines the
illicit and subversive nature of the conversation and intention of the
three men on stage.

   The extract itself falls into three parts: the Cardinal's brief conversation with Ferdinand (ll. 224–31); Ferdinand's instructions to
Bosola (ll. 231–58); and finally, the mutual negotiation and recognition of an arrangement between Bosola and Ferdinand (ll. 258–92).
The tri-partite structural arrangement replicates the shifting relationship between the three men: it physically holds Bosola away
from the Cardinal, whilst representing a visual and narrative link
between them; it helps build to an ascending climax in which Bosola
paradoxically displays political power over the two brothers; and it
displays the power-play between different individuals at different
moments through structural and rhetorical shifts. Structure thence

displays political power as hierarchical and abusive, political processes as open to manipulation, and power as dependent upon knowledge and one's ability to use it.

At the beginning, the two brothers are visually and politically dominant over Bosola, reflecting the conventional social and political hierarchy. But Webster signals the brothers' venality and corruption simultaneously with their status. Their corrupt purposes are dramatically signalled both through their movement to the front of the stage, away from the Duchess's political business, and through the content of their speech. The Cardinal's dominance in their relationship is demonstrated through his rhetoric: he gives orders to his brother, and corrects his views. He sets out his political practice and philosophy. He manipulates men and women behind the scenes, arguing that such manipulation is necessary (ll. 224–5); he insists on keeping clean hands (l. 225); and he suggests that the business of politics is not for honest men (l. 230). This bleak, self-interested, and pragmatic view of politics emerges from a view of human nature as venial, corrupt and fallen. Despite the Cardinal's religious status, theological beliefs and ethics do not inform his political actions and philosophy.

In the second and third parts of the extract Ferdinand and Bosola talk alone at the front of the stage (ll. 231–58), and their relationship is clearly one of dominance and subordination. Ferdinand's political and aristocratic haughtiness assumes Bosola's gratitude for any employment, and this garners our sympathies. The contrast between the two characters in this section is an important indicator of how the audience is asked to respond to the political situation, and the political debate initiated by this covert plot. Let us examine their dialogue, keeping in mind the contrasts invoked through characterisation. Bosola has the most words, but is clearly politically subordinate. His rhetorical dominance contrasts with his political subordination. This inverse opposition between words and power almost defines the malcontent. Bosola never starts speaking at the beginning of a line. His words are always responsive to those of Ferdinand, who maintains political and intellectual dominance in this part: but they have a subversive edge. He signals subservience by not interrupting Ferdinand: but his responses are malcontented and indirectly politicised. Let us look at each of his comments.

His first, after his opening greeting ('Never since he was in my debt', l. 233), is a muttered rejoinder which confirms Delio's earlier rumour that the Cardinal had employed Bosola in a murder, and articulates Bosola's simultaneously resentful and insightful attitude towards the Cardinal. His subordinate status explains both the resentment and the insights.

His second comment is a bolder rejection of the brothers, through criticising the way the Cardinal assesses character. He is sarcastic and doubly emphatic through the extended medical metaphor of urinary diagnostics and the conclusive plain statement ('He did suspect me wrongfully', l. 239).

His third comment, on Ferdinand's arrogant assertion of the natu-ralised power of 'great men' (l. 240), articulates a political aphorism: 'for to suspect a friend unworthily / Instructs him the next way to suspect you, / And prompts him to deceive you' (ll. 244–6). This insight resonates through the political and dramatic action of the play. It is a political and personal warning which Ferdinand fails to hear, and echoes instead in the audience's memory. It has a Machiavellian flavour: illustrating that Bosola is a more perceptive political philosopher than Ferdinand, who believes that power is maintained through natural submission to greatness. By contrast, Bosola suggests that power will only be held successfully over time through negotiation and reciprocity of rewards and patronage. Bosola's actions in the play become the perfect illustration of the folly and errors of Ferdinand's political philosophy.

His fourth comment begins in the last syllable of a line, 'So: / What follows?' in response to Ferdinand's 'There's gold' (ll. 246–7). The 'So', slightly drawn out because falling on the last syllable, sug-gests a thoughtful man adapting circumstances to his own interests. Bosola illustrates his thoughts with the extended metaphor ('Never rained such show'rs as these'), and a sharp, end-stopped question, 'Whose throat must I cut?' (l. 249). His rhetoric utilises both the metaphorical indirection of political-speak favoured by the brothers, and the blunt, bathetic literalism of the common man. Thus he both exposes Ferdinand's actions and language as hypocritical and displays his own knowledge of this.

His fifth comment ('No, sir?') is the shortest and most expressive, indicating a sceptical subordinate's attitude to the vagaries and political protectionism of a superior. This interpretation is reinforced by the grammar and content of Ferdinand's insistent emphasis on his dominance. His pronouns illustrate the way power and knowledge work hand in hand: 'Do not *you* ask the reason: but be satisfied, / *I* say *I* would not' (ll. 257–8). However, it is this arrogant assertion of dominance and its relationship to knowledge and the control of action, which ironically tips the balance of power in this section towards Bosola. He has effectively forced Ferdinand to reveal that his political actions and his intent to spy on his sister are motivated by personal interests (in the repetition of that 'I'). In forcing that revelation, Bosola declares his own power within a subordinate relationship: by intimating knowledge about the brothers and their motivation and remaining in their employment he manipulates political recognition and patronage. Knowledge is power: and this is illustrated by the shift in his relationship with Ferdinand in the final part of the extract.

The final section (ll. 258–92) opens in explicit affirmation of this power shift. Bosola uses intimate pronouns to Ferdinand for the first time, an intimacy underlined by his analogy, 'It seems *you* would create *me* /One of your familiars' (ll. 258–9). Bosola's comments are now directly about Ferdinand and his management of political inferiors. This suggestion initiates Ferdinand's first uncontrolled and surprised response, indicated by his question. From now on Bosola speaks at greater length, and begins three of six speeches at the beginning of the line. The rhetoric and rhythm of the dialogue thus represents a more equal political and intellectual debate. The nature of their dialogue has also changed: it is a negotiation about the work and the reward, an economic equation in which Bosola as employee is both empowered by his economic negotiating power, and disempowered by his economic necessity. In this final part, the relationship between Ferdinand and Bosola is dissected and displayed. Bosola's ethical distaste for spying alongside his perception that the necessity for making a living at a court of patronage may involve villainy illustrates his complex and pragmatic character (ll. 271–5). In complete contrast, Ferdinand has the easy power and self-confidence of a man of wealth, aristocracy and status: and no ethical concerns whatsoever. He has the power of patronage, but abuses it. By contrast, Bosola articulates and acknowledges the possible conflict between ethics and economic necessity. The symbolic and economic contrast between the two men, suggests that powerless men literally cannot afford an ethical politics.

In this extract Bosola establishes himself as a character involved in the corruption central to the tragic action, but one who still criticises its unethical actions and its economic and political structures. His words and images thence resonate as generalised political critique. His vivid picture of courtiers who 'feed in a lord's dish' but 'cut his throat in a dream' (ll. 283–5) furthers neither the plot nor his relationship with Ferdinand, but feeds the overall picture of courtly corruption. All his metaphors emphasise sensual excess and excretion: greedy feeding; horse dung; urinary divination; and whoredom. They paint an image of a corrupted, naturally violent, animalistic and physical world lying beneath courtly games, people and language. His views are emphasised by his habit of using very plain speech after a metaphor: he both rejects the courtly rhetoric and asks the audience to judge its appearance as false. By contrast, Ferdinand's metaphor tries to posit an image of a natural nobility: 'the oft shaking of the cedar tree / Fastens it more at root' (ll. 242–3). The intent behind that metaphor is to assert a belief in a natural political stability dependent upon a social hierarchy: a belief which has already been condemned indirectly by Bosola's words and position, and his criticism that political hierarchy can only be maintained by mutual trust. Bosola de-stabilises a political theory of natural aristocracy, forcing us to ask a set of key political questions which resonate throughout the play. What place do ethics have in a political philosophy? What place does economics have in political practice? To what extent is power dependent upon those who have access to and utilise knowledge? Is corruption endemic to aristocratic political systems? Or is it endemic to any political system?

Bosola's final couplet is interrupted by his own commentary and suggests that, at this stage of the play, Webster leaves these questions open: 'Let good men, for good deeds, covet good fame, / Since place and riches oft are bribes of shame – / Sometimes the devil doth preach' (ll. 289–91). The repetition of 'good' in that first line is ironised: Bosola distinguishes himself from such men, deeds and reputation, and contrasts ideal ethical action with actual political status, wealth and practice. But he also partly distinguishes himself from an involvement in those practices by reminding the audience of his own theatrical status. This self-consciousness, seeing himself as 'devil' (l. 291) and 'villain' (l. 273), marks a character who externalises and thereby comments on the characters and action of the play. By positing himself explicitly as the Vice character he provides a dramatic space for the audience to see and understand the political action within a moralised framework.

Finally, the absent Duchess, in whose presence chamber this plot takes place, is symbolically present all the way through the discussion. Ferdinand's motives and intentions to spy on her are explicit in his employment of Bosola. Covert surveillance of a sister's sexuality and desire is seen to be a politically defensible action, although the dialogue leaves open the suspicion that Ferdinand's motives are sexually ambiguous even to himself (ll. 258–9). The Duchess functions as a political symbol in several ways in this extract: as a sovereign whose trust and court are abused by treacherous plotting; as a female sovereign, whose potential marriage will break or make dynastic connections; and as a female pawn in arrangements made without her consent by men in her family. Webster's dramatic skill is to allow all these symbolic resonances to function together. Each of these raises slightly different political issues and questions. When do men have that right over women? Are women pawns in a political and dynastic power game? When is a sovereign not sovereign?

In summary, this extract provides us with a window on the political shenanigans, methods and views of the two brothers, with Bosola in thrall to the political and social structure as a dramatic focal point. Social and political structures are rigidly hierarchical, and these structures are shown to be decadently corrupt. The Duchess's political practices, and her willingness to marry out of her class set her apart from her brothers' philosophy. Their desire to maintain a closed aristocratic world, through whatever means at their disposal, is exposed as a corrupt and self-defeating political aim. This extract clearly demonstrates and discusses the view that absolutist power corrupts absolutely. Bosola demonstrates this dramatically in three crucial ways. First, through his own practice at court; secondly, through the way he is (ab)used by the brothers; and thirdly, through his commentaries on his own and others' actions as the work of devils and villains. On a more general level, this extract makes two more philosophical points. It shows that political power is dependent upon knowledge and the manipulation and control of knowledge. Finally, it implicitly places political action, ethics and characters within a moralised context. Bosola repeatedly draws attention to, and describes, the actions of others as sinful, himself as a devil, and heaven as an unattainable good (ll. 273–7).

Conclusions

1. In both tragedies the social and political world share several common features:
   • Social hierarchies, fashion, relationships, even family bonds, are seen and described as hypocritical and claustrophobic.
   • Fallen nature is the dominant metaphoric model representing human behaviour, desire and politics. Lust, greed, excretion, feeding, sex and death are the driving forces of all our actions.
   • Corruption is endemic to personal, social and political relationships.
   • Individualism triumphs over collectivism, even the collective purpose of Christian morality.
   • Economics drive and limit human choice.
   • Public behaviour is exposed as hypocritical, in contrast to inner realities.
   • Political, theological and legal hierarchies and order are seen to be ineffectual.
   • Women, visually and narrationally, appear as pawns to a patriarchal imperative to maintain dynastic power. This perception places masculinity, not femininity, under scrutiny.
2. Corrupt human nature informs, creates and perpetuates corrupt political structures. Physical domination, fighting for survival, and individualism validate a rigidly hierarchical political structure, maintained by a police state's surveillance tactics. Power corrupts individuals.

3. *The Duchess of Malfi* posits a radically alternative political model. Both plays demonstrate that closed aristocratic political hierarchies merely perpetuate social and political corruption: but our extract from *The Duchess of Malfi* implicitly raises the possibility of alternative political structures. The Duchess's court and her marriage propose a more democratic, ethical and open form of government and identity: a possibility discussed in the opening of the play by Antonio and Delio. Their ideal is deliberately opposed to the animalistic view of human nature which dominates the views and actions of the politicians. The conflict between the two views forms the tragic crisis of the play. But there are no *successful* models of a 'good' alternative to the corrupt politics we view on stage. The implicit representation of that 'good', through references to Christian redemption and punishment, and to concepts of honour and justice, are reminders of the fragility of ethical action in a fallen world.

4. Webster uses women as symbolic foci for a more general discussion of social and political abuses. Their rare appearances belie their central function. By allowing the audience to see women as victims of corrupt political and economic aristocratic structures, Webster engages the audience in an act of subversive criticism.

5. Webster uses various dramatic means to first engage and then distance our attention in order to engender a politicised critical response. These dramatic means include: tri-partite dialogic structures within scenes to display shifting relationships and ideas and construct dramatic debate; character and thematic oppositions; the internal framing of scenes; and shifting points of view through self-conscious theatrical references.

Methods of Analysis

1. We have focused on rhythm, imagery, sentences, characterisation and metre.
2. We looked at internal scenic structure, dramatic framing, and the symbolic function of different characters.

3. In each analysis we widened our textual analysis to place it in the context of three broader questions: What does this tell us about the political and social structures, attitudes, ideas and ideals of this fictional world? What place does this particular extract have in the wider political debate of the play as a whole? What does Webster want us to think about on a political level?

4. We returned to earlier points and insights, and tried to integrate these with our analysis, aiming to deepen our textual analysis, and contextualise individual dramatic episodes within an interpretative whole.

Suggested Work

1. Look again at the plays' endings, and consider whether the political issues which we have observed in this chapter are resolved.

2. One issue which recurs in both plays is that of the place of religion in both political states and political action. Look at the scenes in which the Cardinals appear, and discuss Webster's picture of established religion. What do characters say about religion as they die? Do you think that Webster's plays criticise the political nature of religious institutions?

3. In *The White Devil* Flamineo exclaims 'O, the rare tricks of a Machiavellian!' (5.iii.190). What role do the explicitly Machiavellian villains have in the political debate of the plays?

4. Look at the whole plot of each play, scene by scene, to determine the overall picture of society and politics. Consider the following:
   - Why are they both set in Italy? How does this affect the audience's understanding of both society and politics?
   - Look at the social and political relationships between the characters. Who is in power where, and why? How is power sustained and seen to be sustained?
   - Which characters stand outside the social order of the plays, and what is their significance?
   - What kinds of political debates are set up by the plays' crisis-points? Do they come to any resolution? What does the audi-

ence learn from any resolution? If Webster leaves us with unresolved dramatic and political issues, why is this?

7

Webster's Theatricality

In the preceding chapters we have noted at least three main areas of Webster's theatricality. First, there are the moments at which characters draw attention to their own fictional and dramatic status: for example, Flamineo at his death; Vittoria's self-conscious rhetorical stances; Bosola's continued references to himself as a devil or villain; and the existence of commentator characters (including Bosola at times). Secondly, Webster marshals visual and physical arrangements of characters in patterns, creating a visible and self-consciously choreographed formality, spectacle and dramatic meaning. And thirdly, we have noted the way he uses large 'set-piece' scenes, which coalesce visual and narrative motifs through self-conscious use of specific visual settings. Self-conscious theatricality is often called 'meta-theatricality': look at the Introduction for a definition of this term.

One of the features of Webster's plays which frequently puzzles modern viewers and readers is the number and variety of dumb shows, masques and dream images in the plots. We shall analyse a few of these in close detail as case-studies of Webster's theatricality. What is the effect and function of the masques and dumb shows within the play as a whole? During our analysis of the turning-point scenes in particular, we noticed Webster's conscious manipulation of visual, iconic and spatial arrangements of characters, props and setting. We need to build on our conclusions about his theatrical skills, and look at how other set-pieces deepen the dramatic meanings of the plays.

*   *   *

Let us turn, first, to the double dumb show in *The White Devil*.

[Act 2, Scene ii]

Conjurer.   I'll show you by my strong-commanding art
                        The circumstance that breaks your duchess' heart.

A dumb show

Enter suspiciously JULIO *and another; they draw a curtain where* BRAC-
CIANO'*s picture is; they put on spectacles of glass, which cover their eyes
and noses, and then burn perfumes afore the picture, and wash the lips
of the picture; that done, quenching the fire, and putting off their spectacles, they depart laughing.*

Enter ISABELLA *in her nightgown as to bed-ward, with lights after her,*
Count LODOVICO, GIOVANNI, *and others waiting on her; she kneels
down as to prayers, then draws the curtain of the picture, does three reverences to it, and kisses it thrice; she faints and will not suffer them to
come near it, dies; sorrow expressed in* GIOVANNI *and in Count*
LODOVICO; *she's conveyed out solemnly.*

Bracciano.	Excellent, then she's dead, –	
Conjurer.	She's poisoned	
	By the fumed picture. 'Twas her custom nightly,	25
	Before she went to bed, to go and visit	
	Your picture, and to feed her eyes and lips	
	On the dead shadow; Doctor Julio,	
	Observing this, infects it with an oil	
	And other poisoned stuff, which presently	30
	Did suffocate her spirits.	
Bracciano.	Methought I saw	
	Count Lodowick there.	
Conjurer.	He was, and by my art	
	I find he did most passionately dote	
	Upon your duchess. Now turn another way	
	And view Camillo's far more politic fate.	35

> Strike louder music from this charmed ground,
> To yield, as fits the act, a tragic sound!

The second dumb show

Enter FLAMINEO, MARCELLO, CAMILLO, *with four more as* Captains; *they drink healths and dance; a vaulting-horse is brought into the room;* MARCELLO *and two more whispered out of the room while* FLAMINEO *and* CAMILLO *strip themselves into their shirts, as to vault; compliment who shall begin; as* CAMILLO *is about to vault,* FLAMINEO *pitcheth him upon his neck, and with the help of the rest writhes his neck about, seems to see if it be broke and lays him folded double, as 'twere under the horse, makes shows to call for help;* MARCELLO *comes in, laments, sends for the* Cardinal *and* Duke, *who comes forth with* armed men; *wonder at the act;* [FRANCISCO] *commands the body to be carried home, appre-hends* FLAMINEO, MARCELLO *and the rest, and go as 'twere to apprehend* VITTORIA.

Bracciano.   'Twas quaintly done, but yet each circumstance
          I taste not fully.

(*The White Devil,* 2, ii, 22–39)

There are several issues to consider here: the framing of the dumb shows by the surrounding narrative, action and dialogue; how the stage directions illuminate visual and physical arrangements of dramatic meaning within the dumb shows; their dramatic function; the way theatricality affects our reading of Bracciano; and finally the way the audience is positioned by Webster. Let us look at each of these in turn.

Both dumb shows are framed within a self-contained scene and by the conjurer's and Bracciano's dialogue. Their actions and the illusion are physically separated from the rest of the play: although the two pictorial stories which are represented are key events in pre-cipitating subsequent events. This physical separation helps it func-tion both as a kind of dream sequence, intimating the metaphorical expression of hidden desires, and as the actual expression of events elsewhere. This sense of physical separation is achieved: by setting (in a private room); by the presence of a conjurer who invokes his 'strong-commanding art' (l. 22) and 'this charmed ground' (l. 36), intimating links to other worlds and devilish magic; by the timing ('dead midnight', 2, ii, 1); by the lighting, which must illuminate the back of the stage for the dumb shows, and show Bracciano and the conjurer barely lit; and by the music which the conjurer summons (ll. 36–7).

Visually, the spectacle is framed by the physical presence of the two men: we literally see the dumb show beyond or through them. This reminds us spatially of how, why and by whom the images are being conjured. The visual framing is made explicit by the dialogue: the conjurer gives an explanatory narrative after each show, replicating what we have already seen. This narrative framing re-situates Bracciano and the conjurer centre-stage for our observation, reminding us of their responsibility for the murders. This change of perspective, from back stage to centre stage, from the violence to those responsible for that violence, re-focuses us on Bracciano. The conjurer's narrative allows us to observe Bracciano dispassionately.

The framing is further created and enhanced through the conjurer's self-conscious theatricality, which draws attention both to his own dramatic arts ('Strike louder music from this charmed ground, / To yield, as fits the act, a tragic sound!', ll. 36–7) and to the illusionary nature of the show. Dramatic action is posited as linked to the dark, deceptive and dangerous arts of the conjurer. This self-conscious theatricality is echoed in the content of the second dumb show, which narrates the failed attempt to perform a fiction. Both dumb shows take art as their subject: in the first, the visual arts are the self-conscious medium of representation and plot; in the second, performance arts. Both devices foreground their illusionary status. This reminds the audience that Bracciano is staging these devices for his pleasure: both to enact and then to observe them: ''Twas quaintly done' (l. 38). Bracciano's behaviour is displayed as artificial, distanced from real emotion and action. The distancing device of the dumb show thence has two complementary but paradoxical effects. It displays Bracciano as shallow, cold, self-interested and voyeuristic. But it allows the audience to view the two-tiered theatrical display (the silent mime and the commenting spectators) and to look at the dumb show in a different, ethical way from Bracciano's amoral voyeurism.

Let us now turn to the staging of the dumb shows. The textual stage directions are extremely explicit, including the opening designation ('dumb show'); details of physical props (the 'spectacles of glass'); the physical movement of individuals (putting on the glasses, washing the portrait's lips, exiting in laughter); and the physical arrangement of the whole scene. They confirm Webster's concern for constructing a visual image as an integral part of his drama. The way the stage directions follow a narrative, but do so via very simplified descriptions of mimed actions and gestures, illustrates Webster's knowledge and use of symbolic blocking and gesture as key dramatic signifiers. This is very clear in two different ways in each dumb show here.

The first one is described and performed as a pageant-like fresco: we see a parade of people crossing the scene, a very formal obeisance as to an icon, and the equally formal taking up of Isabella's body at the end. The action is linear, which echoes the cause-and-effect narrative of Isabella's death, but also creates a sense of ritual formality. The picture we view reminds us of linear visual narratives of heros' lives in renaissance paintings and sculptures. Isabella's death thence reminds the audience visually of her heroic status as victim, and elevates the dumb show to a static work of art with an emotional effect unintended either by the conjurer or by Bracciano. Webster's self-conscious visual artistry in this first dumb show echoes the content. We watch the drama of Bracciano watching a moving picture of Isabella looking at a still picture.

The physical arrangement of the actors in this linear pageant is explicit in the stage directions, including details of the props and how actors should use or respond to them, and of Isabella's dress. In the first approach, the actors hold up the props in exaggerated mime. Webster delineates the burning of perfumes, the washing the lips of the painting, the dousing of the fire, the taking off the spectacles, and their laughing departure. Each is a separate, exaggerated mimed act or gesture, slowing down the action and engendering a magical, ritualistic atmosphere, highlighted by the dark setting. The mimed laughing departure adds an intimate horror, particularly since it is accompanied by music. The second formal approach to the painting is equally linear. Isabella enters first ('in her night-gown'), followed by lights. The details of the physical arrangement of her courtiers behind Isabella, how many reverences and kisses she does to the picture, and of her death, demand mimed actions. Her adoration of her husband's portrait is a parody of religious worship, but one which becomes imbued with pathos as the kiss of love becomes for her the kiss of death.

Each physical detail has a crucial place within a simple visual narrative and does not require dialogue. In this first dumb show the two emotions expressed ('they depart laughing' and 'sorrow expressed in GIOVANNI') are capable of being simply mimed. Their departure ('she's conveyed out solemnly') provides a final visual image of the formal ritual. From 'JULIO and another' entering *suspiciously* to the final conveyance of Isabella *solemnly*, the absence of dialogue, and mimed gestures to music, heighten the ritualistic atmosphere. Webster gives the mime emotion, horror, ritual, and visual embodiment

The second dumb show has a different visual arrangement and effect. It stages a more versatile and open physical action than the first, and takes place in the light rather than the dark. Its visual parallel is the physically expressive, active and demanding circus or dance, not the static, ritualised sculptural or painted linear narrative of the first dumb show. The physical arrangement of actors, setting, dress and props are again very detailed. The gymnasium is depicted as a place of physical competition and of the expression of masculine prowess: 'they drink healths and dance', posits an exuberant, though naturalistic, setting and movement. The mimed actions (drinking, dancing, 'whispered out of the room', and the preparations for the vaulting competition) are informal and physically expressive, and maximise narrative meaning through the simplest of physical movements. The details of the physical rituals surrounding the gymnastic competition are very exact, providing a clear choreography of the action, from their stripping of shirts, through the 'compliment who shall begin', to the way in which Flamineo manoeuvres the killing and subsequent arrangement of the body to appear as an accident. As the conjurer notes, Camillo's death is 'far more politic' (l. 35) than that of Isabella, literally staged as an accident, a theatrical illusion, which attempts but fails to mask the death as unpremeditated. The second dumb show represents both the physical exuberance and careful arrangement of dramatic action and its fragile status as illusion.

In Jacobean drama, dumb shows were used as an efficient way of compressing action into a short visual and narrative time frame, of indicating different spatial or time frames, of acting as prologues, or symbolic commentaries on subsequent actions. Many dumb shows, in their self-conscious and self-referential artistry, have the effect of partially distancing the audience from the main action: making them sceptical of dramatic illusions; or creating a sense of displacement, like a dream-sequence in a film, aiding a sense of psychological or interpretative depth; or creating a sense of awe, of events as fated, inevitable actions beyond human intervention. What specific dramatic effects do these two dumb shows produce? They propel the narrative plot, and make visual the murder plots of both Bracciano and Vittoria. In making them visual and ritualised, Webster ensures a change of pace from the previous scenes. They force the audience to see the dark consequences of the lustful desires of the first Act. The dumb shows are the first direct visual intimation of the actual dark deeds which propel the play, and much of its imagery. Their silent delivery reinforces our sense of a claustrophobic, self-interested political world that is propelled by inner desires and demons which remain hidden by the surface world of courtiers and politics. Finally, the ritualistic representation of death enhances the horror of the action, a horror reinforced by the framing.

How does this scene affect our reading of Bracciano? His characterisation firmly establishes his link with the dark forces of evil. The scene follows immediately from that of his public divorce from Isabella. The juxtaposition of legal divorce and unnecessary murder shows Bracciano drunk with the belief that he is above the law, an interpretation echoed in the internal structure, both through his arrangement of the deaths, and through his visible response. By arranging to murder Isabella immediately after the divorce, Bracciano undertakes evil for pleasure. His comments before and after the visions reinforce this reading: 'Excellent, then, she's dead'

(l. 24). His response to the drama is appropriate to a game or a business arrangement, not a murder. His unfeeling response to the ritualised, slow death which is physically caused by Isabella's kiss of his portrait, sets him apart from the audience. We watch and are moved: he watches and is unmoved. We thereby look askance at his motives and character. When the ending of his second dumb show does not proceed according to the plan (that is, Francisco arranges the arrest of Flamineo and Vittoria), Bracciano does not react emotionally. Our response to the mime is exactly counterpointed to Bracciano's. Where he is amused, we are shocked; where he applauds, we watch in horror; where he is cold, we are saddened; where he is the gleeful voyeur, we are made critical of voyeurism and asked to place it in a moral context. Theatricality thus functions doubly: as visual drama and as an effective way of engendering a thinking and feeling audience. This leads to our final point, how the audience is positioned by Webster.

The external scenic juxtaposition, internal setting and commentary create a separated, demonised space for Bracciano on stage, in which he appears isolated visually from an anchored morality, from us and from the actions he has ordered: he abuses the magic arts to order murder, and enjoys watching violence. However, we also see that his grand self-confidence is a mistake: for while Francisco and his men arrange for the arrest of Vittoria, Bracciano admires the artistry of the display. The contrast between the shows' content, in each of which a woman whom he loved or loves is threatened, and his unmoved response raises the audience's horrific understanding of his unfeeling amorality. Throughout the scene Webster engenders a judgemental audience through contrasts: of this scene with the previous; of the shows with Bracciano's response; of Bracciano as audience, with us as audience. This judgement remains with us through the next short scene, into the trial scene (Act 3, Scene ii) when we next see Bracciano maintaining his distance from political and moral responsibility. The dumb shows are thus crucially placed this early in the play to create criticism of Bracciano. We see *him* as the manipulator of action, emotion and intent, rather than Vittoria. Bracciano's impunity, emphasised by his theatrical observation of the shows, is one of the central political and gendered themes of the play.

*   *   *

This dumb show in *The Duchess of Malfi* immediately follows the
Cardinal's initial preparations to go to war, and Bosola's news that
the Duchess has fled.

[Act 3, Scene iv]
    Enter two Pilgrims *to the Shrine of Our Lady of Loretto*

First Pilgrim.	I have not seen a goodlier shrine than this,
	Yet I have visited many.
Second Pilgrim.	The Cardinal of Aragon
	Is this day to resign his cardinal's hat;
	His sister Duchess likewise is arrived 5
	To pay her vow of pilgrimage. I expect
	A noble ceremony.
First Pilgrim.	No question. – They come.

Here the ceremony of the Cardinal's *instalment in the habit of a soldier,
performed in delivering up his cross, hat, robes, and ring at the shrine,
and investing him with sword, helmet, shield and spurs. Then*
ANTONIO, *the* Duchess, *and their* children, *having presented themselves
at the shrine, are (by a form of banishment in dumb show expressed
towards them by the* Cardinal *and the state of Ancona) banished.
During all which ceremony, this ditty is sung to very solemn music, by
divers* Churchmen; *and then exeunt.*
    [The author disclaims this ditty to be his.] . . .

First Pilgrim.	Here's a strange turn of state! Who would have
	thought
	So great a lady would have matched herself 25
	Unto so mean a person? Yet the Cardinal
	Bears himself much too cruel.
Second Pilgrim.	They are banished.
First Pilgrim.	But I would ask what power hath this state
	Of Ancona to determine of a free prince?

Second Pilgrim.   They are a free state, sir, and her brother
                              showed   30
                     How that the Pope, fore-hearing of her
                         looseness,
                     Hath seized into the protection of the church
                     The dukedom which she held as dowager.
First Pilgrim.   But by what justice?
Second Pilgrim.   Sure, I think, by none,
                     Only her brother's instigation.   35
First Pilgrim.   What was it with such violence he took
                     Off from her finger?
Second Pilgrim.   'Twas her wedding ring,
                     Which he vowed shortly he would sacrifice
                     To his revenge.
First Pilgrim.   Alas Antonio!
                     If that a man be thrust into a well,   40
                     No matter who sets hand to't, his own weight
                     Will bring him sooner to th'bottom. Come,
                         let's hence.
                     Fortune makes this conclusion general:
                     All things do help th'unhappy man to fall.
                                                            Exeunt.
                          (*The Duchess of Malfi*, 3, iv, 1–44)

This dumb show shares several distinctive features with that in *The
White Devil*. It is mimed action, which speeds up the amount of
information represented to the audience, whilst retaining visual
interest and attention. It is also a doubled narrative: we see the set of
events and we witness a subsequent commentary upon them.
Finally, the dumb show is clearly framed by other narrative and dramatic devices which ask us to think critically.

    Let us first consider the framing of the dumb shows in this scene.
This is achieved by setting, narrative position, dialogue and music.
The setting is religious: a shrine visited by pilgrims, Cardinals and
petitioning believers. The visual setting is underlined by both the
costume and the opening words of the first pilgrim ('I have not seen
a goodlier shrine than this, / Yet I have visited many', ll. 1–2). On a

narrative level, the pilgrims remind the audience that both Cardinal and Duchess arrive at the same shrine: a comparative framing device which ironically draws attention both to the manipulation of religion and to its protective inefficacy in this world. Finally, within the action of the scene itself, the pilgrims' dialogue frames what we see. The difference between their 'before' and 'after' reactions leads the audience to a particular interpretation. Before the mime, the second pilgrim anticipates 'A noble ceremony' (l. 7). Afterwards, their dialogue is disjointed, consisting in disbelieving exclamations and questions. Their immediate response raises questions which the audience share. What will everyone think of the Duchess's marriage to a man of meaner status (ll. 24–5)? What power does another state have to banish a free prince (ll. 28–9)? Does the play's action deny a place for justice in its political states (ll. 35–6)? The pilgrims' dialogue implies that the Cardinal's actions exceed the bounds of natural justice and the bonds of family. Their characterisation as sceptical observers of the political and familial conflict is central. They have no individual identity, they are unnamed and uninvolved in the rest of the play's action or corruption, and they do not appear again in the play. These three attributes establish a physical bond with the audience, which encourages us to believe in their objectivity: they observe and depart, as we do. Their anonymity and function are choral: like the choruses of Greek tragedy, they objectify and comment on the action, distancing and interpreting. Their function suggests that the play asks us to criticise the Duchess's actions, but equally, the brothers' abuse of patriarchal power. Finally, the pilgrims play one further crucial role as commentators and elucidators of the banishment. The stage directions do not fully describe the action of the dumb show. The pilgrims tell us that the Duchess's ring has been taken 'with violence' from her finger (ll. 36–9), and that the Cardinal has sworn revenge on it.

The framing of the dumb show displays and draws our critical attention to its narrative function as a shocking visual display of the abuse of power and the transgression of familial, political and religious bonds. Framing is thus a meta-theatrical device to engender a critical audience, but creates sympathy with the first-level viewers, unlike those in *The White Devil*. Let us now turn to the dumb show proper.

Music is integral to the performance: 'During all which ceremony, this ditty is sung to very solemn music, by divers Churchmen', intimating the playing and performance of sacred music. In the published version of the play, Webster corrected the manuscript, disclaiming the lyrics as his work (which are consequently omitted here). Music satisfies our aural senses whilst we observe the visual mime. The sacred music, in combination with the setting, creates a dissonant frame when contrasted with the visual action. The dissonance between sound, setting, and action underlines further the disparity between the cardinal's religious office and his military and civil actions, against other political states and against his sister.

The mime itself falls into two halves: the first showing the formal disrobing of the Cardinal's religious costume, and his arming as a military leader; the second, the arrival of the Duchess's family to worship at the shrine, in their search for sanctuary, and their subsequent political banishment by the Cardinal. In slow motion, we are presented with visual metaphors of key themes.

The play's theme of fashion and clothing as dissimulation, of outer masks disguising the inner self, is given another turn: does either garb (military man or chuchman) display the real Cardinal?

The thematic and political opposition between moral, theological and other-worldly values, on the one hand, and military, worldly or civil ones, on the other, is invoked. The Cardinal's disrobing and rearming suggests the victory of worldly values. The pilgrims' later outrage at his actions reasserts the opposition in a transposed form, with the Duchess, justice, truth and morality on the one hand, and corrupt religious, patriarchal self-interest on the other.

Furthermore, the literal re-fashioning of the Cardinal invokes the broader theme of identity which the play addresses. Bosola is continually hiding his identity behind masks and disguises. The brothers mask their intentions in courteous words. The Duchess asks the question 'Who am I?' before her death (4, ii, 122), and shortly answers it with 'I am the Duchess of Malfi still' (4, ii, 141). Her struggle to maintain an identity which fuses her public role with her private domestic happiness is finally physically lost. However, her resurrection as echoing voice and moral icon in Act 5 suggests her identity is recognised *in memoriam* by the audience. The Cardinal's appropriation of different clothing displays an opaque, chameleon-like and shallow character. Masking and disguise, dress and fashion thence become markers of political chicanery.

The Cardinal's arming in sword, shield and spurs builds a visual and physical picture of military masculinity. The phallic symbols of sword and spurs are physically draped about his body. These phallic symbols have previously appeared in the play, in the risqué sexual banter Ferdinand addressed to the Duchess in Act 1, in the celebration of military prowess in that Act, and in Ferdinand's manipulation of his poniard as phallus.

The second part of the dumb show acts as a visual contrast to the Cardinal's military investiture. In contrast to the masculine and martial images, we are shown the arrival of a family in distress. Their arrival at a shrine creates a visual parallel with the Holy Family, transposing the moral and religious symbolism from the Cardinal (who has literally divested himself of it by taking off his religious robes) to them. The private domestic circle of the family, within the safety of the shrine, is visually destroyed by the mimed act of banishment and the taking of the Duchess's ring. The violence of the action is intensified by the contrast with the religious setting, by the familial relationship of Duchess to Cardinal, and by the visual image of a domestic family destroyed. Their physical departure from the stage contrasts markedly with their hopeful arrival at the sanctuary. They have lost the public protection of their political status and lands, and the private security of their marriage. Their abject departure visually draws attention to the extremity of their situation: they leave without home, money, status or protection. The resulting pathos is echoed in the pilgrims' choral commentary, and reinforces the Duchess's status as tragic victim.

Finally, the wedding ring is a central visual prop in the play as a whole. In the first Act, the Duchess used it to cure Antonio's sorrow, and to marry them. It signifies both the privacy and sanctity of her marriage and vows to Antonio. Its circular shape symbolises their private domestic family. The ripping of it from her finger, illustrates her brothers' violent invasion into the sanctity of her marriage and personal privacy. Finally, the symbolic metonymic function of a ring for a woman's sexuality propels the audience into seeing this violence as a near rape, a parallel image to that of Ferdinand invading her private chamber in Act 3, Scene ii. The visual taking and transfer of the ring is a mimed, exaggerated physical action which coalesces verbal and narrative imagery into a single visual icon. This action is the only one which is chorically repeated by the two pilgrims: a verbal reminder of the visual transgression.

In this dumb show, theatricality serves somewhat different ends from the manipulation of theatrical devices in *The White Devil*. Instead of distancing us from the action, it serves to bind us emotionally closer to the Duchess and her plight, mainly through contrasting visual imagery and the clever dramatic use of visual symbolism which echoes earlier symbols. Tragic theatre is literally displayed before the eyes of a secondary audience (the pilgrims) and we see them moved, asking questions and coming to a moral judgement, an illustration of how tragedy works on an audience. The pilgrims validate our own response to the play. Self-conscious theatricality thence creates an objective visual, aural and narrative symbolic microcosm of the whole play. By placing this microcosm at one remove from the audience, displaced through the independent eyes and words of the pilgrims, Webster uses theatricality to ask us to come to both moral and emotional judgements. Theatricality is shown to be an effective and succinct means of imparting crucial political debates and conflicts, and of encouraging an engaged and thinking audience.

Let us now move on to a different example of theatrical self-consciousness in *The Duchess of Malfi*.

Here the Duchess is imprisoned in her own castle by her brothers and Bosola. Ferdinand orders Bosola to ask the Duchess to see him, in the dark. This extract begins as he arrives.

[Act 4, Scene i]
Duchess.   At his pleasure;
            Take hence the lights. He's come.
Ferdinand.   Where are you?
Duchess.   Here, sir.

Ferdinand.	This darkness suits you well.
Duchess.	I would ask your pardon.
Ferdinand.	You have it;

Ferdinand.   You have it;   30

For I account it the honourabl'st revenge,

Where I may kill, to pardon. Where are your cubs?

Duchess.   Whom?

Ferdinand.   Call them your children;   35

For though our national law distinguish bastards

From true legitimate issue, compassionate nature

Makes them all equal.

Duchess.   Do you visit me for this?

You violate a sacrament o'th'church

Shall make you howl in hell for't.

Ferdinand.   It had been well   40

Could you have lived thus always, for indeed

You were too much i'th'light. But no more;

I come to seal my peace with you. Here's a hand

       Gives her a dead man's hand

To which you have vowed much love; the ring upon't

You gave.

Duchess.   I affectionately kiss it.   45

Ferdinand.   Pray do, and bury the print of it in your heart.

I will leave this ring with you for a love token,

And the hand, as sure as the ring; and do not doubt

But you shall have the heart too. When you need a

     friend,

Send it to him that owed it; you shall see   50

Whether he can aid you.

Duchess.   You are very cold.

I fear you are not well after your travel. –

Hah! Lights! – O, horrible!

Ferdinand.   Let her have lights enough.

                               Exit.

Duchess.   What witchcraft doth he practice that he hath left

A dead man's hand here?   55

Here is discovered, behind a traverse, the artificial figures of

ANTONIO *and his children, appearing as if they were dead.*

Bosola.	Look you, here's the piece from which 'twas ta'en.
	He doth present you this sad spectacle
	That, now you know directly they are dead,
	Hereafter you may wisely cease to grieve
	For that which cannot be recovered. 60
Duchess.	There is not between heaven and earth one wish
	I stay for after this: it wastes me more
	Than were 't my picture, fashioned out of wax,
	Stuck with a magical needle and then buried
	In some foul dunghill; and yon's an excellent
	property 65
	For a tyrant, which I would account mercy.

(*The Duchess of Malfi*, 4, i, 28–66)

Here self-conscious theatricality is integrated into the action. The visible theatricality (the use of the 'hand' stage prop and the waxen figures) is doubly framed, first by Ferdinand's plot, and secondly by the Duchess's and Bosola's experience. However, the audience is kept from full knowledge of the nature of the second framing until the end of the scene (sixty lines later). During the main action of this extract, theatricality is invoked naturalistically as part of the action. In sharp contrast, Ferdinand's final admission that he has used the wax dummies as a lie 'to bring her to despair' (4, i, 16) displaces and objectifies theatricality for critical analysis.

Let us first consider the double dramatic framing, which creates a visual and conceptual hierarchy of four separate layers of experience. As the audience, we are in the outermost tier; the second is Ferdinand's plot to torment the Duchess; the third is the experience of the Duchess throughout the scene; and the fourth is the visual wax sculpture of Antonio and the children. However, unlike the double frame in the dumb show of *The White Devil*, the audience is not aware of the dramatic illusionary trick until afterwards. This has an important interpretative effect: during the viewing of the wax works we share the Duchess's horror and grief at the loss of her family, but we and Bosola are then displaced from that by becoming privy to the illusion which Ferdinand has fashioned to torment her.

The framing functions as a dramatic means of changing points of view: from tragic sorrow to relieved laughter; from emotional sympathy to critical analysis. It allows the audience to experience pity, but not to be disabled by that pity. Such relief is not allowed the Duchess, who continues to believe her family has been killed, until moments before her death in the next scene. In being removed from the intense experience of pathos, which Bosola articulates (l. 88), and through being allowed to see Ferdinand's illusion *as* illusion, we literally watch the brothers trying to control the Duchess's life and emotions.

The second way in which theatricality functions is through the use of stage props, which work at two levels for the audience. First, during the main part of the action, we accept the convention that the stage props signify normally: that is, that they really do represent a dead hand, and a transported image of the Duchess's dead family. However, by the end of the scene, the illusion of verisimilitude is destroyed, and the stage props are revealed as literal stage props.

Ferdinand's manner and rhetoric as he presents the hand to the Duchess intimates betrayal. He demands darkness, and he uses doubled, ambiguous words: 'here's a hand / To which you have vowed much love' (ll. 43–4). The stage is dark, so the audience does not always see that the hand is detached from his body, although the ambiguous language makes us suspect it. The suspicion, combined with our knowledge that Ferdinand planned something with Bosola, raises the tension, which is further enhanced by the Duchess's expressed concern for her brother's well-being – she worries he is not well, because the hand is cold. This increases our horror at Ferdinand's grotesque imagination. When the Duchess registers that she has been left with a dead man's hand, we still believe it to be Antonio's, carrying his ring. This is equally the case with the waxen tableau. Waxen figures were frequently used on stage as an alternative to a dumb show, to convey narrative information, and were a well-worn theatrical convention in revenge tragedies. The audience think that they recognise the convention, and the players on stage accept the illusion as a valid way of imparting information. We thus believe that her family is dead. Bosola reinforces this in chorally interpreting the tableau: 'Look you, here's the piece from which 'twas ta'en. / He doth present you this sad spectacle / That, now you know directly they are dead' (ll. 56–8).

There are two key questions here. Why does Webster draw attention to Ferdinand's deception through exposing the fake stage props? And why does he use theatricality to achieve it? We shall consider the question of self-referential theatricality in a moment. By exposing Ferdinand's lies and actions to the Duchess as an illusionary, theatrical art, Webster achieves a paradoxical two-fold effect. The first result is 'to bring her to despair'. We literally see and understand that theatrical art (stage props and spectacle) creates, distils and heightens tragic emotional responses. However, the second effect throws a negative shadow on illusion and theatricality. Ferdinand as the producer, writer, director and chief actor of the evil action and spectacle is demonised, and so is fictional theatre. By contrast, the Duchess's naive acceptance of the illusions places her outside fiction, in opposition to game-playing, masked identities, theatricality and spectacle. Self-conscious theatricality thus condemns Ferdinand and allows us to believe that the Duchess's integrity resonates beyond the fictional illusion of the play.

Finally, let us turn to the Duchess's theatrical and illusionary *references*. The way she uses these is interesting given the context of the whole scene, which is about false, perhaps devilish, illusions. Her first reference 'what witchcraft doth he practice . . . ?' (l. 54) implies that she means the question to be taken literally. She is unaware of the joke about the stage prop and the irony perceived by the audience in the reference to devilish illusions. She really is worried that he is practising witchcraft. Her second reference (ll. 63–6) is to wish herself to be a cold waxen figure, wrapped with those of her family: and again she means this literally. Twenty lines later she analogises her position to an actor in a 'tedious theatre/ For I do play a part in't 'gainst my will' (ll. 84–5). She does not use theatrical metaphor self-consciously: she employs it 'straight'. Ferdinand comments that she is completely deceived by his fiction, a belief confirmed and ironised by her innocent use of language.

However, the audience is made conscious of the metaphors, illusions and stage props, by the setting, structure, framing and revelations of the scene. This achieves several ends. First it enables us to experience the full range of horror, dread, and dark emotion which is inflicted upon the Duchess. Secondly, by subsequently making us aware of the theatrical illusion, Webster distances us from emotion and defamiliarises us from the action. This succeeds in allowing us intellectual judgement about the political manipulation of the Duchess by her brother. Thirdly, and linked to this point, it raises dramatic tension by giving the audience more information than the characters. Fourthly, by placing the Duchess alone outside and in contrast to the negative connotations of illusion, fiction and dramatic spectacle, Webster allies her spatially with the audience: we too are outside the illusion. Fifthly, the self-referential theatricality is often funny: in the way in which extreme special effects in a horror movie can make us laugh, so do the severed hand and the waxen figures. Our laughter partly eases our emotional tension: and it is another means by which Webster changes the pace and point of view within a very short space of performed time. This changed perspective does not lessen the tragedy: that level of response remains with us, but it enables us to acknowledge other, additional responses. These include a pleasure in extreme special effects; an enjoyment in being shocked; and as a result of seeing these, by our laughter and pleasure we come to an ethical self-questioning about the nature of our pleasures and enjoyment.

Conclusions

1. Webster's theatricality is three-fold: first, his awareness of the performability and visual nature of his drama; secondly, his awareness of theatre's artificiality; and thirdly, the manipulation of these two abilities and perceptions in his dumb shows, theatrical 'set-pieces' and masques.
2. Features of the dumb shows and self-conscious theatrical set-pieces include:
   - The establishment of double frames which create different playing and observing spaces. The audience participates emotionally with central characters, and objectifies them in the context of other characters and actions. Our natural reaction to

a play is to both feel and judge: Webster uses stagecraft to maximise these responses, and to make us aware of them.

- Mime and gesture, which slow down the action and raise overall dramatic tension.
- The combination of music and visual effects in meaningful spectacle.
- The reappearance of more general themes and symbolic props within the dumb shows.
- The physical bodies and movements of the actors, which are carefully choreographed. This illustrates Webster's hands-on dramatic skills: the implicit and explicit symbolic blocking and three-dimensional movement of bodies on stage are crucial bearers and makers of dramatic meaning. Theatricality is not just about verbal self-references, visual spectacle, or plays-within-plays: but about the acknowledgement of gesture, action and actor as key vehicles of expression.
- The individual function of each self-conscious theatrical episode is appropriate to its place within the overall plot. In *The White Devil* the dumb shows are not necessary for the furtherance of the narrative: however, they are essential in illustrating Bracciano's character. In *The Duchess of Malfi* the dumb show furthers the plot, but does not illuminate character. In *The White Devil*, the dumb shows objectify characters and events; whilst in *The Duchess of Malfi*, it intensifies audience involvement.
- Some of the dumb shows display the appearance of cinematic or dramatic dream-sequences, which give psychological depth to characterisation and motive.

3. The effects of this form of theatricality include:
   - The creation of a sense of awe and horror in the audience through the combination of silence and mimed violence.
   - Audience defamiliarisation from the actions and characters on stage, creating shifting points of view and shifting perspectives. The aesthetic shape of such changing points of view may be described as cinematic: we are used to juxtaposed scenes and sudden changes of view in film. These juxtapositional aesthetics can be labelled 'baroque' or 'mannerist', the artistic

movement of early seventeenth-century Europe in which visual and sculptural art often mismatched and juxtaposed perspectives, shapes, and points of view to de-stabilise the viewer's perceptions. Webster uses such techniques to engender a critical, sceptical and thinking audience.

- By making the nature of illusion an explicit subject on stage, Webster defuses the argument about the dangerous, diabolical nature of tragedy. He shows us evil illusions, produced by Bracciano and Ferdinand, and the potentially dangerous emotive effect of art (driving the Duchess mad). However, by making us *see* these as illusions, and the way evil art actually reinforces the Duchess's sense of integrity and order, Webster posits his own drama as a 'good' illusion.

4. Webster is critical of the unethical and uncommitted spectator and drama. Bracciano's diabolic illusions are the demonised version of their opposite: an ethical and political theatre. This opposite remains implicit throughout the play in the mind and ideas of the audience, invoked by the condemnation of Bracciano. Webster's theatricality self-consciously acknowledges the dangers of fiction, but poses an alternative where evil can be debated but not endorsed.

5. All the set-pieces demonstrate Webster's lucid visual and theatrical imagination. They illustrate how Webster fuses the visual, physical setting, physical movement, and stage properties with the verbal text and metaphors of the play. The resulting drama can only be meaningful in performance.

Methods of Analysis

In addition to the methods used in previous chapters, this chapter has:

1. Specifically considered the way stage directions choreograph actors and construct visual images.
2. Considered the integration of visual images, stage props, and verbal metaphors with broader themes and actions of the plot.

3. Looked at the way the audience is manipulated by staging techniques.
4. Considered how the stage space is used by different characters and in different situations.
5. Introduced and used new analytical terms, including 'meta-theatricality', 'double frame' and 'distancing'.

Suggested Work

You should look at other aspects of meta-theatricality in the plays.

The White Devil
1. One good place to start is Isabella's 'public' divorce from Bracciano (2, i, 146–265). Here she repeats the words he has used to privately divorce her. What is the effect of the repetition on the audience?
2. Act 4, Scene iii shows the formal election and initiation of the Cardinal as Pope. Comment on the visual function of this scene, its relationship to the surrounding dialogue, and its overall place within the narrative.
3. Act 5 opens with the marriage of Vittoria and Bracciano. How is it framed? Comment on its place within the plot, and its visual theatrical meaning.
4. Act 5, Scene iii is a courtly military tournament to celebrate Vittoria's marriage, at which Bracciano is poisoned by Francisco. Comment on its odd mixture of formality and apparent confusion.
5. Finally, look at the opening of Act 5, Scene vi: here Flamineo tries to murder his sister in a double suicide, in which he pretends to die, whilst she and Zanche try to double-cross him. What is the dramatic effect of the double pretences? Do they distance the audience or intensify our engagement?

The Duchess of Malfi
1. Look at the whole of Act 4, Scene ii, the Duchess's death scene. The scene falls into a clear number of sections: what are these

and what relationship do they have to each other? Why does Bosola disguise himself as a number of different characters? What is the point and performative effect of the dance and conversation of the madmen? Does the Duchess still remain aloof from theatricality? What is the effect of this?

2. Almost every scene in Act 5 betrays an exaggerated theatricality: Scene ii sees Fedinand as a wolf, and includes the Cardinal's plot to kill Julia; Scene iii is the echo scene in the graveyard; Scene iv shows Bosola's accidental killing of Antonio in the dark; and Scene v, Bosola's killing of the Cardinal and Ferdinand. Theatricality becomes linked with excessive violence, coincidence, and evil, except for the Duchess's disembodied echoing voice. Look at each scene and consider the way the audience is asked to think about, and through, theatricality.

8

Iconography and Imagery

The same, or similar, images, symbols and visual icons appear repeatedly in both plays. Furthermore, Webster integrates visual images of action on stage (including pageantry, masques, and the blocking of actors) with setting, costume and props and the more extensive themes of the play, coalescing and concentrating dramatic meaning and conflict through imagery and iconography as well as verbal conflict. For example, visual setting and blocking in the trial scene of *The White Devil* are used to signify a confusion and abuse of roles.

Before we move on, you should remind yourselves of the definition of 'imagery' in the Introduction. In this chapter we shall look at a few of Webster's recurring images and icons within some specific short extracts, considering their significance within the play as a whole. There will be other images in the play that you have noticed, but that we do not have time and space to analyse. The 'Suggested Work' section will give you additional pointers. In each extract we will be analysing explicitly the relationship between visual staging, stage-prop symbolism and verbal imagery, and considering the way in which that relationship resonates within the play as a whole. Let us now turn to *The White Devil*.

*   *   *

The first speech we shall look at comes at the very end of Act 4, sandwiched between the formal election of the Pope, and the marriage of Bracciano and Vittoria at the very beginning of Act 5. Both events are clearly staged as spectacular pageants across the stage.

These two iconic ceremonies are deliberately juxtaposed by Webster in order to further the dramatic ironies inherent in the plot and to suggest the continued corruption of public office and public events. The two events are hinged by Lodovico's comments.

The election of the Pope is attended by the ambassadors, paralleling the trial scene, in which Monticelso was also visually and politically central. The ambassadors' clothes are the opening topic of conversation between Gasparo and Lodovico: some of the colours and their symbolic crosses explicitly delineated: black with a silver cross for the Knight of Rhodes, and red with a white cross for the English ambassador, dedicated to St George. Dialogue emphasises what we see, drawing attention to Christian icons, appropriate to the election of a Pope. Monticelso's election is displayed to the audience when he appears in the white Papal robes on stage 'in state' (4, iii, 58). Visually, the formal costumes of state representatives dominate the scene.

However, the formal, visual, Christian icons and colours, representing spiritual purity, are undermined by both the action and the dialogue of the other characters on stage. Lodovico is present throughout, and functions as both commentator on the action, and servant at the Pope's court (he examines food to check for concealed letters, or bribes for advancement). This actor will be the closest to the audience, and we view the other action, both physically and verbally, past and through him. As a convicted, but pardoned, murderer, his presence and function comment on the visual images, suggesting that outer icons of Christianity accommodate and conceal a dark interior. The audience see this even more clearly through the continued contrast between visual icons and setting and the remaining action of the scene. News is delivered to Francisco of Bracciano's, and Vittoria's escape and pending marriage, at the very moment Monticelso emerges in state. Francisco's whispered communication of the news to Monticelso graphically illustrates the continuation of covert and unethical political chicanery. This covert corruption is made visible by the symbolic gap between visual icons and the real-time action and dialogue on the stage. As we know, the contrast between an exterior and public appearance and inner, corrupt realities is a central theme of the play. It is often the action and dialogue of the play which displays the corruption, whilst setting, costume and stage props proffer a contrasting visual display of pomp, glory and rectitude. The dramatic manipulation of the visual icons thence literally, as well as symbolically, unveils a political, theological and social truth about the world of the play.

The iconography of a theological sacred event is juxtaposed with that of marriage at the opening of Act 5. We see many of the same actors, a similar action (a crowning and a commitment) and the same colour imagery. Thus, the same ambassadors cross the stage, in the same costumes, and Vittoria appears as a bride dressed in white, as the Pope would have been. The procession across the stage intimates celebratory renewal and harmony, symbolised in the social function of marriage and by the colours of purity. However, this image is belied both by the audience's knowledge and Vittoria's social status as a publicly condemned whore. The scenic and visual juxtaposition, combined with the ironic symbolism, illustrates that hypocrisy is criticised from within the plot, as well as externally by the audience. Her white costume echoes Monticelso's in the previous scene: we see two devils visibly re-dressed in symbolic white.

The imagery of colour and dress in these two scenes overall is used to signify that external appearance does not tell us the truth, and further, that we need to be sceptical about any judgements based on external appearance. In addition, the pageantry of these images carries a political message. We see that the trappings of power can be easily manipulated, using conventional symbols (for example, that white means purity and chastity) in order to achieve base political and personal ends. Nevertheless, we have already been positioned as a sceptical audience, and this along with Lodovico's verbal intervention and effective commentary on the symbols, ensures we 'read' the imagery as hypocrisy.

What place does Lodovico's imagery have, juxtaposed as it is between two key iconic scenes? He has just been told by Monticelso not to seek revenge, but given money by Francisco to do so secretly: he believes that despite Monticelso's public words, the money has come from him. Let us read through this brief extract.

[Act 4, Scene iii]
Lodovico.   . . . O the art,
    The modest form of greatness! That do sit
    Like brides at wedding dinners, with their looks
       turned   145
    From the least wanton jests, their puling stomach
    Sick of the modesty, when their thoughts are loose,
    Even acting of those hot and lustful sports
    Are to ensue about midnight; such his cunning!
    He sounds my depth thus with a golden
       plummet,   150
    I am doubly armed now. Now to th'act of blood;
    There's but three Furies found in spacious hell,
    But in a great man's breast three thousand dwell.
                (*The White Devil*, 4,iii, 143–53)

Lodovico makes explicit the thematic and visual link between Monticelso and Vittoria, which is first established at the trial scene. Let us look at his language in detail. He first uses an extended metaphor to comment upon the nature of external visual images ('the art / The modest form') in a political society. The tenor of the simile is Monticelso himself, as well as all great men: the vehicle an extended image of a bride at her wedding dinner, appearing virginal and modest, her appearance and actions masking her thoughts ('loose / Even acting of those hot and lustful sports'). Monticelso's election as Pope is simultaneously, and conventionally, paralleled to marriage and then diminished (through metaphor) to selfish lust. This has several effects.

First, through the ironically delivered vehicle, he describes the exterior behaviour and appearance of those in public office as an 'art' (l. 143) with established exterior behavioural conventions ('*modest form* of greatness'). Secondly, the tenor of the metaphor suggests that exterior forms mask an inner and dark lust. And thirdly, through the linking of both tenor and vehicle, he argues that political and sexual behaviour stem from the same sources of greed, desire and self-interest. The metaphor spells out key dramatic themes: the disparity between outer appearance and inner corrupt reality; the endemic nature of political and theological corruption; the perceived excessive lust of women; the analytical centrality of female sexuality as symbolic of both the external workings of patriarchy and their inner corruption; and the bestial nature of all human endeavours. These themes are ones we find again and again in our analyses, often supplemented by images of fashion and clothing. This linguistic image reappears literally on stage here in the parading of the visual icons of costume and colour, contrasting what we know is underneath.

Lodovico's metaphor thus resonates as a symbolic commentary on the action we have just witnessed and an anticipatory one on the subsequent marriage. His imagery intensifies and draws attention to what the juxtaposition of image and dialogue has already told us in one scene, and is about to do in the subsequent one.

He uses three further metaphors, the last in the closing couplet. The first analogises his inner self to the depths of an ocean or river (l. 150); the second uses a military analogy to justify his motivation ('doubly armed', l. 151). Each of these metaphors echoes both literal actions and metaphorical frames of reference elsewhere in the play. Vittoria describes her death as a shipwreck. Military and gaming metaphors and actions feature in all accounts of masculine courtly behaviour, intimating the odd intermixture of danger, corruption and play. Lodovico's images thus anchor him firmly within the world he inhabits.

His final couplet, and third metaphor, initiates a comparison between hell and a great man's breast, in which by a paradoxical combination of diminution (the Pope's breast is far smaller than 'spacious hell', l. 152) and multiplication (three thousand furies, not three) he creates an image of the evil intensity of Monticelso's anger. The acknowledgement of Monticelso's devilry by one of his own men echoes and confirms all previous such accusations and analogies. The simultaneous characterisation of him as a devil with his visual appearance in white, literally and physically displays his character as the titular 'white devil'. Why are we shown this *before* seeing Vittoria in white? Monticelso's white devilry is literally seen as prior, and more lethal. His devilish reputation and actions are more dangerous than hers, because Lodovico's murderous revenge is half 'armed' by his belief that Monticelso has authorised his actions.

Imagery literally displays this to us, a reinforcement of all the other dramatic modes through which Monticelso's evil is demonstrated.

Imagery is thence two-fold: it is visual (iconic) and verbal (metaphoric). Iconic imagery is used in this part of the play to intensify and clarify moral judgement, to remind us of colour images and their function and to emphasise the theme of the gap between appearance and reality. Verbal imagery is used to link Monticelso and Vittoria, to argue that femininity is a deceitful performance, and suggest that hidden sexuality drives all human behaviour, whilst appearances of propriety and modesty dominate social conventions.

Lodovico's language is also typical of the play in using imagery to paint and describe other characters, rather than himself. It is through his images that we learn about Monticelso's and Francisco's characters and motivations. This is an interesting dramatic technique, because while it creates an atmosphere of distrust and evil at court, we are never completely sure of the reliability of a commentator character. The imagery used by commentator characters keeps the audience aware of corruption in the courtiers and politicians they observe. But because we are continually aware of their commentator status, we can never be objectively certain whether the motivations and inner lives objectified through imagery are just the commentator's perceptions, or an approximation at truth. This uncertainty, both in us and in the drama, ensures that Monticelso and Francisco remain partly opaque. This method of characterisation is a key dramatic technique: our uncertainty about their future actions at the close of the play leaves us with a sense of amorphous political corruption. Additionally, the fact that characters mostly use imagery to describe others rather than themselves displays a world where identity is both worldly and relational, rather than interior. By relational, I mean that identity is displayed to us in relation to circumstance, action and the commentaries of others.

The exceptions to this lie in the imagery that characters use as they move towards death or a major crisis, the only point at which Webster allows them some self-knowledge. We have looked at both Vittoria's and Flamineo's language at the end of Act 5, in Chapter 2. Let us now briefly consider a slightly earlier speech by Flamineo. He has just observed his mother distracted and driven mad by his killing

of his brother Marcello, and dressing his corpse with flowers. She
gives Flamineo rosemary, rue and heartsease (5, iv, 77–8), but mis-
takes him for 'the gravemaker'. On her exit, he speaks the following
lines, alone on stage, which are then immediately followed by his
confrontation with Bracciano's ghost.

[Act 5, Scene iv]
Flamineo.   I have a strange thing in me, to th'which
               I cannot give a name, without it be   115
               Compassion. I pray leave me.   *Exit Francisco.*
               This night I'll know the utmost of my fate;
               I'll be resolved what my rich sister means
               T'assign me for my service. I have lived
               Riotously ill, like some that live in court;   120
               And sometimes, when my face was full of smiles,
               Have felt the maze of conscience in my breast.
               Oft gay and honoured robes those tortures try;
               We think caged birds sing, when indeed they cry.
                               (*The White Devil*, 5, iv, 114–24)

Flamineo here comes close to self-knowledge. The language in which
this is expressed is paradigmatic of the way imagery and language
function in the play. Literal words haltingly speak truths: metaphor
and images flow thick and fast, eloquently positing images of feelings and interior life, which aim at clarity, but often obscure as
much as they reveal. Flamineo's words fall into two parts: the halting
start, and then his succession of four metaphors in five lines.

    He begins by stating that there is no language for his feelings: 'I
have a *strange* thing in me', to which 'I cannot give a name, without
it be / Compassion'. This last word is propelled from his mouth,
shot out at the beginning of a line, and then end stopped, indicating
a pause. His inability to name an emotion, to articulate, and the
stuttering rhythm with which it is pronounced, paradoxically intimates a more intense emotional response than elsewhere. The surfeit
of words and images with which Flamineo usually bombards us is
absent. Verbosity and cumulative imagery are part of the excess and
deceitful display of courtly life, as we saw in the play's opening use

of imagistic language, conveying a world of circumlocution and deceit. Here, Flamineo's stumbling response and actual words replicate that insight. Ironically, then language and images both reveal and conceal. Flamineo, the master of metaphors, is first lost for words, and when forced to speak of his feelings, speaks literally.

The second part of his speech (ll. 120–4) contains four metaphors, the overall tenors suggesting the gap between courtly appearance and interior life, between gaudy exterior and dark reality. His first metaphor, 'I have lived / *Riotously* ill, like some that live at court,' analogises his life and that of other courtiers to 'riots'. This paints an image of a world turned from its proper path, a world of excess and violence, where respect, authority and order are ignored. His analytical view of the political world concurs with our own observations and makes us believe his expression of momentary remorse. The combination of analytical commentary and self-awareness is typical of the malcontent-type figure which Flamineo has played throughout the play. Thus, whilst we distrust his eloquence, we believe what he says: our response delicately balanced between scepticism and belief.

The second metaphor's vehicle ('when my face was full of smiles, / Have felt the *maze* of conscience in my breast') tries to map a description of inner life, by using the analogy of a maze. The image is almost a pun: the winding maze conjures up both a physical image and a physical feeling of being lost, of not knowing the way forward or back. But the noun 'maze' also means astonishment or confusion, so Webster utilises both literal and metaphorical senses. This image then names both his bewildered sensibility, and a sense of his physical and spiritual interior. The tenor of the metaphor is again the absolute divide between exterior forms and inward feelings.

The final couplet here consists of one metaphor to each line. The first uses the metonymy of clothes to denominate great men ('gay and honoured robes') and their glorious exterior appearance, and to suggest that, by contrast, their interior life, like his, is tortured. The clothes imagery works on several levels. It continues the theme of the gap between outer appearance and inner truths. It also works on a political level, suggesting that political and courtly finery in particular is a disguise. Finally, it invokes the theatrical imagery and theme used elsewhere in the play to suggest that all identity is the performance of a role in costume. The second line of the couplet ('We think caged birds sing, when indeed they cry') is an evocative and conclusive summary of his whole speech, personalising his generalisations and his political commentary.

The vehicle of the metaphor has two parts to it: the caged birds, and the real meaning of their singing. The whole line is a commentary on the previous one, so we know he is analogising courtiers to caged birds, whilst the tenor is the conduct and meaning of courtiers' lives. This analogy re-figures a political life of service as a claustrophobic entrapment in which one is expected to perform (or sing) for the entertainment of one's owners. Courtiers are cruelly anatomised as subservient pets. The second half of the image ('when indeed they cry') works at two levels: first, it suggests that political language always means something other than what it says ('*indeed*'). However, its broader meaning proposes a deeply sceptical view about all language and performance: what we see and hear is not the truth. Singing does not signify an expressive joy but a terrified sorrow. His metaphor creates a despairing image of how language itself cannot tell the truth. Flamineo suggests that we can never really know another's feelings or thoughts.

In summary, his metaphors reiterate images and themes which recur elsewhere in the play. But they go one step further than that: they engender in us a despairing sense that language cannot name our experiences. Language clothes our thoughts in the way in which dress clothes our body: and the play has made us distrust all such outward signs. In the end, the vehicle, tenor and function of his imagery all combine at different levels to tell us to be sceptical about what we see and hear. The extensive use of theatrical, clothing and animalistic metaphors, joined with the surplus of metaphoric language, constructs a paradoxical world. It is a world of performance, of the parade of appearance and role and speech: but we are continually told to mistrust the exterior performance, and that underneath our exterior lies a bestial interior. We are left with an open question: where is truth? It is a question which is not answered by the play.

Let us move on now to *The Duchess of Malfi*.

*   *   *

You could choose almost any speech in the play and find imagery which resonates with the overall themes and visual icons. If you return, for example, to Chapter 5, and look at Bosola's speech to the old lady, the metaphors of sickness, health, bodily functions and excretion, witchcraft and animalism dominate. The continual presence of these metaphors spreads a sense of sickness and corruption over political courts and the actions of politicians. By contrast, interestingly, the Duchess rarely uses imagery at all. Where she does use metaphor, she uses theatrical or religious images, rather than those of the body or debased animals, which tend to be used by Bosola, Ferdinand and other courtiers.

I have chosen three images to comment on, two of which utilise animal imagery in different ways to suggest a commentary on the present fallen and corrupt world, and posit an impossible image of an ideal one. The third also uses images from the natural world, to suggest the integration of the human with both the physical and spiritual worlds.

The first comes from Act 1, at a point where Antonio and Delio are conversing for the second time about the political situation in Italy and specifically about the political characters on stage. Ferdinand's Machiavellian, manipulative and performative character is sketched by Antonio: 'If he laugh heartily, it is to laugh / All honesty out of fashion' (ll. 171–2) and 'Dooms men to death by information / Rewards by hearsay' (ll. 176–7). Delio then uses an extended metaphor to comment on the nature of the political state he has heard described:

[Act 1, Scene i]
Delio. Then the law to him
  Is like a foul black cobweb to a spider:
  He makes it his dwelling and a prison
  To entangle those shall feed him.
  (*The Duchess of Malfi*, 1, i, 177–80)

Both tenor and vehicle of this extended simile are central to the images and themes of the play. The vehicle paints a picture of a malevolent spider sitting in the middle of a thick cobweb. The image is redolent of evil, menace and calculation, and of unkempt disorder. The spider sits in his sticky web and both awaits and controls his prey. The extended simile is taken further in the two subsequent lines, the delivery and rhetoric intensifying the moral judgement implied by the overall comparison of a web to the law, and Ferdinand to a spider. First, Delio outlines the web's double and paradoxical function in the description 'dwelling and a prison': intimating dark and claustrophobic associations with dungeons and entrapment, which resonate later in the play when the Duchess herself is imprisoned in her own dwelling by her brothers. Secondly, he continues the exposition of the mutual dependence of perpetrator and victim, 'To entangle those shall feed him', by positing an inversion and transgression of normal laws of hospitality, and implying that the law under Ferdinand will consume and not protect. The world the simile denotes is one of darkness, inversion, feeding, capture, greed, imprisonment and poison. It is a world dominated and determined by physical appetites.

The tenor of the extended simile is Ferdinand's character and abuse of the law: Delio's image graphically conjures animalistic inversion long before we hear Ferdinand himself give voice to such thoughts, and presages his final descent into the bestial lycanthropia. Images surrounding the court and the brothers thence prefigure and help create an atmosphere of excessive appetites, inversion, darkness and abuse. The brothers' political and fraternal manipulation of their sister, which becomes the action of the play, is placed within this context from the very opening of the play.

Finally, the character making this judgement is himself an outsider. Delio is an adviser and confidant of Antonio's, he never initiates action himself, and is usually standing on the edge of the stage, or at the margins of a more important event or scene. In addition, he is the character who leads the Duchess's son onto the stage at the end. He is thus physically and structurally a character whom we are encouraged to trust. We thence tend to see his metaphors as reliable, providing an accurate, moralised description of the brothers' politics.

Animal omens figure literally as well metaphorically in the play. Examples include the owl hooting before the Duchess's first confinement; Ferdinand's attack on the Duchess as 'screech-owl' (3, iii, 88), and wish to banish Antonio to the company of monkeys (3, iii, 100–7); Bosola's hangman's song, which invokes all creatures of the night; and Ferdinand's own mad descent into a wolf's identity. Bestiality literally becomes our final, possibly terrifying, identity underneath the veneer of conventional socialised behaviour, prefigured in Delio's image of Ferdinand as a spider, and of supposedly independent institutions, such as the law, as his cobweb.

The second extract also uses natural imagery, but tenor, vehicle and speaker all point in a completely different direction to the example we have just analysed. The words are spoken by the Duchess to Antonio in the scene succeeding their banishment, during a disbelieving discussion about their loss of status, followers, and home. Her words are followed by the sudden entry of Bosola, summoning Antonio to Ferdinand. She allows herself to be taken back, whilst Antonio flees. The tone of this comment is somewhat whimsical, but the context gives her fanciful desire the status and resonance of a utopian dream, expressed in sharp contrast to the hard, double-dealing of the masculine political world she has offended.

[Act 3, Scene v]
Duchess.   The birds that live i'th'field
On the wild benefit of nature live
Happier than we; for they may choose their mates,
And carol their sweet pleasures to the spring.
(*The Duchess of Malfi*, 3, v, 18–21)

Again, both tenor and vehicle enhance and supplement the meaning of the whole scene and resonate throughout the play. The tenor is the analogy between wild birds and humans: but it is an analogy which is raised only to be denied. This denial of the viability of a human/animal analogy tells us much about the Duchess's pragmatic understanding of the political and familial conflict in which she is embroiled. The way her metaphor both asserts and rejects a naturalistic idealism self-consciously exposes her escapist desire as solely a wishful fiction: wouldn't it be nice if . . . ?

The vehicle paints an image of unfettered natural freedom,

invoking ideas of the classical golden age when nature provided abundant food, and conflict was unknown. However, her comparison goes further than the description of an ecological paradise: after setting the physical scene, her key point is about animals being free to choose their own mates and the consequent freedom of their 'pleasure'. Here she conveys a vision of an alternative world: where free will and natural desire, not status or political negotiation or family, determine one's path, sexuality, love and actions. She is only able to articulate this desire for freedom indirectly, through an image which she has to admit is a dream. However, the image reminds the audience of the pleasure she found in the private world she and Antonio created, and which we glimpsed briefly at the beginning of Act 3. It is an image which is set in absolute thematic and dramatic opposition to the actions and beliefs of her brothers. The audience see and feel the various aspects of this opposition: between pleasure and duty, women and patriarchal control, love and politics, privacy and surveillance, freedom and entrapment. This metaphor's vehicle is therefore a key building block in giving words and pictures to the alternative the Duchess represents.

However, the tenor of the metaphor effectively illustrates, to both the Duchess and the audience, that the imagined, idealistic alternative of pursuing an unfettered naturalism is impossible: our world is not like this imagined one, for these imagined birds are 'happier'. By stating a comparison, but denying its validity, the Duchess uses the workings of imagery to literally express her impossible situation. We in the present are not in this imagined unfettered animalist world. This comparison has two crucial opposite effects. First, it distinguishes humans from animals absolutely, allying her with a spiritual rather than a physical realm, against the bestial descent of her brothers. Secondly, it also suggests, indirectly, to the audience, that the fallen, evil world she experiences is a constructed world: it is not 'natural' (unlike the birds). This crucial perception suggests that her brothers' world may be changed: it is neither natural nor inevitable. Her negative comparison places herself and the play firmly within the realm of a human political world, defined in opposition to the natural, by ideas, social and familial structure and economics created by men. Nevertheless, her image, placed in absolute opposition to the world in the play, functions as a powerful utopian critique of that corrupt unnatural world. Paradoxically, then, although her image resonates tragically (for it is impossible to achieve within the play), it produces a critique of the political and social customs and the workings of state and familial power in the play as temporal, unnatural human constructs.

Let us now look at the final extract. This speech occurs after the Duchess, Cariola and the children have all been strangled. Ferdinand has left the stage to Bosola and the Duchess's body. After this speech, she briefly revives before death, rousing and dashing the hopes of both Bosola and the audience. There are seven metaphors, conceptually and coherently linked in both tenor and vehicle. Let us read through the passage, and then list the metaphors.

Bosola.	. . . Off, my painted honour!	335
	While with vain hopes our faculties we tire,	
	We seem to sweat in ice and freeze in fire.	
	What would I do, were this to do again?	
	I would not change my peace of conscience	
	For all the wealth of Europe. She stirs; here's life!	340
	Return, fair soul, from darkness, and lead mine	
	Out of this sensible hell. She's warm, she breathes!	
	Upon thy pale lips I will melt my heart	
	To store them with fresh colour. – Who's there?	
	Some cordial drink! – Alas! I dare not call.	
	So pity would destroy pity. – Her eye opes,	345
	And heaven in it seems to ope, that was late shut,	
	To take me up to mercy.	

(*The Duchess of Malfi*, 4, ii, 335–8)

We have observed Bosola's dense metaphorical language in previous chapters, so the presence of seven separate metaphors in twelve lines is not particularly unusual for him. In the face of this death, and his subsequent confrontation with both damnation and salvation, his linguistic delivery does not change much. However, the subject matter he deals with is very different from his usual vein. Let us list each metaphor.

1. Political honour as cosmetic or costume (l. 335)
2. Current physical experience described as 'to sweat in ice and freeze in fire' (l. 337)
3. A clear conscience analogised to political peace (l. 339)
4. Death as darkness (l. 341)
5. The current situation as 'sensible hell' (l. 342)
6. His heart will literally melt to give fresh colour (blood) to her lips (ll. 343–4)
7. The Duchess's open eyes, and metonymically her body, analogised to heaven (ll. 346–7)

The vehicles of this succession of metaphors are interesting: painted honour, icy sweat, freezing fire, peace, darkness, sensible hell, melting hearts, and heaven. They set up a semantic oppositional field between hell and heaven. Hell is linked literally to Bosola's own physically described experience; heaven literally to the body of the Duchess. The tenors linked to each symbolic place spell this out. Hell's words are painting, freezing fire and burning ice, and darkness. A 'sensible' hell is one that is literally felt. Heaven's words are peace, the ability to melt hearts and open eyes. Bosola's metaphors additionally link heaven and hell in his own body. His belief that she may be breathing still, precipitates his offer to melt his heart to colour her lips. The heat from the hellish image of sweating in ice and freezing in fire, is transposed to a positive physical force: it can enliven her dead lips. This is an astonishing and emotive image: a melting heart is a metaphorical commonplace, but Bosola seems to imagine it literally. His melting (and therefore bleeding) heart will colour her lips: his heart literally destroyed to save her life. His metaphor expresses repentance directly through an image of self-sacrifice. Instead of telling us he has repented, his imagery plays out the physical evidence of it. His repentance is confirmed in his belief that her eyes will 'take me up to mercy'·(l. 348).

The tenors are actually less interesting than the vehicles: as we have seen the latter delineate the sensual pain and terrors of living in hell on earth. The tenor is the continued theme of the fallen nature of our present, painted and corrupt world, and the idea of salvation through mercy. There is much critical debate about whether Webster does provide an idea of salvation in this play. This particular extract shows that he does. The semantic oppositions and metaphors here work in conjunction with the action: the Duchess's death shocks the audience, but shocks Bosola more. His emotional reaction takes him by surprise, and seems to precipitate the nature and content of the metaphoric language. We recognise the Duchess's function as symbolising the possibility of salvation through Bosola's response and his language. The physically descriptive and sensuous tenors, invoking conventional and recognisable images and concepts of hell and heaven and their conventional denotations, are here given new meaning. The action credibly displays Bosola moving from one state (of hell) to a new state (of melting mercy). It is both the opposition of the two sets of metaphors and their connection through Bosola's change of character that posits the possibility and experience of redemption and hope: both for him and for the audience.

Conclusions

1. Webster's imagery is reiterative and replicative: he uses both recurrent and patterned images throughout the play. Reiterative images forcefully register on the audience and create a consistent visual and conceptual world. Replicative images (that is, a tapestry of different metaphors whose subject matter is similar) appeal to many conceptual senses, intensifying our sense of a claustrophobic physical setting.
2. Verbal and visual images greatly extend and deepen our sensory and intellectual understanding of Webster's political and social world. However, they go further than merely deepening our understanding: they sharpen our sense of dramatic crisis and conflict, often prefiguring actual tragic events. They raise dramatic tension in varying ways. For example, they can slow down the action, creating an anticipatory sense of future events. By contrast, they can illuminate a conceptual insight by expressly coinciding with a character's self-knowledge, or with other themes, as we saw in both of the last extracts from *The Duchess of Malfi*. Finally, imagery can significantly develop the action in a non-

verbal way: this is clearest in Wesbter's use of colour imagery in the successive formal ceremonies of *The White Devil.*

3. Visual and verbal imagery echo and reinforce each other in both plays. Colour imagery in *The White Devil*, from the title through to the last scene, is intensified and made literal by costume. In *The Duchess of Malfi* rings are an integral part of the textual reference and symbolic action, and as stage props they become physical emblems of the secure world that is eventually lost. Animals and natural disasters are used as metaphors throughout. These metaphors are also visual: the action often occurs in the dark, we hear the crying of animals and the coming of storms, and we eventually watch Ferdinand's act as a wolf-man.

4. All images use a tenor and vehicle: Webster's consider both extremely carefully, and they are structurally clustered in each play. The world of images and ideas raised by the vehicles of his metaphors construct a consistent picture of a world turned awry; dark; plagued or poisoned by sickness, deformity and witchcraft; gaudily painted and performative; and reduced to purely physical functions. The consistent world created by the imagistic vehicles is the way Webster creates a dramatic, sensory idea of the corruption and evil of the world he paints. The tenor of the images is equally systematic: the spiritually sick, fallen political and social world.

5. The natural basis of many of Webster's images suggests a world-view in which the microcosm is intimately connected with the macrocosm. However, the characters frequently suggest that this connection has broken down: despite the gaudy appearances of the courtly world, in reality it stinks of corruption and decay. The Duchess's image of the wild birds is perhaps the most poignant example of this radical division between ideal universal harmony and the actual human world.

6. Clusters of images, using either similar vehicles or the same tenor, are often used by the same types of characters. For example, images of death, sickness, decay, bestiality and deformity are used by malcontent figures, such as Lodovico, Flamineo, Bosola, and Ferdinand. Images of truth and justice are used mainly by women.

7. Imagery is most often used to describe other characters, or a desire, rather than an internal state of emotion. It thus tends to reflect and help create a sense of how identity is fashioned in and by the world.

Methods of Analysis

In this chapter we have chosen a few key images from each play, from scenes which we have looked at or mentioned previously, and then proceeded in the following way:

1. Looked separately at both tenor and vehicle: the language of the comparison and the overall meaning of it.
2. Considered the immediate dramatic place and function of the image, through relating it to its dramatic and conceptual context.
3. Related the image to other similar ones in the play, considering the cumulative effect of such images on the audience.
4. Asked whether the image was being used differently to previous examples.
5. Tried to recall other images with similar semantic fields: linking, for example, images of fashion with costume and theatricality.
6. Thought about the effect of the reiteration of images, icons and image patterns on the audience.
7. Integrated our thinking and perceptions about verbal imagery with that about visual imagery and theatricality.

Suggested Work

There has not been space within this chapter to follow through the continuity of a single image, for example, black and white, or poison in *The White Devil*, and bestiality in *The Duchess of Malfi*. However, you should try to note down recurrences of patterned and repeated images, and begin to undertake that kind of more extensive analysis yourself. Pick any image which has stayed in your mind from the analyses in this book, and trace its recurrence and function within the play. Try doing this with a single word and examine its recurrence. Look at which character speaks it, when and why. Recurring images which you find in both plays include: poisoning, medical imagery, masking and playing, bestial imagery, and food. Here are a few additional ideas.

The White Devil

1. Look at one of the first images Flamineo uses about sex: 'If the buttery hatch at court stood continually open, there would be nothing so passionate crowding, nor hot suit after beverage' (1, ii, 23–6). Comment on tenor and vehicle, and the linkage of feeding, sex and politics. Where else and why does this type of imagery recur?

2. Look at the way the word 'devil' recurs: for example, 1, ii, 251 (Flamineo's aside about Vittoria's dream); 3, ii, 217 (Monticelso's accusation that Vittoria is a devil); 3, iii, 16–17 (Flamineo links the characters of devils, politicians and actors); 4, ii, 57 (Flamineo claims there are degrees of devils in the world); 5, i, 86–90 (Marcello and Flamineo call Zanche a devil); 5, iii, 103 (Bracciano believes Flamineo is the devil) and 5, iii, 154–70 (Lodovico links Bracciano to the devil); and 5, vi, 18 (Flamineo accuses Vittoria of having the devil in her). Comment on who speaks the accusations. How does each relate to the title? How does other imagery in the play relate to this word?

The Duchess of Malfi

1. Analyse the language and image of Bosola's tale of an old lady: 'There was a lady in France, that having had the smallpox, flayed the skin off her face' (2, i, 28–32). How do the different vehicles here resonate within the action and atmosphere of the play? What themes are echoed by it?

2. Look at the repeated imagery of eyes: Antonio's weeping eye mended by the Duchess's sovereign ring in Act 1; his reference to her eyes weeping pearls, in 3, v, 16–17; Bosola's watching of her eyes before and after she dies (Act 4, Scene ii); and Ferdinand's 'Cover her face, mine eyes dazzle', in the same scene (4, ii, 263), a motif he repeats when he cries 'I have cruel sore eyes' (5, ii, 64).

What is the symbolic function of eyes? Where else do we have a sense of watching eyes? Are there other images in the play which supplement the semantic frame established by the vehicle? Examples you might find include stars, brightness, and sight.

3. Look at the visual and verbal image of the ring.

General Conclusions to Part 1

1. Webster's tragic world is explicitly social and political: individuals are seen to be trapped by conventions, corrupt practices, social and political hierarchies, and socialised gender norms, as much as by their own *hubris*, evil or actions. Tragedy is seen to result from the mis-match between individual desire or action, and social, familial or political constraints. Such constraints are themselves characterised as corrupt: but conversely, individual rights and liberties are not necessarily represented as 'good'. Webster does not set up black-and-white moral values in this conflict, but asks us to debate the issues.

2. The world which Webster's main characters inhabit is one characterised by decay, corruption, amorality, bestiality, and chaos, and this is intimately linked through metaphors and action to the political and theological institutions. Order and virtue lie, for the most part, outside the realm of the play, and thereby appear as unattainable ideals.

3. The heroines and heroes are in visible conflict with dominant ideas or power relations, rather than engaged in an internal conflict (as are Shakespearean protagonists). This conflict informs the overall structure of the plays, as well as the internal structure of scenes and dialogues.

4. The plays are structured to engender particular sympathy for, and understanding of, the tragic heroines and their situation. Our understanding is created by scenic juxtapositions, and dramatic structure, as much as by the content of their speeches and characterisation.

5. Webster's plays are typically dialogic and open-ended: he sets up debates on political and social subjects which are taken up by the audience.

6. His sense of the theatrical nature and performability of his plays is evident throughout, and we need to attend to the meanings and manipulations of three-dimensional narrative and iconic symbols as much as to the more conventional verbal text of the plays.

PART 2

THE CONTEXT
AND THE CRITICS

9

Webster's Plays

John Webster was born in about 1578 and died in 1634, his life spanning the reigns of Elizabeth I, James I and Charles I. The first records of his working life as a playwright begin in 1602, at the very end of Elizabeth's reign. His plays continued to be performed in repertory until and beyond his death, although the last play he wrote was in 1627 (*Appius and Virginia*). The range and nature of the plays he wrote across his career can illuminate his two tragedies. He only wrote one other play as a sole author: his others were all collaborative, written jointly with other playwrights. His other sole-authored play, *The Devil's Law Case*, is a tragicomedy, setting up potentially tragic situations and conflict, which are magically resolved and transformed by a surprise ending. He wrote this play after his two tragedies, in 1617 or 1618, and its combination of tragic intensity, with comic closure and a burlesque, often macabre, jokiness has similarities with both the structure and content of the two tragedies. We shall return to these similarities in a moment, when we come to discuss the relationship of the two tragedies to his whole career's work. However, let us first have a look at a probable chronology of his work, and comment on both his working methods and the range and types of writing in which he was engaged over twenty-five years of writing.

Before we look at his writing career, it is useful to look at the Elizabethan and Jacobean theatrical world. There were three main theatre companies in London during the later part of Elizabeth's reign: The Chamberlain's Men (the company with whom

Shakespeare worked); the Admiral's Men (who held the copyright of Marlowe's plays); and Worcester's Men. These companies consisted of adult men and teenage boys (there were no women actors on the public stage until after the Restoration), and during the 1590s and early 1600s the three adult companies played in outdoor theatres, seating about 3000 people. In 1599 the adult companies were supplemented by the establishment of a boys' acting company, St Paul's Boys, who played in a small indoor theatre, seating about 200. The price of admission was far greater than for the larger theatres, and this tended to produce a wealthier, narrower audience than that of the outdoor arena theatres. The drama written for the boys was more stylised and satirical than that hitherto performed by adults. At the accession of James I, the three adult companies all gained new royal patrons and became, respectively, The King's Men, Prince Henry's Men and Queen Anne's Men. Later a fourth major company was formed, from the merging of a small adult company with St Paul's Boys, and named the Lady Elizabeth's Company.

Several writers held shares in one company, or were continually employed by them, others wrote for different companies as and when commissioned. Thus, Shakespeare held a major share in The King's Men and wrote all his work for them. Marston was commissioned by St Paul's Boys to write all his early plays for them. By contrast, Middleton wrote for The King's Men, Prince Henry's Men and Lady Elizabeth's Company. The King's Men had established themselves as the leading company by gaining the monarch's patronage, and they consequently played most often at court. They built the new outdoor Globe theatre on the South Bank, moving there in 1599, and played most of their repertory there. In 1609 they additionally began playing at an indoor theatre called Blackfriars, allowing themselves both a summer and winter season. The other two companies played at the Fortune Theatre or The Red Bull, near Smithfield and Clerkenwell, both open-air theatres attracting diverse audiences, and both of which also hosted other entertainments such as bear baiting.

Critical history in the past has argued that there were two 'rival traditions' in Jacobean theatre: the private and the public. The former was played indoors to elite and educated audiences, and tended to be satirical and meta-theatrical; and the latter played out-doors to populist mass audiences, catering to their tastes with stories of romance and swashbuckling adventure, and history. In recent years, this view has been challenged on various fronts: audiences have been shown to have been equally diverse in their tastes in both theatres; satirical plays also played in public theatres; and the influence of the boy actors on adult companies and repertories was great. The history of The King's Men is a good example of how the rival traditions blurred. They began playing at The Theatre and The Globe in public outdoor theatres, in the 1590s, and their repertory included all of Shakespeare's comedies and histories, as well as Ben Jonson's early comedies. In 1604 they commissioned Webster to write a new Induction to a play to which they had bought the copy-right from St Paul's Boys, John Marston's *The Malcontent*, which drew explicit attention to its meta-theatrical framing. The suppos-edly elite content of the play (given it was written for a boys' company) was happily received by the Globe's plebeian audience. The King's Men's subsequent purchase of an indoor theatre in 1608 proved that a single company could perform in different types of staging spaces, to different audiences, with the same plays, and remain successful. This illustrates that, whilst there were two dif-ferent types of theatre, and therefore different staging spaces and conventions within these, we ignore the cross-fertilisation between these two experiences if we rigidly define them as 'rival' traditions. Finally, many writers collaborated on the writing and production of plays, even Shakespeare, for example with Fletcher in both *Henry VIII* and *The Two Noble Kinsmen*. Jonson wrote *Eastward Ho!* with Marston, and so on. Collaborative writing was an accepted way of dividing up the labour to speed up production time, and to enable theatre companies to perform plays combining the different strengths of major authors. Many television comedies today are written by teams of writers, or two writers who together produce something distinctive and different. The way in which plays were both commissioned and written in Webster's period was very similar to the way television scripts today are commissioned, written and produced by a diverse number of production companies for several different channels, which cater for slightly different audiences.

Where does Webster's work belong in this brief outline? The following chronology gives the first dates of his theatrical productions, or other pieces of writing, the company which commissioned the play, the place of its performance, its genre, and Webster's collaborators. Take time to familiarise yourself with his career, before moving on to the rest of the chapter.

Date	Commissioned by	Place performed	Authors	Genre	Title
1602	Lord Admiral's Men	Rose Theatre	Dekker Middleton Munday Webster	Roman	*Caesar's Fall* [lost]
1602	Lord Admiral's Men	Rose Theatre	Heywood Webster	History play	*Lady Jane* (later pub. as *The Famous History of Sir Thomas Wyatt*)
1602/3	Worcester's Men	Rose Theatre	Chettle Dekker Heywood Smith Webster	Revels comedy	*Christmas Comes but Once a Year* [lost]
1604	The King's Men	The Globe	Webster [Marston's play]	Tragi-comedy	Revision of and Induction to Marston's *The Malcontent*
1604	St Paul's Boys	St Paul's Boys' indoor theatre	Dekker Webster	City comedy	*Westward Ho!*
1605	St Paul's Boys	St Paul's Boys' indoor theatre	Dekker Webster	City comedy	*Northward Ho!*
1612	Queen Anne's Men	Red Bull	Webster	Tragedy	*The White Devil*
1613				Elegiac poem	Elegy to Prince of Wales on his death; prefatory poem to Heywood's *Apology for Actors*

Date	Commissioned by	Place performed	Authors	Genre	Title
1614	The King's Men	Blackfriars, then The Globe	Webster	Tragedy	*The Duchess of Malfi*
1615				Essays	Contributed to Overbury's *Characters*
1619	Queen Anne's Men	The Cockpit (indoor theatre built in 1616)	Webster	Tragi-comedy	*The Devil's Law Case*
1620/1	The King's Men	Blackfriars	Middleton Webster	City comedy	*Anything for a Quiet Life*
1623					*The Duchess of Malfi* and *The Devil's Law Case* published
1624	Red Bull Company (formerly Queen Anne's Men, until her death in 1619)	The Red Bull	Dekker Ford Rowley Webster	Reportage tragedy	*The Late Murder of the Son upon the Mother* [lost]
1624	Merchant Taylor's Company	A pageant in London streets, for the Lord Mayor's inaugural banquet	Webster	Pageant	*Monuments of Honour*
1624/5	Unknown	Unknown	Rowley Webster	Tragi-comedy	*A Cure for a Cuckold*
1625/6	The King's Men	Blackfriars	Fletcher Ford Massinger Webster	Tragi-comedy	*The Fair Maid of the Inn*
*c.*1627	Unknown	Unknown	Heywood	Roman history/ tragedy	*Appius and Virginia*

A few of these dates are conjectural, most based on evidence from lists in The Stationer's Register, where all plays had to be registered as having successfully passed the censor's official pen.

Several points of interest emerge from this chronology. Webster's writing career spanned twenty-five years, a similar length to that of Shakespeare's. He began his writing career collaborating with well-known populist writers: his association with Dekker culminating in the immensely successful and popular 'Ho!' plays of 1604 and 1605. The plays he wrote or shared the writing of represent a broad generic range: including English history plays, revels entertainments, city comedies, tragedies, tragicomedies, and Roman history. This undoubtedly enabled an experimental dramatic apprenticeship. His linguistic and dramatic versatility and reliability cannot be in doubt: he was commissioned to write both on his own and collaboratively in a range of genres. There is no evidence about how he spent his 'gap years', most particularly those between 1605, when *Northward Ho!* was performed, and the first performance of *The White Devil* in 1612. We shall return to this gap in a moment. Although he did not collaborate with either Shakespeare or Jonson, he did write with all the other major dramatist of the Jacobean and early Caroline period: Dekker, Middleton, Heywood, Rowley, Ford, Massinger and Fletcher. Finally, his two tragedies were produced after a decade of apprenticeship to respected writers and companies, and apparently written and performed within two or three years of each other.

We must see him therefore as embedded fully in the contemporary commercial and aesthetic practices of the theatre, sharing the available commissions with leading fellow writers. The production of plays to commission, as he and his contemporaries did, means that we should be careful about using concepts such as 'artistic freedom' and 'authorial control'. Webster's writing is clearly beholden to several interest groups, all of whom he would have had to accommodate in order to make his play successful. These included: the company and manager commissioning the play, the exact specifications of the commission, the type of audience who came to the theatre in which it was to be performed, and the differing skills of the writers with whom he worked. So, for example, in collaborative work, Rowley usually wrote comic scenes, characters and sub-plots. Thus, in the tragicomedies he wrote with Webster, it is likely that Webster provided the high tragedy, whilst Rowley provided the transformative comic scenes. Nevertheless, in such collaboration, both writers would have to come to an agreement about the relationship of individual scenes to each other, the preparation for and nature of the denouement, and issues such as continuity of characterisation.

Webster's non-dramatic life can be summarised swiftly. He attended the Merchant Taylor's School in London as a boy, and probably proceeded from there to the Middle Temple, one of the Inns of Court, in 1598. The Inns of Court were the place of study, qualification and practice for young, aspiring middle-class lawyers. However, many students did not actually fully qualify, using their time to experience the pleasures of London life. Webster's contemporaries at the Middle Temple included the playwrights Marston and Ford. Many other contemporary poets and writers attended one of the Inns of Court, including John Donne and George Herbert. Webster's father was a master coach-maker, the family business based near Smithfield. His business provided carts and wagons for plays and pageants, hearses for funerals, and carts for the conveyance of condemned prisoners to Tyburn. As a local businessman with religious leanings, his father was one of the signatories to a benefice appointing a minister to provide for the spiritual needs of condemned prisoners awaiting execution at Newgate in 1605. Webster married in 1606, his wife giving birth to their son two months later. His biography thus suggests evidence of his personal familiarity with the business and workings of theatre; the trappings of both violent and natural deaths; the workings, philosophy and rhetoric of the law; and of the asymmetrical relationship between sexual conduct and socialised gender norms (that is, pre-marital sex being accommodated into legitimate marriage).

Let us now turn to discuss the writing and performing context of the two tragedies. We have already noted the seven-year gap between his work on *Northward Ho!* and the first performance of *The White Devil*. During this period he got married and had his first child. He applied for and became a Master of the Merchant Taylor's Guild Company, suggesting that he practised as a coach-maker in the family business. He may have written part or all of a lost tragedy, based on the life of one of the Medici brothers. The Italianate, Renaissance subject matter of this tragedy (of which only a fragment survives) certainly makes a plausible precursor to both *The White Devil* and *The Duchess of Malfi*. The only other evidence we have of his activities during these years is the hint he gives in the address 'To the Reader', prefaced to the published version of *The White Devil* in 1612, after the play's unsuccessful performance at The Red Bull. They are both a defence and an apology of the nature of his tragedy. His defensive response acknowledges, and simultaneously explains, his lack of output in the years between 1605 and 1612. He writes:

> To those who report I was a long time in finishing this tragedy, I confess I do not write with a goose-quill winged, with two feathers; and if they will needs make it my fault, I must answer them with that of Euripides to Alcestides, a tragic writer: Alcestides, objecting that Euripides had only in three days composed three verses, whereas himself had written three hundred, 'Thou tell'st truth', quoth he, 'but here's the difference: thine shall only be read for three days, whereas mine shall continue three ages.'

At the same time that he defends the length of time he has taken to write the play, he positions himself as a great tragedian, citing an affinity with one of the greatest Greek writers, Euripides, arguing that minimal output can produce plays of lasting worth.

It is possible to identify at least five specific features of his work, prior to 1612, which influenced the shape of his tragedies. The first is his first extant play, written with Thomas Heywood, *Lady Jane, part I*. This history play tells the tragic story of the attempted accession of Lady Jane Grey to the throne after the death of Edward VI, Elizabeth I's brother. It focuses on the way in which political plotting intersects with, and is destroyed by, self-interest, and how women with dynastic power become the pawns both of their patriarchal families and of political back-stabbing. The characterisation of Jane, ensconced and then imprisoned in the Tower of London, and finally executed, engenders pathos and is consequently politically and emotionally powerful. Attacks are occasionally made upon the abuse of political position and the law in a manner reminiscent of the later plays. For example, 'great men like great flies, through law's cobwebs break', is the almost exact replica of Delio's comment on Ferdinand's abuse of the law which we analysed in Chapter 8. Webster's early involvement in this play illustrates an abiding dramatic interest in the personal drama of political and public women, and the dramatic ways of representing political corruption.

The second feature is the necessarily complex and tight plotting which is required of a successful city comedy. His work with Dekker provided him with good experience of dramatic structure and dramatic turning points, both of which he uses to intense and novel tragic effects in *The White Devil*, as we have seen.

The third aspect is the nature of the influence of his collaboration with Dekker and Heywood on his work. Both writers had significant, though different, impacts on developments in Jacobean drama. Dekker was an artisan's son, and originated and perfected the citizen comedy of gentle humour and gullible though loveable city artisans (as, most famously, in *The Shoemaker's Holiday*). He wrote several entertainments for the London mayor, and later prose satires on London life. In the prologue to *If This Be Not a Good Play*, Dekker wrote that a good writer should ensure an audience 'applaud what [his] charmed soul scarce understands'. His populism, combined with this explicit intention to charm an audience with magic, guaranteed his success, and possibly influenced Webster. Thomas Heywood, by contrast, wrote history plays and romances, as well as citizen comedies. He was educated at Cambridge, and had a writing career spanning nearly forty years. He wrote the only dedicated work on actors in the period. *An Apology for Actors*, published in 1612. He described the fusion of a good play with an effective actor as a production of 'lively and well spirited action' that could 'bewitch' an audience. Webster's association with both these working playwrights suggests a common concern for, and belief in, the magical function and effects of theatre, its physical nature and the centrality of audience reception in both critical and dramatic understanding.

The fourth area of influence is Webster's working association with Marston on *The Malcontent*, in 1604. Marston single-handedly initiated the tradition of Italian revenge and political plays at the turn of the century and *The Malcontent* is arguably his best play. It has an

Italianate setting, involves Machiavellian characters plotting power and revenge, uses a malcontent central figure to comment on political corruption and action, combines excessive violence with burlesque humour, and has a tragic closure which is partly mitigated by a surprising reconciliation at the end. With the exception of the tragicomic closure, this outline of its features could describe Webster's tragedies. In 1604 Webster re-worked the play for The King's Men to perform at The Globe, adding an Induction. His work with Marston, and undoubted debt to his imagination and political perceptions, clearly shaped and influenced the tragedies we know.

Finally, Webster shared with his contemporaries a common intellectual interest in Italian and Roman history, and its application to contemporary political debates. The political philosopher Machiavelli was read in conjunction with the Roman historians Tacitus and Suetonius, who wrote about the political corruptions and excesses of the Roman empire. Many contemporary intellectuals wrote closet plays based on Roman history, whilst both Shakespeare and Jonson wrote Roman history plays during this period. *Timon of Athens* was performed in 1605, Marston's *Sophonisba* and *Antony and Cleopatra* in 1606, *Coriolanus* in 1608, and Jonson's *Catiline, his conspiracy* in 1611. The political historians and philosophers were often quoted in fierce parliamentary debates about the political prerogative of the monarch and the rights of the subject. The use of Italian settings and examples was thus a contemporary intellectual interest, fashionably current and politically contentious. Webster's choice of subject matter and an appropriate dramatic form in which to display and discuss such issues placed him at the forefront of Jacobean intellectual, cultural and philosophic debate. His probable work on the lost tragedy about Alessandro de Medici during this period suggests that from *The Malcontent* onwards he was engaged in working on and thinking through dramatic ways of realising and making relevant Italian intrigue and tragedy on stage.

Webster's work prior to the writing and performance of his two tragedies thus illustrates a demonstrable developmental continuity of thematic and dramaturgical interests.

On a less individual level, there was a contemporary debate about the proper conduct of women. There were also two major contemporary scandals involving public women, which made the issues of gender politics current. The first was the secret elopement and marriage of the King's cousin, Arbella Stuart, with her lover. She married against the King's express wishes, because he was worried about claims to the throne from her and any potential legitimate children she might produce. He fetched her back from France and imprisoned her as a result of her disobedience. Her story lucidly demonstrates at the highest political level in the land the power of patriarchal heads of families to impose their personal will and judgement through public and apparently legitimate means on women in their extended family. There were other public examples of families fighting over the rights of daughters to choose their own lives: the former Lord Chief Justice, Edward Coke, kidnapped his own estranged daughter in 1617 in order to force her to marry someone of his choice.

The second sexual scandal of the Jacobean court was the divorce of the Countess of Essex from her husband, much gossiped about in 1613. The countess claimed divorce on the grounds of non-consummation, arguing that she was still a virgin, and wished to marry Somerset, one of the King's favourites. The divorce was decided by a public commission, and the examination of the countess's body by midwives was a matter of public news. The main opponent of the marriage, Thomas Overbury, was imprisoned on trumped up charges and later murdered. Two years later, the new husband and wife faced trial for his murder. However, in 1613, the year before *The Duchess of Malfi* was performed, there were only rumours and suspicions of the chicanery and corruption many courtiers had engaged in to achieve the divorce and marriage. One famous contemporary commentator, John Chamberlain, wrote in 1613: '[it] makes me somewhat to stagger and to think that great folks, to compass their own ends, have neither respect to friends or followers.' Chamberlain's words echo those of Antonio or Delio, Flamineo or Bosola. Both these examples illustrate that female sexuality was publicly perceived as dangerous and even murderous, and that it was also visibly seen to be subject to systematic patriarchal control and potential abuse.

Webster fused his dramatic working experience with relevant contemporary issues in his two tragedies. He finds a form which combines the intensity of characterisation and theatrical symmetry we find in Shakespeare's tragedies, with the convoluted plotting and setting of Marston, and a focus on feminine heroism and political relevance all of his own.

Finally, what about those first productions? Throughout this book we have noticed that Webster consciously conceives of his drama as performative and three-dimensional. He wanted his plays performed in public, and to receive public acclaim. Unfortunately, the first performance of *The White Devil* was a complete failure, acknowledged in the published preface. It was performed at The Red Bull in the open air, and Webster had this to say about the event:

> Only since it was acted in so dull a time of winter, presented in so open and black a theatre, that it wanted (that which is the only grace and setting out of a tragedy) a full and understanding auditory; and that since that time I have noted, most of the people that come to that playhouse resemble ignorant asses.

It is clear that the audience hated it, but that Webster blamed location, weather and an unsophisticated audience for this failure. Webster's decision to rush the play into print, and to supervise the manuscript's transition into print, displays his intense ambition that the play's excellence be recognised by a more understanding 'auditory'. The Red Bull's audience had a reputation for demanding spectacle, fighting, clowns, and topical references, most of which appear in Webster's play. However, its subject matter is not local to Clerkenwell's economy or politics, but concerns the lives and tribulations of the great. In 1618 some satirical verses about Webster were printed in which he was labelled a 'playwright-cartwright', suggesting that class betrayal was a reason for local resentment. Nevertheless, the play's inauspicious opening belied its future success: it was played during the 1630s by Queen Henrietta's Men; revived during the Restoration, and it has been particularly popular in the twentieth century.

The performance and reception of *The Duchess of Malfi* was

immediately, and has been consistently, celebrated. It was commissioned by The King's Men, suggesting Webster's theatrical peers felt that *The White Devil* had not received its due. The play was performed at both their indoor and outdoor theatres, thence guaranteeing a wide audience. The commendatory verses attached to the publication of the play in 1623, at which point it had been recently revived, tell us something about contemporary responses to it. Middleton, Ford and Rowley all contributed laudations. Middleton's words are perhaps the most eloquent, and their content is echoed by the poems of the others. He wrote: 'Thy monument is raised in thy lifetime', and 'For whoe'er saw this duchess live and die / That could get off under a bleeding eye?' Their praise intimates that both the play and its live performance produced the fame and critical acknowledgement as well as an engaged, emotional audience that Webster desired in his own time.

10

Contexts

In the previous chapter we discussed the performing contexts for Webster's plays, including their original place and time of performance, and touched on the possible influences of other writers on his work. In this chapter, we shall broaden that approach by considering what other writers, both theorists and dramatic practitioners, thought about 'tragedy' as a genre. The purpose of talking about tragedy in this more theoretical way is to enable us to consider how general and historical ideas about the form of tragedy, and its expressed purposes, help us to understand what Webster was doing. We shall also discuss some tragic generic conventions, and the broader political and philosophical contexts to which we have referred elsewhere in the book.

Theories of Tragedy

There are three views on tragedy which we should consider, and which influenced Webster and Jacobean tragedy. These are: Greek tragedy and theory; the Medieval Mystery and Morality Plays; and the impact of dramatic tragic practice during Webster's own lifetime. Let us consider each of these in turn.

One of the most famous, and the first, theorist about tragedy was Aristotle, who wrote his *Poetics* in the fourth century BC, an account of drama describing and analysing the great tragedies of his time. His account of tragedy is not timeless: genre is a set of conventions, which alter through time and are influenced by the social, political and cultural issues and changes of history. Nevertheless, Aristotle's work, as it was transmitted to the Renaissance through Italian commentators, was influential on some English writers. However, modern critics have often interpreted *The Poetics* in a rigid way and, unfortunately, it is their terminology that dominates discussions of tragedy. We need to avoid using an inappropriate terminology: but it is useful to acknowledge the aspects of Aristotle's work and thinking which were influential and certainly current amongst Webster's contemporaries. The main misuse of the *Poetics* is the theory of the 'unities'; using Aristotle's term 'unity of action', neo-classic critics claimed that tragedies had to conform to the 'unities' of time, place and action. These were: that the action represented on stage should take no more time in fiction than it took for the actors to play it (unity of time); that given the stage was one single space, the play should represent only one setting (unity of place); and that there should be a single main character and one plotline (unity of action). The theory of the unities was first expounded in the Renaissance by the famous Italian critical theorist Scaliger. His writing greatly influenced some of the aristocratic writers who were contemporaries or near contemporaries of Webster, who wrote 'closet drama' (drama that was for reading rather than performance) but often failed to recognise that effective drama could transcend the constraints of realism and decorum because of its fictional status.

Webster's address to the reader, appended to *The White Devil*, positions himself in the line of Greek tragedians, comparing himself to Euripides, and citing Greek tragic conventions. It is therefore both legitimate and essential to re-examine his view of tragedy. Let us look at Webster's view of and understanding of Aristotelian ideas on tragedy. He writes:

> If it be objected this is no true dramatic poem, I shall easily confess it . . . willingly, and not ignorantly, in this kind have I faulted; for should a man present to such an auditory the most sententious tragedy that ever was written, observing all the critical laws, as height of style, and gravity of person, enrich it with the sententious *Chorus*, and as it were lifen death, in the passionate and weighty *Nuntius*; yet after all this divine rapture . . . the breath that comes from the uncapable multitude is able to poison it.

He acknowledges that his tragedy does not match the critics' definition of a 'true dramatic poem', making two crucial points: first, he
acknowledges the critical generic laws stemming from Aristotle; and
secondly, that he has flouted them, partly because of his contemporary audience ('such an auditory'). His implicit account of tragic
theory combines both Greek and Roman tragedy. He refers to
several key features: sententiousness; height of style; gravity of
person; the presence of a chorus and a messenger, or commentator
(the 'Nuntius'). Let us look, in turn, then, at the Aristotelian and
Roman traditions.

Aristotle's view on tragedy was several-fold. He articulated both a
structure and an appropriate linguistic mode. In the *Poetics* he writes:

> Tragedy, then, is an imitation of an action that is serious, complete, and
> of a certain magnitude, the several kinds being found in separate parts of
> the play; in the form of action, not of narrative; through pity and fear
> effecting proper purgation of these means. . . . Every tragedy therefore,
> must have six parts, which parts determine its quality: namely, plot,
> character, diction, thought, spectacle, song. . . . But most important of
> all is the structure of incidents. For tragedy is an imitation not of men,
> but of an action and of life, and life consists in action. . . . Dramatic
> action, therefore, is not with a view to the representation of character:
> character comes in as subsidiary to the actions.   (*Poetics*, chapter 6)

There are several points made here, which may be clearer as a list:

1. Tragic action should be 'serious' and 'of a certain magnitude': this
   later developed into a theory of 'decorum', which argued that
   tragedies could only represent those of high birth as their central
   characters.
2. The action should be 'complete', by which he means that the plot
   should have a beginning, middle and end: all loose ends should
   be tied up and explained in the closing resolution.
3. It should be enacted, not narrated.
4. The audience should be aroused to both pity and fear, but the
   action of the plot should close by purging these emotions.
5. Plot and the structure of incidents are the key units of writing
   and analysing drama, and these create characters.

In summary, Aristotle's view of tragedy comprises an acknowledgement of its performative nature, of plot as a set of interlocking structural units, of character as determined by action and plot, and of the audience and its response as essential parts of the meaning and definition of tragedy. Each of these conclusions replicates conclusions we have come to about Webster's own practice.

In Webster's address to the reader, then, he invokes a recognition of certain aspects of Greek tragedy. The first aspect is to do with decorum and content: he could, he says, have observed the laws about height of style and gravity of persons. Secondly, he also recognises the structural function of the chorus, a function which we have noted he transposes in his plays onto characters like Bosola, who comment upon the action and motives of the great in the same way as the chorus does in Greek tragedies. Thirdly, he could have 'lifen death' with the characterisation of a messenger figure, bringing news of tragic deaths. However, despite the implicit tribute he effectively pays to both Aristotle and the Greek tragedians, Webster implies that such tragic drama is not fit for the audience for whom he is writing. He argues that the tragic mode has to adapt to the circumstances of dramatic performance and production in his own time. None the less, there are three key areas shared by Aristotle and Webster. The first is the centrality of plot and its structural arrangement in tragedy. The second is the construction of characterisation through action and the development of plot. Thirdly, the messenger who would 'lifen death' by narrating on stage the off-stage tragic denouement, is brought literally onto the stage by Webster and his contemporaries: the passion and weight he attributes to the messenger's narration, becomes part of the action observed and felt directly by the audience.

Let us now turn to his invocation of the Roman tragic tradition. Seneca was the tragedian most studied in English schools during the Elizabethan and Jacobean period. All nine of his plays were translated in the first twenty years of Elizabeth I's reign. His tragedies were written to be read rather than performed. They followed a strict formal pattern: focusing on the protagonist's revenge for an act of dishonour against himself or his family, and usually ending in everyone's death. The stated aim of such tragedies was to learn political and personal stoicism: fortune can throw endless disasters at us, but acquiescence, detachment and submission to one's fate produced a wiser 'man'. Sententiae (that is, succinct proverbial phrases) littered Seneca's own plays, and those of his imitators. 'Sententious tragedy' (Webster's phrase) is therefore one conforming to such models, and there are aspects of both Senecan form and rhetoric in Webster's work. His characters invoke the revenge tradition, and many of their speeches are littered with sententiae. However, reference to both Aristotle and Seneca does not 'explain' Webster's drama. Instead, Webster's self-conscious placing of his own work within this tradition shows that he is critically and creatively aware of the tragic dramaturgical tradition and modes, claiming equality for his own work with that tradition. For these two reasons, we should understand both his references to Aristotle and his distance from him.

Let us now move on to the second major area of influence on both the practical development and theoretical account of tragedy in English Renaissance drama. This was the practice of tragedy within the Christian Morality and Mystery tradition, through both interpretative narrative about Biblical events and their translation into a wide range of stories which bore only incidental relationship to their original Christian context. Within this interpretative framework, tragedy was the story of the Fall, and by analogy, any temptation, which could eventually be redeemed through repentance and rebirth. The English Morality Plays performed didactic, allegorised tales about the temptations of the devil (as Vice) on Mankind, his embroilment in corruption, and the eventual punishment of Vice and reward for a virtuous Mankind. Chaucer, in his 'Prologue to The Monk's Tale', combines a Senecan view of tragedy with the Christian:

> Tragedie is to seyn a certayn storie,
> As olde books maken us memorie,
> Of hym that stood in greet prosperitee,
> And is yfallen out of high degree
> Into myserie and endeth wretchedly.

Tragedy was thence seen and defended as a moral mode: a necessary defence when it was so frequently attacked as a form which encouraged men and women to evil acts through representing them on stage. The debate still rages today about whether the representation of death and violence is innately immoral or moral, in discussions about the effect of violence on television and film. It is clear from both their endings that Webster presented his tragedies within this morality context, although it is equally clear that he suggested that such a context for understanding evil was too black and white. Thus, for example, when Flamineo dies at the end of *The White Devil* he acknowledges his complicity with the 'villains' of the world in which he has lived, and that his life has been a 'black charnel'. Jacobean audiences would have understood Webster's use of the convention of the Vice figure's defeat in Morality Plays. Similarly, at the end of *The Duchess of Malfi*, Bosola also articulates a consciousness of a descent into hell.

The third area to consider is the impact and influence of contemporary dramatists on Webster. This is a matter for conjecture, of course, but it is helpful to summarise schematically traditions and developments in tragic writing and theory, and posit some connections to Webster's drama. Heroic tragedies were not written for the public stage until the late 1580s, and were popular in the 1590s, the last decade of Elizabeth I's reign. As we have already noted, the translation and performance in private of Senecan tragedies, and English plays imitating Seneca, was a commonplace activity at the universities, Inns of Court, and private houses. Philip Sidney wrote one of the most famous English Renaissance treatises on poetry, *A Defence of Poetry*, in about 1580. He defined poetry very broadly as any fictional writing, including drama as 'dramatic poesy', as Webster was to call *The White Devil* a 'dramatic poem' thirty years later. The courtly writers' educated view of tragedy was rigidly Aristotelian, and exemplifies their scorn for popular native traditions of drama. It is illuminating to quote Sidney at length:

> The right use of comedy will (I think) by nobody be blamed, and much less the high and excellent tragedy, that openeth the greatest wounds, and showeth forth the ulcers that are covered with tissue; that maketh kings fear to be tyrants, and tyrants manifest their tyrannical humours; that, with stirring the affects of admiration and commiseration, teacheth

the uncertainty of this world, and upon how weak foundations gilden roofs are builded; that maketh us know,

> *Qui sceptra saevus duro imperio regit,*
> *Timet timentes, metus in auctorem redit*

[He who rules harshly and with tyranny, fears those who fear him, and terror recoils upon the author]

But how much it can move, Plutarch yieldeth a notable testimony of the abominable tyrant Alexander Pheraeus; from whose eyes a tragedy well made and represented, drew aboundance of tears, who, without all pity, had murdered infinite numbers, and some of his own blood. So, as he, that was not ashamed to make matters for tragedies, yet could not resist the sweet violence of a tragedy. And if it wrought no further good in him, it was that he, in despite of himself, withdrew himself from harkening to that which might mollify his hardened heart. . . .

Our tragedies and comedies (not without cause cried out against), observing rules neither of honest civility nor skilful poetry... [are] faulty both in place and time, the two necessary companions of all corporal actions. For where the stage should always represent but one place, and the uttermost time presupposed in it should be, both by Aristotle's precept and common reason, but one day, there is both many days and many places inartificially imagined . . . where you shall have Asia of the one side and Afric of the other, and so many other under-kingdoms, that the player, when he cometh in, must ever begin with telling where he is, or else the tale will not be conceived. Now ye shall have three ladies walk to gather flowers, and then we must believe the stage to be a garden. By and by, we hear news of shipwreck in the same place, and then we are to blame if we accept it not for a rock. Upon the back of that comes out a hideous monster, with fire and smoke, and then the miserable beholders are bound to take it for a cave. While in the meantime two armies fly in, represented with four swords and bucklers, and then what hard heart will not receive it for a pitched field?   (*A Defence of Poetry*, ed. J. Van Dorsten, Oxford University Press, 1966, pp. 45, 65)

Sidney's parodic account of how the audience's disbelief must be suspended when watching a play is both funny and misleading. He misses the absolutely central point about drama which the popular dramatists grasped. In contrast to the neo-classical view, contemporary drama was the medium where space and time conventions could be flouted; where new means of representing ideas, plots, and the passage of time could be explored; where fantasy could be juxtaposed with realism in order to tell a story in a particular manner.

There are a couple of other points that Sidney makes which suggest a continuity with Webster. First, they both cite Greek tragedy as a benchmark: although Sidney adheres to it as a template, Webster acknowledges it, and then politely veers in his own direction. Secondly, Sidney also concentrates on the centrality of the effect of tragedy on the audience, citing the tyrant who is more moved by fiction than by reality. This belief in the power of tragic dramatic action to move us and even change our minds, outlines a theory of drama which is dialogic: that is, in continued debate with its audiences. Webster continually raises this question of the mutual dependence of the power of fiction and the response of the viewer (see Chapter 7). The Jacobean 'theory of tragedy' necessarily included an audience. This suggests a couple of important conclusion: that drama is therefore by nature open-ended, positing questions rather than answering them, leaving an audience to judge, be moved, or decide; and that this has consequences for overall dramatic structure.

Three different forms of tragedy developed in the 1580s and 1590s: revenge tragedy, heroic tragedy, and domestic tragedy. Revenge tragedy was adapted to the English stage from the Senecan influence we have discussed, the first and most famous of such plays being Thomas Kyd's *The Spanish Tragedy*. The features of revenge tragedy were: a Spanish or Italianate setting; political intrigue and corruption superseding the rule of law; the exacting of private revenge against acts of dishonour; and a denouement in which whilst private revenge is the means that indirectly ends public corruption, the rule of public law is reasserted. The plays typically ended with a stage littered with bloody bodies. Shakespeare's early *Titus Andronicus* imitated Kyd's play, whilst his later *Hamlet* (1600) focuses more on the protagonist than on the revenge conventions.

At the same time as revenge tragedy flourished, Marlowe developed the form of a new heroic tragedy, in *Tamburlaine* and *Dr Faustus*, in which the ambition of a single heroic man was pursued for the action of the play, and in which that ambition became the cause of his fall. Simultaneously there developed a form of tragedy which focused on tragedy within a domestic environment, beginning with *Arden of Faversham* in about 1588, a realistic play based on a true story of a wife's murder of her husband, and raising key questions about gender politics. All three types of tragedy enabled the exploration of both general and specific political and social issues. They raise such questions as: What happens when the rule of law fails? What is the relationship between private duties and public responsibilities, especially when they conflict? What place does individual ambition have in a political state? To what extent does power corrupt? What kinds of political conflict are dangerous to the peace of the state? The dramatic tradition of raising these kinds of issues on the public stage in the 1590s and early 1600s through the formal and structural means offered by tragedy was well established by the time Webster was writing. It is also coincident with the acknowledgement of its debating, open-ended nature we discussed in the previous paragraph. In the Jacobean period these three traditions continued to be identifiable in a range of authors, from Jonson to Middleton.

In addition, explicit theories of tragedy emphasised its didactic function (that is, its teaching of a moral lesson). In Jonson's address to the readers which he attached to his tragedy *Sejanus* (first acted in 1603, and published soon after) he wrote:

> If it be objected that what I publish is no true poem, in the strict laws of time, I confess it; as also in the want of a proper chorus, whose habits and moods are such and so difficult, as not any whom I have seen since the ancients, no, not they who have most presently affected laws, have come in the way of. Nor is it needful, or almost possible in these our times and to such auditors as commonly things are presented, to observe the old state and splendour of dramatic poems, with preservation of any popular delight. . . . If in truth of argument, dignity of persons, gravity and height of elocution, fullness and frequency of sentence, I have discharged the other offices of a tragic writer, let not the absence of these forms be imputed to me.

Jonson, like Webster, acknowledges the importance and status of Greek tragedy, but argues that it needs up-dating and revising for 'preservation of any popular delight'. Thomas Heywood, also a tragedian and good friend of Webtser, published *An Apology for Actors* in 1612, the same year as the first performance of *The White Devil*. Webster collaborated with Heywood on *Lady Jane* and *Christmas Comes But Once a Year*, and acknowledged his debt to him in the preface to the reader when he published *The White Devil*. Heywood wrote:

> Comedies begin in trouble and end in peace; tragedies begin in calm and end in tempests. . . .
>
> If we present a tragedy, we include the fatal and abortive ends of such as commit notorious murders, which is aggravated and acted with all the art that may be, to terrify men from the like abhorred practices. If we present a foreign history, the subject is so intended that in the lives of Romans, Grecians, or others, either the virtues of our countrymen are extolled, or their vices reproved. . . . If a moral, it is to persuade men to humanity and good life, to instruct them in civility and good manners, showing them the fruits of honesty and the end of villainy.

Thus tragedy has a clear structure (begins in peace, ends in tempest), a violent content, a contemporary relevance, and a moral closure and reception.

However, equally importantly, during this period, a number of formal developments are identifiable in the work of other playwrights, which Webster can be said to have incorporated into his work. The first of these is an intensified interest in the psychology and interior life of characters trapped by circumstance and the consequences of their actions. The best known examples of this interest come from Shakespeare's plays, for example, *Hamlet* and *Macbeth*, but also *Antony and Cleopatra* or *Coriolanus*. The second area of development was formal: an increased use of framing and distancing devices, including prologues, masques, and juxtapositioning of scenes which create different viewpoints on the action, and thence encourage the audience to develop their own judgement on events and characters. Marston's *Antonio's Revenge* and *The Malcontent*, Middleton's *The Revenger's Tragedy*, and Chapman's *Bussy D'Ambois* are good examples of this formal development. All these plays were first performed in the first eight years of the century. The third development was an increasing experimentation with form: incorporating comic elements in order to disturb the audience's expectations, initiating the use of sub-plots in tragedy, or inventing the tragicomedy to incorporate an explicitly redemptive ending. The fourth development was the increased use of Italian and Spanish settings to symbolically indicate political and social corruption and decadence, and simultaneously enable the playwrights to discuss such issues in a setting that, because it was not London, gave them greater artistic and political freedom.

The Political Context of the Tragedies

Throughout this book we have discussed how various political issues are debated within Webster's two tragedies. Issues such as: How can tyrants ignore and over-rule the rule of law? Is a system of patronage necessarily corrupt? How can you get political leaders to take impartial advice? Does power corrupt? What kind of independence is a woman allowed in a patriarchal society? To whom should an individual be loyal, self, family, honour or state? Do old-fashioned notions, such as honour and chastity, have a place in a competitive urban world? Does anarchy rule if we do not establish agreed codes of civil laws? What place, if any, does the Church have in politics?

All these questions belong to the realm of political philosophy, and are not solely specific to Jacobean England. Nevertheless, in Jacobean England these questions did gain a particular intensity, and carried a wider popular currency than in many other times. Let us look at each question in turn, and the way it participated in a national debate in the first two decades of the seventeenth century.

The first question we noted concerned how, and to what extent, a tyrant can ignore the rule of law. This issue was one the parliaments of James I's reign repeatedly raised. They confronted the King on the abuse of his 'prerogative' to over-rule and by-pass Parliament and the Commons. James I's articulation of the theory of 'divine right', for example in a speech to Parliament in 1610, the year before audiences watched the antics of a Monticelso, said:

Kings are justly called gods for that they exercise a manner of resemblance of divine power upon earth. For if you will consider the attributes to God you shall see how they agree in the person of a King. God hath power to create or destroy, make or unmake, at his pleasure, to give life or send death, to judge all, and to be judged nor accountable to none, to raise low things, and to make high things low at his pleasure, and to God are both soul and body due. And the like power have Kings: they make and unmake their subjects; they have power of raising up and casting down; of life and death; judges over all their subjects and in all causes, and yet accountable to none but God only.

Here he sets out in a public speech to Parliament the theory of 'divine right' and of the unaccountable status of a monarch in the seventeenth century. Parliament tried to defend the supremacy of the common law against the monarch's prerogative.

The second question (that of the potential corruption engendered by a system of patronage) was equally debated, both by Parliament, the Privy Council, and court gossips throughout James' and Charles's reigns. James I was renowned for choosing favourites, usually attractive young men, whom he advanced both politically and socially. The best known example is Robert Carr, who was made Viscount Rochester, and later Duke of Somerset. He was replaced by George Villiers, who became Duke of Buckingham, a member of the Privy Council, and fiercely disliked by many members of parliament. Conversely, a talented man who failed to gain elite patronage could end up financially ruined. Francis Bacon failed to gain patronage under Elizabeth I, but did so under James I, eventually becoming Lord Chancellor. However, he was impeached by Parliament in 1621 for taking bribes. Unfortunately, patronage was the only way in which a man could be paid for public service. Advancement at court depended on either a private income or patronage. Ambitious young men, like Bosola or Flamineo, really did have to sell themselves to get a job or recognition.

The third question (of the status and influence of advisers) was also a matter for debate in Parliament, and gossip amongst the letter writers of the time. The debate had two aspects: first, they argued that the monarch should use Parliament as his advisers and do so more frequently, something James I usually refused. Secondly, they complained about his over-dependence on the self-interested advice of his counsellors, members of the Privy Council, who were appointed by the monarch, thereby, as Parliament argued, creating a political cabal of private, unrepresentative interests.

The fourth question (Does power corrupt?) was equally part of the contemporary and public political debate about the monarch's prerogative, and James I's studied ignorance of the checks and balances of the legal and parliamentary systems. Satire abounded in the late 1590s and early 1600s, which presented the court and its power as decadent, flashy and corrupt.

The fifth question (What kind of independence is a woman allowed in a patriarchal society?) was one which had barely begun to be articulated elsewhere than on the stage, although much debate had surrounded Elizabeth I's right to reign as a woman. There were, however, pamphlets about the supposed growing threat of independent-minded women, and defences against such assertions. The first woman to publish her work as a poet did so in 1611 (Amelia Lanyer). And there were some very public law cases in which noble women challenged their estranged husbands' rights to access their property, and to inherit land from their fathers. We discussed two examples of Jacobean men unilaterally and physically taking charge of their female relatives' lives and marriages in Chapter 9.

The sixth question (To whom should an individual be loyal, self, family, honour or state?) is a perennial one, but had an added intensity in an era still embedded in family and local networks, which occasionally came into conflict with the demands of the state. Several rebellions during the early part of Elizabeth I's reign arose out of such conflicts. Loyalty to locality, family, state or cause was a key determining issue of commitment during the Civil War itself (1642–9). The huge increase in power, size and subsequent influence of the nation-state during the sixteenth and seventeenth centuries meant that the more general philosophical issue of ethical and political loyalty became contentious.

The seventh question (Do old-fashioned notions, such as honour and chastity, have a place in a competitive urban world?) was again one much debated in social and political conduct books of the period. Philip Stubbes, for example, in *Anatomy of Abuses* (1578), argued that all the old 'English' virtues such as frugality, modesty, chastity, honour, and manliness had been swallowed up by the greedy competitive consumerism of the new urban centres, particularly capitalist London.

The eighth question (Does anarchy rule if we do not establish agreed codes of civil laws?) is linked to the first three, and was the ground for Parliament's attack on both 'divine right' and the monarch's use of his 'prerogative'. They argued that the power of a monarch would be that of a tyrant unless he or she was checked by two representative counterbalances: a representative parliament and an independent judiciary. The abusive power of the Star Chamber during James I's and then Charles I's reigns was fiercely debated in both Parliament and contemporary pamphlets.

The ninth question (What place, if any, does the Church have in politics?) was one of the central political and theological debates of the seventeenth century. The establishment of the Church of England in 1559, on Elizabeth I's accession, and its intimate connection to the state, opened a debate between radical puritans and the established Church. The former, who became increasingly influential and persuasive in the early seventeenth century, argued that religion was a matter for the individual, and that the hierarchy and political institutionalisation of the Church was potentially and actually corrupt and contrary to the simplicity and ethics of Christianity. Webster's plays certainly display the corruption attendant upon the elision of church and political power.

Whilst it would be simplistic to say that Webster's tragedies reflect these issues, they certainly debate them in a political and dramatic context, which has specific historical relevance to Jacobean England. Whether he comes to absolute conclusions, or merely leaves the debate open, is for each audience to decide.

The Reformation, Renaissance and Scientific Revolution

In the period between 1500 and 1700 Europe began to become recognisably 'modern'. Nation-states emerged with attendant powerful leaders, armies and bureaucracies, encouraging increasing centralisation. Economic changes presaged the later development of capitalism, both in the early development of industrial production and in terms of the organisation of capital in large financial centres such as Amsterdam and London. The economy began to be dominated by international trade and the urban consumer, rather than being an agricultural subsistence economy. The invention of the compass and gunpowder stimulated the expansion of imperial power and trade, aiding a growing optimistic sense that anything could be achieved. Nevertheless, for the poor, these changes often made things worse. A series of bad harvests in the sixteenth and seventeenth centuries exacerbated the transition from a feudal economy to an urban one, leaving many peasants without a livelihood. Vagrancy was seen as a major social and political problem. These and other social changes precipitated debates on social and economic change and poverty.

The Italian Renaissance saw both a rebirth of art and a new focus on the individual, and helped establish a cultural climate in which challenging old authorities was the norm. In many ways such artistic changes paralleled scientific ones: most famously in the figure of Leonardo da Vinci, who was both eccentric scientist and artistic genius. The new science relied on 'objective' and empirical observation of the natural world, rather than on old authorities. The increasing popularity of public anatomies, in which the body of a man or woman was publicly laid bare to view bones, sinews, and bodily structure, graphically illustrates the new interest in investigative and empirical science. Both the new art and science shared the view that the individual experience was more important and more objective than the general. The intellectual outlook was therefore increasingly sceptical and detached in its observation of the world.

In 1492 Columbus 'discovered' America, opening up new trade links, the purchase of new goods and the import of gold. During the sixteenth century Copernicus first argued that the sun, not the earth, was the centre of our universe. In 1517 Luther pinned his treatises to the Church in Wittenburg and initiated the Protestant break from the Catholic Church (known as the Reformation). These three changes presaged a cultural shift away from a Euro-centric perspective, and encouraged people to think of geographical, outer and spiritual space as more diverse and less predictable. Equally, all three changes challenged old authorities: that of intellectuals and classical geographers who claimed that the known Indo-European world was the whole world; of scientists and theologians who claimed the earth was the centre of the universe; and of the Catholic Church, who claimed to be the sole authority and interpreter of religion and faith. Knowledge of the world shifted. John Donne wrote *An Anatomy of the World* in 1611, the year before the performance of *The White Devil*. In it he expresses an emotional response to the scientific and intellectual changes we have sketched:

> And new philosophy calls all in doubt,
> The element of fire is quite put out;
> The sun is lost, and th'earth, and no man's wit
> Can well direct him where to look for it.
> And freely men confess that this world's spent,
> When in the planets and the firmament
> They seek so many new; they see that this
> Is crumbled out again to his atomies.
> 'Tis all in pieces, all coherence gone.

The philosophical and psychological uncertainty attendant upon intellectual and theological re-definitions of the world and the self is something we find in Webster's tragedies.

In England the Reformation was firmly established in 1559 with the establishment of the Church of England. Its tenets were Calvinist: predestination, the fallen and abject state of mankind and the mortal world, the physical reality of both damnation and redemption, were realities which were expounded weekly in churches across the land. The fatalism of many of Webster's characters, and the sense of a corrupt and fallen world, have often been attributed to a Calvinist outlook.

With the combined changes of the decline of the universal authority of the Catholic Church and the increasing power of nation-states, a new kind of political philosophy was outlined. Most famously, this was articulated by Machiavelli, who wrote *The Prince* in 1516. He advised pragmatism and various practical ways in which a leader should maintain power, which might involve either actual or pretended use of unethical means. His work was widely seen in England as a corrupting influence, although statesmen such as Francis Bacon and William Cecil cited and used his advice. The English drama contains many references to Machiavelli: either as 'Machiavel' characters, or even, in the case of Marlowe's *The Jew of Malta*, appearing as a character. Such characters were explicitly linked to the 'Vice' characters of the Morality Play tradition, and were habitually defeated or exposed at the close of the play. Nevertheless, they also became crucial dramatic mouthpieces for the debate of a different and new kind of pragmatic political philosophy, and particularly when linked to the malcontent figure, could stand to one side on the stage and voice effective political criticisms of authoritarian and feudal politics. Dissatisfaction with the aristocratic patronage system and other economic changes fuelled the creation of a new dramatic character: the malcontent. Marston named his 1604 play after this type, a play on which Webster himself worked. The malcontent exhibited a particular melancholic psychology which was meant to indicate a fusion of political and social discontent with a 'naturally' bitter disposition.

The figure of the Machiavel retained a certain ambiguity: although within the play they often make what seem to the audience to be valid critical points, their advocacy of pragmatism and change merges into self-interest and complete civic anarchy, and their final destiny is always punishment for evil. In *The White Devil* Flamineo both links himself to this tradition and indicates its acceptability in the world Webster portrays when he says of Francisco's convoluted plot to kill Bracciano, 'O the rare tricks of a Machiavellian!' (5, iii, 194). Webster's portrayal of Machiavellianism is ambiguous: he shows us a world in which idealism is exposed as naive, and in which we need an ethical pragmatism to survive. However, the Machiavellian leaders in *The White Devil* (Monticelso and Francisco) survive, whilst the less noble 'malcontents', such as Lodovico and Flamineo, are severely and publicly punished. Webster seems to be suggesting that pragmatic self-interest works for those in power, but creates scapegoats of those who are not. This cynical and deeply depressing view of political power is somewhat mitigated in *The Duchess of Malfi*, where the Machiavellianism of the Cardinal is both exposed and defeated, and counterbalanced by the actions of the Duchess. The Duchess herself is not a naïve ruler: she refuses to expose her marriage to her brothers, keeping it secret for years. Webster's view of a 'good ruler' is therefore one that rules with pragmatism.

It is clear from the brief outline in this chapter that Webster's tragedies participate in both cultural and political debates of his time. He acknowledges the literary and dramatic inheritance of Greek tragedy and the theory of tragedy, but self-consciously makes a claim for a modern tragedy which will speak to its own audiences. He fuses several traditions of English tragedy: the revenge, the heroic and the domestic. Finally, he debates and transforms into dramatic conflict and narrative many central political and social issues of his time. This perception should be carried into our discussion, in the next chapter, of the way in which different critics and directors have interpreted and presented Webster's tragedies.

11

Sample Critical Views

Your own analyses, built up gradually throughout this book, will have provided you with a strong and individual interpretation of the plays. So long as these are based upon the plays and justified by close readings, they are as valid as those of any academic critic. Nevertheless, your own ideas and interpretation will be stimulated by engaging with other readers and critics of Webster's plays, just as they are by discussing them with fellow students and teachers. You should always look on the writings and arguments of critics as part of a process of developmental discussion, rather than a visit to an all-knowing oracle. If you approach critical argument in this fashion you will be much better equipped to be sceptical and thoughtful about critics' arguments, and come to your own decisions about the validity and importance of their approach.

This chapter presents both conventional literary critical views and accounts of several performances. The aim is to introduce you to some of the critical debates about, and approaches to, Webster's work, and to ask you to think about these in the light of our preceding analysis.

The following sample is not representative of all possible approaches to Webster's plays: there is neither time nor space for that kind of survey in this book. The bibliography at the end of this book will guide you to further reading.

*   *   *

Our first critic is Travis Bogard, whose *The Tragic Satire of John*

Webster was published in 1955. His major contention is that Webster's tragedies are political, and that their fusion of satire and tragedy is a unique achievement, and distinctively different from Shakespeare's tragedies. Let us examine more closely how his argument proceeds, and what he means by a fusion of tragedy and satire.

His first point is that Webster uses his sources in a more journalistic way than Shakespeare, aiding a sense of contemporaneity. He writes:

> *The White Devil* is an intensely contemporary play. It is explicitly concerned with political ethics, and seeks to find some rationale of behaviour in a realistically depicted court society. *The Duchess of Malfi* is much broader in its implications. The political background is still present, but now the individuals must face not merely a society, but a mortal world – the terror of a dying universe.   (p. 16)

General atmosphere, an accurate depiction of the milieu, and the specific debates of the plays appear to invoke contemporary sexual and political scandals.

Bogard then examines the structural organisation of Webster's tragedies. Dramatic conflict is enacted between the stoic protagonist and the Machiavellian antagonist. This clarifies the nature of the political conflict (between stoicism and Machiavellianism); of the dramatic conflict (protagonist and antagonist); and characterisation (oppositional and emergent through action). In contrast to most previous critics, Bogard argued that Webster's characterisation was *social*, although identity was adherence to 'integrity of life' in the face of formless and fearful mortality. Webster's plays are thus fundamentally different from Shakespearean tragedy: they do not focus on interior life, or psychological decay and regret. Bogard demonstrates his thesis by looking at the way dialogue, characterisation and motivation tend to be both generalised and demonstrated through social and political situations:

> Webster, then, took a general view of man and his world and tried to depict the forces which played destructively upon individuality. His characters do not possess an inner reality. Only their outer nature is revealed, and even this is frequently absorbed into the panorama of

general forces. . . . The soliloquy which Shakespeare used to permit the audience deep insight into his characters, is used by Webster for expository purposes only. . . . Finally, by removing the inner nature of man from his tragic picture, Webster indicates that he is not showing the development of his characters through suffering to an affirmation of moral good. Not development but stubborn consistency to self is the distinguishing element of Webster's tragic action.   (p. 55)

Bogard looks at characterisation in detail, summarising thus:

Their individuality diminishes when viewed against the panoramic background Webster painted. They have the qualities of good and evil which men and women have in life. But oppression and struggle mount beyond what they are in life, and consequently are lifted out of the normal atmosphere. Behind the figures on the stage lie forces of which they are the agents, and it is these forces, unseen in the world of ordinary reality, that impress the audience as being of general concern. *The White Devil* and *The Duchess of Malfi* together depict a world that is horrifying. But it is the world, rather than any individual in it, which apparently interested Webster most vitally.   (p. 80)

Bogard's argument examines how Webster incorporates that 'world' through literary and dramatic means. This is the central plank of his argument: Webster fuses the satiric with the tragic in order to provide a unique spin on that world.

He discusses Webster's debt to Marston's *The Malcontent* (which we discussed briefly in Chapter 9), where the figure of a satiric outsider comments upon dramatic action, as well as participating in it. Marston fused the satiric persona with the Machiavellian, a figure who credibly enacted vice. Nevertheless, Marston's play was not itself a tragedy, but a satiric tragi-comedy in which the satiric impulse dominates over any spiritual or moral seriousness. Bogard summarises the problem in this way, simultaneously voicing his own tragic theory:

To write tragedy that is also satire presents, on the face of it, an almost insoluble problem. For tragedy depends on belief in the fullest potential spiritual achievement of man. Because the potential is unrealised in any world, the tragic ideal must carry with it some of the evanescence of illusion. But it is the especial power of tragedy that it tests the capabilities of men by the strength of their faith in the ideal. Pity, to be sure, lies in the spectacle of a man's world shattering about him, and there is terror in the sense of godlike capabilities wasted by the death of a tragic hero. But his heroism – and indeed the greatness of tragedy – lies in his triumphant assertion of faith in the potentialities of man's spirit, whatever the condition of the mortal world. . . .

The essential difference between satire and tragedy may simply be that satire is not required to make such a case, positively. It may offer its ideal condition by the implication of strong negative statement. . . . Satire, like tragedy, knows pity and terror, for it too concerns itself with man's spiritual potential and with man in 'actuality', surrounded by the limiting bonds of the flesh. But whereas tragedy attempts to bring the two together, satire measures the gulf between, finding in such measurement material for mockery.   (p. 96)

Bogard shows how Webster finds dramaturgical and technical solutions to the problem of their fusion. He succeeds in simultaneously displaying the heroic qualities of the men and women of the Italian Renaissance, at the same time as displaying the illusory quality not only of their political lives and systems, but of life itself:

Their heroic quality, their capacity for magnificent struggle in the assertion of their individuality, made them fit subjects for the heightened action of tragedy.

The tragedies, however, are concerned not only with vigorous individualistic action. They show also the pernicious inroads which the world of actuality makes on the lives of the heroic protagonists. Consequently the heightened action is subjected to unrelenting satirical analysis, designed to reveal the full meaning of individualistic action in its relation to society and to exhibit the heroic for what it is in terms common to all mankind. The contemporary allusions and the details of local colour only serve to emphasise the presence of the actual in the heroic world.

By exhibiting his action from two points of view, Webster could show not only how splendid individuals can be, ideally, but also to what they are brought in actuality. Man, the satire shows, even at his most wilful, is not the master of his fate. His power is restricted by death; disease limits his body; the wrath of man and the laws of society check his course.   (pp. 99–100)

Bogard illustrates this argument through an analysis of the function of the satiric personae (for example, Flamineo and Bosola) as both commentators on the action and participants in it. He examines the changes in tone created by scenic juxtapositions and character contrasts within scenes (for example, Bosola's misogynist address to the midwife in Act 2, compared with the rest of the scene). He shows how sententiae are both appropriate to the speaking characters and ironic juxtapositions against the action and reality we see on stage. The aim of Webster's juxtapositional dramatic technique is predominantly satirical, providing a commentating 'counterpoint' to the main tragic action.

Finally, Bogard argues that Webster's fundamental 'philosophy' is nihilistic, neither play providing a conventional moral closure or message.

> Life, as it appears to Webster, is a moral chaos. . . . Unable to find a solution to the problems he raises, and yet unable to effect a compromise with the terrifying world of his vision, Webster tries to present the ugliness beneath the artificial glory. Every character of importance, every situation, the noblest ethical statement, is attacked by Webster's relentless analysis.   (p. 118)

His tragedies are not didactic: they can 'only arouse men to a concern for their world' (p. 120). *The White Devil* establishes its central theme of 'courtly reward and punishment', and its three branches: 'the rotten prodigality of court life; . . . the evils of a social system in which sycophants flatter a lord for an uncertain living; . . . the treachery of a prince's capricious justice' (p. 120) from its opening. The play's structure, characterisation and techniques show that these do not change through time, nor under the impact of the actions of good men, nor by the end of the play. Thus the satiric impulse demonstrates the futility of heroism and the ethics of conventional tragedy in the real political world. Bogard identifies a central theme, with three strands, in *The Duchess of Malfi*: 'natural evil', divided into the bestiality of man; the conception of the rotting body, accompanied by images of sexuality and widespread corruption; and the dignity of death. The first two are satiric commonplaces; the third is a new departure. All the major characters welcome death as part of the process of natural decay. In *The White Devil*, despite its attack on worldly corruption, the major characters display 'a quality of grandeur', in their individualism. The play shows that evil is man-made: so man may still control it. In *The Duchess of Malfi* corruption is endemic, and therefore man is power-less to control its work. 'Such a view of the world, more profound than one of disillusion, leads to despair' (p. 142).

Bogard's approach has three particular strengths. First, his percep-tion that satire and tragedy are fused and work juxtapositionally in Webster's plays provides an analytic framework for understanding how and why we experience his plays as political. Secondly, his ana-lytic account of characterisation as social and political, rather than internal, broadens and deepens previous approaches. Thirdly, he refuses to condemn Webster for not writing a conventional 'moral' tragedy, a long-standing critical condemnation. These insights have been born out by our analysis in this book. However, there are weak-nesses in his approach. First, his insistence on Webster's nihilistic vision and the primacy of the individual's assertion against the world echoes the philosophical and political concerns of 1950s existen-tialism rather than those of the 1600s. This leads to the second point. Bogard's assertion that *The Duchess of Malfi* 'leads to despair' does not sufficiently take account of the character of the Duchess, her death, or the play's symbolic closure on her son. You need to decide for yourself how accurate Bogard is in this interpretation. Thirdly, despite Bogard's insistence on the Jacobean contempo-raneity of the plays, he does not address this explicitly. This leaves a central weakness in his argument: for example, had he acknowledged the influence and power of Calvinism, he might have been able to contextualise his references to decay and death. Fourthly, although his close textual analysis is convincing, he does not open his conclu-sions to a consideration of audience response and dramatic theory. As he notes, the plays' plots end unresolved, but such dramatic irres-olution does not necessarily entail Webster's personal irresolution. Instead it may indicate a radical confidence in the political educata-bility of his audiences. This is the central point of our next critic.

*   *   *

Our second critic is Jonathon Dollimore, whose *Radical Tragedy: Religion, Ideology and Power in the Drama of Shakespeare and his Contemporaries* was first published in 1984. The second edition (1989) included an important preface, setting forth the theoretical arguments underpinning his approach. It is useful to look first at this preface, before discussing his chapter on Webster.

He argues that there are two critical views about tragedy. First, that tragedy is a religious and metaphysical genre, demonstrating that human suffering is inevitable but ennobling. This theory combines a conservative belief in the status quo on earth (suffering) with a transcendent belief in the transformative power of individual suffering (future redemption). Dollimore argues that this theory places tragedy *outside* history and context, ignoring the specificity of individual tragedies in individual and different cultures. The second approach is characterised by J. W. Lever, to whose *Tragedy of State* (1971) Dollimore's own work is much indebted. Lever argued that Jacobean tragedy concentrates on the social and political milieu rather than the characters, and how these entrap and constrain individual action, belief and identity. The focus of tragedy is not the individual 'but the society which assails him, that stands condemned'. Some recent critics (new historicists) have contested Lever's view that tragedy is oppositional, arguing that tragedy displays disorder merely to show its defeat by the tragic closure and re-establishment of political order. Nevertheless, his premise about tragedy's political and social nature is generally accepted.

Dollimore himself acknowledges that the endings of many tragedies demonstrate the defeat of subversion or transgression, but nevertheless, that the conceptualisation and representation of alternatives during the performance of the plays has raised radical alternatives. His argument is therefore two-fold: that tragedy is radical because subversive ideas and actions are staged as oppositional possibilities to the political and social status quo; and secondly, that tragedy is specifically a social and political genre, emerging from and intimately related to the local culture. His approach is called 'materialist criticism'.

He addresses the tragedies' context and content and form to illustrate his thesis, beginning with contemporary philosophical and political contexts. The writings of Machiavelli, Bacon and Hobbes show that contemporary political philosophy introduced concepts of relativism, demystified the process of political government and legal process, and effectively instituted our modern secular and sceptical attitude to authority, the social order, politics, and religion. This new kind of oppositional attitude fostered new dramatic techniques, for example, parody, dislocation and 'structural disjunction'. He cites Flamineo's self-description 'more lecherous, more courteous by far' (*The White Devil*, 1, ii, 315–16) as a good example of the typical dramatic method of 'interrogative irony' which interrogates conventional contemporary concepts of courts and their politics. The typical Jacobean tragedy displays structural dislocation rather than resolution of conflicts. Dramatic structure reflects the breakdown of political and religious certainties and helps construct a sceptical view about a providential and beneficent universe.

This theoretical outline is applied to *The White Devil* (chapter 15):

> In no other play is the identity of the individual shown to depend so much on social interaction; even as they speak protagonists are, as it were, off-centre. It is a process of displacement which shifts attention from individuals to their context and above all to a dominating power structure which constructs them as either agents or victims of power, or both. (p. 231)

Dramatic and textual analysis reveals how religion is exposed as 'an instrument of state power': Monticelso's formal entry 'in state' is juxtaposed with his orders to excommunicate Vittoria and Bracciano for private and personal revenge. Content and visual metaphors construct a radical commentary.

He uses the character of Cornelia to illustrate how he radicalises his audience. Her attack on her daughter Vittoria and articulation of the philosophy of 'the virtue of princes' are shown to be naïve and gullible. The audience is placed in a privileged position, by seeing that Cornelia takes at face value the manipulations and self-presentation of princes. Dollimore argues that Webster uses her character to show how power works in the way described by Machiavelli: by creating appearances of virtue and truth through any means possible, and ensuring that the people believe in the fiction. By showing that Cornelia both believes in the fiction and is wrong, Webster creates a powerful and radical criticism of authoritarian ideology.

Webster's critique extends to an attack on the marginalisation of women and other subordinate groups, which Dollimore illustrates by the triangular relationship between Flamineo, Vittoria and Bracciano. Both Vittoria and Flamineo desire Bracciano's patronage, respectively, through legitimate marriage, and political preferment. By creating a triangle in which both Flamineo and Vittoria can achieve this solely through the exploitation of female sexuality, and by contrasting the ways in which each does and does not have access to power, Webster suggests simultaneously the interlinked corruption of the political and sexual worlds. Webster neither condones nor judges either Vittoria or Flamineo: this is not conservative drama which judges any kind of transgression as 'morally defective'. Webster also shows that Vittoria's representation as an 'unruly woman' by other characters in the play links the exploitation of women to wider fears of social and political disorder in Jacobean England. The voice of the 'dispossessed intellectual', found in the words of a Flamineo or Bosola, echo the political criticisms of many contemporary courtiers and political aspirants.

Finally, Dollimore argues that the play's closure does not display the individual's triumph over suffering, and fashioning of a coherent identity. He argues, in contrast to Bogard, that:

> It is in the death scene that we see fully the play's sense of how individuals can actually be constituted by the destructive social forces working upon them. We have already seen how Cornelia and Isabella internalised roles of subservience with the consequence that they revere that which exploits and destroys them. Conversely, Vittoria and Flamineo refuse subservience even as they serve and, in so doing, are destroyed as much by their rebellion as that which they rebel against. Perhaps the most powerful contradiction lies in this simple fact: their stubborn, mindless self-affirmation at the point of death is made with the same life-energy which, up to that point, had been life-destructive.   (p. 246)

In summary, then, Dollimore's critical focus is on the political and critical nature of tragedy in specific historical circumstances. His approach emerges from the Marxist literary critical and political movements of the 1960s and 1970s. There are undoubtedly great strengths in this approach, for it enables us to see both the plays within their material context, and to understand how formal dramatic techniques can be manipulated to political and critical ends. Nevertheless, there are also several weaknesses in his book. He does not really discuss the local complexities and details of Jacobean politics and philosophy, preferring a broad-sweep approach incorporating a century of different debates under one umbrella. Subsequent critics have tried to re-focus on the specific years when Webster was writing to illustrate and discuss the plays' politics. Secondly, he omits a feminist critique of Jacobean patriarchy from his examination of challenges to the status quo; although this is a criticism he acknowledges in his 1989 preface. Thirdly, his omission of *The Duchess of Malfi* skews his argument. Its representation of individual suffering may illustrate how an iconic female victim can become a redemptive symbol, central to the tragic genre. This is an explicit argument of our next critic.

*   *   *

Our final critic is Dympna Callaghan, whose *Woman and Gender in Renaissance Tragedy* was published in 1989. She acknowledges her indebtedness to Dollimore's cultural materialism, applying this specifically to gender. She combines psychoanalytic analysis, which argues that the icon of the 'phallus' is imbued with symbolic and actual power in all patriarchal societies, having the power of labelling gender and sexual difference, with specific citation of Jacobean writings about women. Her use of psychoanalytic analysis is actually rather cursory; students should look instead at Coppelia Kahn's *Man's Estate*, or Janet Adelman's *Suffocating Mothers*, although these concentrate on Shakespeare. The value of Callaghan's work is its focus on Jacobean debates about femininity and masculinity; her insistence that such debates, whilst focusing on femininity, necessarily entail ideas about masculinity, in demonstrating how femininity is other or inferior; and in her ability to integrate debates and theory to an analysis of her chosen plays (*King*

Lear, *Othello*, *The White Devil* and *The Duchess of Malfi*). She summarises thus:

> My analysis extends the fundamental premise of feminism, namely that gender is a crucial category of analysis . . . by positing that gender opposition is probably the most significant dynamic of Renaissance tragedy, and that the gender categories produced both within and outside the dramatic text are precarious and problematic.   (pp. 2–3)

Rather than following previous feminist critics in examining female characters, she looks at broader 'discourses' which construct, determine and delimit gender and sexual identities. By 'discourses', she means the language and rhetoric of religion, physiology, education, conduct and self-improvement manuals. During the Elizabethan and Jacobean period these discourses all differently, but in combination, construct an image of woman as subordinate to man, of femininity as weak and vulnerable, of feminine sexuality as dangerous and in need of control, and of masculinity continually threatened by feminine wiles. Callaghan argues that this binary gendered conceptualisation was central to other political discourses. For example, the family was used as a conceptual unit of political ideology by James I, who described his divine right to rule in terms of fatherhood. Subservience to monarch, father and husband were invoked as the rule of political order in order to suggest a 'natural' obedience and conformity to the status quo. Gender was thus part and parcel of the contemporary political debate.

Tragedy is an 'ideological construct' with crucial implications for gender, because female transgression is central to the action and symbolic meanings of the tragedies (by 'ideological construct' she means a system of belief which was socially and politically constructed). The way tragedies demonise and then expel female sexuality, for example, echoes pulpit attacks and advice on how to control your daughters', wives' and widows' sexual proclivities. Such attacks equated all women with Eve, her original temptation of Adam being used as a causal model for man's loss of communion with God. All women became the original cause of tragic fall for all mankind. However, since transgressive acts are central to tragedy, which tests and questions the boundaries of social and political norms, gendered transgression can become a sceptical means of criticising those norms. In particular, female transgression questions male transcendence, and de-centres the tragic hero. 'Seen as transgressors, female characters cease to be passive victims who exist primarily to embellish the downfall of the tragic hero' (p. 63). The plays display contradictory views of the same women: for example, in *The Duchess of Malfi*, the brothers are seen to construct the Duchess as the archetypal lusty widow, whilst Antonio constructs her as the idealised love object, and her courtiers construct her as an ideal prince, and later as an ideal mother. The existence of multiple meanings for femininity within the play and within single characters de-stabilises conventional views on gender.

The de-stabilising and de-centring of masculine heroes, and the concomitant critical questioning of the function of woman in Renaissance tragedy, is achieved through various dramatic techniques. Callaghan examines the way silence and absence are used dramatically to construct women, and draws attention to the masculine construction of a public/private divide where women who speak in public are labelled aberrants or whores. Similarly, in looking at the deaths of female protagonists, she argues that their presence on stage and under our gaze problematises masculine identity and actions which have put them there. In summary she writes:

> As the instigator of tragic action through transgression and as the dead centre of the denouement, woman has a unique and crucial relation to tragedy. Her death undermines notions of transcendence so beloved of humanist criticism, and her progress from transgressor to saint demolishes neat schematisations of tragic form. . . . Major female characters in these plays may indeed repeat the historic transgression of Eve, but if they do, their transgression does not bring the downfall of humanity but rather . . . discloses the limitations of moral and social codes.
>
> (pp. 96–7)

She examines the plays' exposure of misogynistic discourse – including the demonisation of female sexuality as monstrous – as one abused by men in order to distance themselves from their own mortality, and as the discourse which leads directly to the death of the female protagonists. The audience is placed in an ambiguous position by the language of misogyny, because it is usually spoken by the malcontent figure with whom we are led to sympathise. The narrative eventually exposes the malcontent's 'reading' of femininity through the prism of misogyny as a mis-reading. Thus, the dramatic techniques and structure re-focus us on masculinity and male honour as objects of criticism.

In summary, then, Callaghan's approach radically changes the way we look at both femininity *and* masculinity in these plays, illustrating how the conceptualisation of gender is dependent on both terms, and thence illustrating the instability and impermanence of their supposed givens. She enables us to see the plays as radical engagements with contemporary debates about gender. Her analysis of gender identity as constructed, and her analysis of how the plays display this, enables us to see that femininity and masculinity in Jacobean drama was not 'natural', but contested and a matter for political debate.

*   *   *

Let us now turn to consider some performances which reflect or develop these critical responses. Two performances in the 1970s shared a similar approach to Webster's plays: Peter Gill's *The Duchess of Malfi*, performed at the Royal Court Theatre in 1971, and Michael Lindsay-Hogg's *The White Devil* at the Old Vic in 1976.

Gill's *Duchess* made the most of the Royal Court's intimate stage space, eschewing conventional stage scenery and props for a bare stage, a bricked back wall, and peeling doors. Plain deal chairs were used to seat the characters. The lighting was stark, and everyone was dressed in acid yellow. The visual appearance of the set and performance reminded many critics of Peter Brook's *Marat–Sade*, in which grey bare boards and simple monochromatic clothes produced the atmospherics of the mad-house. Gill's idea was to use the austere 'empty space' of the stage to allow the language, actors and action to dominate the theatrical experience, as well as to suggest visual thematic echoes of the madness and entrapment of the play's themes. The levelling effect of the monochromatic costumes attacked the Cardinal's and Ferdinand's social pretensions of rank.

The production's central focus was on the love affair between Antonio and the Duchess the tragic centre of the play. The intimate setting of the Royal Court aided this emphasis on domestic tragedy, fuelling the play's claustrophobia. Actors who were not participants in a scene stood around the edge of the stage, acting as a chorus, including producing music. The 'chorus' carried the Duchess and her brothers onto the stage in the opening Act, an image of a cohesive family and state, acquiescent in the higher rank of the Duchess and her brothers. Later, the chorus stood aside from the action (for example, in the wooing scene), looking on. This furthered and enhanced a sense of entrapment: our perception of the Duchess as continually spied upon, and of the characters as isolated and lonely. This increased the tragic tension, for the audience could see that discovery was inevitable. The chorus thus acted as an ironic Brechtian commentary upon the self-deception of the central characters.

The performances of the Duchess and Antonio (Judy Parfitt and Desmond Gill) created a credible picture of lovers snatching a new kind of marriage out of the jaws of convention, privilege and family history. Their sensitivity to the language, particularly in the intimate and loving bedroom scene and the subsequent contrasted panic as they agree to flee, ensured the audience's commitment to their cause. Audience sympathy was clearly sought on the side of impulsive young love, and against the more archaic court and the Duchess's brothers. Its political 'message' meshed with the rebellious generation of the late 1960s. The production's emphasis on the characters' psychology was central, which helped highlight the intimate domestic relationships, but was also a central tenet of the radical movement of the 1960s and 1970s.

Let us now turn to Michael Lindsay-Hogg's *The White Devil*. Here again, simplicity was a key visual motif, although the emphasis was on elegance. The setting was the present day, the stage representing a large, expensive hotel, with revolving doors at each side of the stage. Costumes looked expensive and chic, monochromatically brown. Bracciano, Isabella, Francisco and Monticelso were played and visually represented as privileged members of a protected, rich elite. Vittoria (played by Glenda Jackson) and Flamineo were 'outsiders'. This visual and staging division illustrates the production's central interpretation of the play as a drama about the abuse of privilege and power by closed elites.

Many critics found the production too 'cool', lacking the 'decadence' expected of a Websterian production. However, the cool approach allowed the audience to see corruption as internal to the characters. Watching these cool exteriors suddenly consumed by lust or greed, we were given a privileged psychological window on the costs, terrors, and vulnerability of the rich. James Villiers (Bracciano) gave a genuinely shocking performance, when his face genuinely appeared to be half eaten away by poison. The visual image brought alive the verbal imagery of clothing/unclothing, masking/unmasking, which dominates the play. It validated Lindsay-Hogg's decision to clothe the characters in such wealthy-looking costumes: the contrast between Bracciano's ravaged face and his costume made mortality and decay tangible and real.

Two actors in particular contributed significant weight to the production: Glenda Jackson as Vittoria, and Frances de la Tour as Isabella. The latter gave a heart-rending performance in the divorce scene, rousing audience antipathy against Bracciano from early in the play. His lack of interest in Isabella was echoed in Act 4, Scene ii in his treatment of Vittoria. Glenda Jackson's performance as Vittoria was both positive and radical: she played her as a strong, intelligent woman, who gradually perceives that she has been trapped by the manipulative machinations of men. Her performance in the trial scene and in Act 4, Scene ii illustrated a woman who was thinking faster than Monticelso or Bracciano, and whose language spoke her feelings and views clearly. This contrasted explicitly with Bracciano's language and actions, which were continually portrayed as Machiavellian. When she and Zanche trample on Flamineo, believing him to be dead, in Act 5, Scene vi, the audience sympathise with her violence against all the men in her life. The theme of a 'sex war' was echoed in Lodovico's final on-stage action: he stabbed Vittoria's dead body in the genitals with his sword. The audience left having seen the play as a critique of patriarchal violence.

The script was prepared for performance by Edward Bond, whose links to the theatre of cruelty, and political realism, led him to emphasise these aspects of the play. His only major alteration to the script was that the dialogue at the very end was mainly obscured by the violent sounds of the attempted entry, finally achieved with machine guns, which shot Lodovico in the back. The future legal trial was thus eliminated, and with it all hopes of a return to the rule of law. His final words, delivered as he crawled among his own and his victims' blood, emphatically enhanced the criticism of masculine violence. But his death on stage by retaliatory, if authorised, violence denied the audience any naive optimism about its final eradication. You might want to go back to Chapter 2, and reconsider your own responses to the end of the play in the light of this production.

Let us now turn to two more recent performances, both in 1996: Gale Edwards' *The White Devil* at the Swan, and Declan Donellan's *The Duchess of Malfi* at the Wyndham Theatre.

The Swan theatre is a small, intimate theatre with an apron stage, and this was used to enhance both the play's intimate themes and its inclusion of the audience. In the trial scene, for example, the audience were used as jury and spectators, an interpretation which deepens our involvement in the debate and outcome of that scene. But the major theme of the production was the mutual destructiveness of lust: for both Vittoria and Bracciano. Despite programme notes which argued that women like Vittoria were little 'other than manipulated pawns in the power games of powerful male relatives', the performance and costuming of Vittoria suggested otherwise. She and Zanche were clothed in full skirts, with bodices slit to the waist, but completely naked underneath. In scenes such as those with Bracciano and with her brother, Vittoria would bare her breasts in self-confessed wantonness. Her frank avowal of sexual desire dominated her actions. Bracciano and Lodovico wore black leather. The theme of sexual excess was emphasised in Flamineo's relationship with his sister. When, with Camillo watching, he pretended to encourage her back to her husband, whilst actually pandering her to Bracciano, he put his hand down the front of her bodice, and groped her genitals. Both siblings were seen to enjoy this. In Act 4, Scene ii, when he persuaded Bracciano to believe Vittoria, the brother and sister kissed. Finally, in Act 5, Scene vi, he persuaded Vittoria of the need for their death by thrusting his pistol between her legs. This was an almost exact echo of the 1976 performance when Lodovico did this to Vittoria: but its meaning was very different. In the 1976 version, it signalled the continued triumphalism of masculine aggression, in which women were posited as victims. In the 1996 performance, it signalled the mutual dependence and mutual lust of Vittoria and Flamineo. Their death showed them entwined as lovers, beneath pouring stage-rain: and this image closed the play.

In the first lovers' scene between Bracciano and Vittoria, the production clearly showed both Flamineo and Cornelia watching. The scene was explicitly erotic, if not pornographic, and in combination with the visible voyeurs, made the audience aware of its own ambiguous voyeurism.

The insertion of an incest theme into this production was interesting, if finally untenable. The presence of an incest theme certainly emphasised the close relationship between Flamineo and Vittoria, which is essential to the play. However, by reducing that relationship solely to sexuality, Edwards denied some of the play's other themes: the question of masculine political patronage; the workings of masculine honour; the way in which other women are victimised by the play's misogyny; and the presence of such misogyny in the words and action of the play. Nevertheless, this production was a valid contribution to debates about Vittoria. You might want to return to Chapter 4 to reconsider what you have thought and written about Vittoria in the light of the two very different performances we have discussed.

Declan Donellan's production of *The Duchess of Malfi* emphasised the action and milieu of the play, rather than the psychology of individual characters. This was achieved in several ways. First, by setting and lighting, which was simple, bare and stark. A chequered floor posited a sense of characters as chess-pieces. Blue drapes made up the walls. Orange light lit the court scenes, but this was bisected at moments of crisis (for example the onset of the Duchess's labour) by green light. Blackness surrounded the lit parts of the stage.

Secondly, by costume: most were black lounge-suits or military-style garb. The two exceptions to this were the Cardinal's crimson robe, which he wore in Act 2, Scene v, and Ferdinand's white asylum gown in Act 5, Scene ii. Bosola was dressed as a fascist storm-trooper.

Thirdly, Donellan used 'freeze-frames' at key points, which had the effect of allowing the audience to see the characters as pawns in a political system that was larger than any one individual. It also allowed the production to emphasise the juxtapositional nature of many scenes, encouraging the audience to make judgements about one set of characters or actions in contrast to the previous or subsequent set.

Fourthly, stage properties, which in the main were kept to a minimum, where used, gained particular significance. There were two chairs, with an occasional third brought out for court scenes. They were always placed in a straight line facing the audience: and the external visual order acted as a tonal and intellectual contrast to the internal turmoil at court. A trunk was brought into the Duchess's chamber in Act 2, Scene iii, and covered with a cloth. In Act 4, when her chamber becomes her prison, this trunk was revealed as her coffin.

Finally, stage business used action to emphasise theme and emotion. The company built the Duchess's bedroom around her at the opening of Act 3, Scene ii. We gradually watched her confined by the building, even whilst celebrating the freedom of her private marriage. This then presaged its later conversion to her prison and coffin. Another innovative piece of stage business was the manner of killing in the final scene. Bosola and Ferdinand stood ten yards apart, and mimed their mutual stabbing. This served to alter and widen the audience's interpretation of the scene, reminding us that tragic responsibility lies not just with Bosola, or with Ferdinand, but with the system which supported and nurtured them. Donellan also made some scenes overlap, with characters passing each other without acknowledgement. This enhanced a sense of the interconnections and juxtapositional contrasts between scenes in a very effective visual way. Many actors sat at the side of the stage, observing the action, drawing attention to the play's theatricality. Many of Donellan's techniques share this theatrical effect: aiming, in a Brechtian way, at making the audience conscious of the broader political and philosophical debates of the play, rather than individual psychology.

In the main, the acting was subservient to the milieu. The

Cardinal was a sadist to Julia, and an indifferent brother to Ferdinand's distress (who lay weeping on his lap, ignored). Antonio was presented as a weak man, dominated and led by the Duchess and his own venal ambition. None of the characters seemed to 'connect', and this created a sense of emotional dislocation. The Duchess (played by Anastasia Hill) did not ask for or play for sympathy. She was shown to be careless of the consequences of her action, and even foolishly self-involved: for example, ignoring Ferdinand's threats with his father's poniard, she seized it and dismissed him. Nevertheless, the acting was more than balanced by the theatrical techniques used to arouse the audience's awareness of characters as trapped, isolated individuals enmeshed in political and social systems over which they have no control.

*   *   *

Before we end this chapter, it is useful to consider what the critics and performances have in common.

One of the major attributes they all share is an insistence on Webster's theatricality, including visual and staging effects as a central and critical dramatic tool. They all also argue or display the way in which he uses such techniques in a complex juxtapositional way to engender a complex audience response. The second approach that they all share is the perception that tragedy is predicated on fundamental and oppositional conflict, although each critic or director differs slightly in what they identify as the central conflict. The third common approach is the perception that Webster's tragedy differs fundamentally from Shakespeare's in his focus on character as social and political, as dependent on external forces, as much as on internal ones. Finally, they see political and social order as fragile and possibly unattainable. The four common threads are shared by the main part of our critical analysis in Part I. You may now wish to return to some parts of that analysis to match your own interpretations against those of these critics and directors.

Further Reading

Throughout this book you have engaged in detailed reading of the original texts. We have tried to enable you to develop your own independent interpretations, reinforced by close, analytical readings. If you read and discuss a play, using the approaches suggested in this book, you should be able to write essays which are original, analytical and convincing. You may feel that you would like to engage with what other critics have written about your chosen texts: but it is best to do this when you have already formed your own opinions. If you read other critics before you read and think about the play yourself, you will find it harder to develop your own personal ideas and feelings about the play, and it will also make the whole process far less pleasurable.

The suggestions made here for further reading are necessarily curtailed: both by space and by my own selection. All good editions of the plays will have additional suggestions for reading, as will the catalogue of a good library. You will also find that the footnotes and bibliographies of some of the books or articles recommended below, point you to other texts that will interest you.

Reading Webster's Contemporaries

We have mentioned several plays and writers in this book which would give you a good sense of the dramatic context in which Webster wrote. Shakespeare's 'Roman' tragedies, written some years before Webster's plays, are a good comparison: *Coriolanus* and *Antony and Cleopatra*. Marston's *The Malcontent* (which we discussed briefly in Chapter 9) is an excellent comparison, particularly as Webster was closely associated with revising its script for public performance. Middleton's revenge and Italianate tragedies are very close to Webster's in style, form and theme. Look particularly at *The Revenger's Tragedy*, *The Changeling* and *Women Beware Women*. You should also look at Webster's other plays, in particular the collaborative *Westward Ho!* and his tragicomedy, written a few years after *The Duchess of Malfi*, *The Devil's Law Case*.

It is helpful and illuminating to look at some non-dramatic contemporary texts which discuss and address many of the issues with which Webster was concerned. Look at Machiavelli's *The Prince*, in any edition; Francis Bacon's *Essays* (any edition); and other political and social debates in the relevant sections of my book *The English Renaissance: An Anthology of Documents and Sources* (Routledge, 1998).

Historical and Social Contexts

This Stage-Play World: English Literature and its Background, 1580–1625 by Julia Briggs (Oxford University Press, 2nd edition, 1997) is excellent on the background to all of the period's drama, and the up-dated version considers issues such as gender and travel, as well as the political and social context. G. P. V. Akrigg's *The Jacobean Pageant* (London: Hamish Hamilton, 1962) discusses the specific social and political world of the Jacobean court. J. W. Lever's *The Tragedy of State* (1971) is an indispensable account of the political nature and content of tragedy and tragic form in the Jacobean period. David Scott Kastan and Peter Stallybrass's *Staging the Renaissance: Interpretations of Elizabethan and Jacobean Drama* (London: Routledge, 1993) contains extracts from some of the key current critical writers on Renaissance drama, as well as individual essays on both plays.

Criticism

The critical works which we discussed in Chapter 11 were: Travis Bogard, *The Tragic Satire of John Webster* (Berkeley and Los Angeles: University of California Press, 1955); Jonathon Dollimore, *Radical Tragedy: Religion, Ideology and Power in the Drama of Shakespeare and his Contemporaries* (Brighton: Harvester Wheatsheaf, 1989); and

Dympna Callaghan, *Woman and Gender in Renaissance Tragedy* (Brighton: Harvester Wheatsheaf, 1989).

There are a few anthologies of Websterian criticism, although most collections are now quite dated. *John Webster: A Critical Anthology* edited by G. K. and S. K. Hunter (Harmondsworth: Penguin, 1969) is the best of the earlier ones. R. V. Holdsworth has edited the casebook *Webster, 'The White Devil' and 'The Duchess of Malfi': A Casebook* (London: Macmillan, 1975), and Harold Bloom *John Webster's 'The Duchess of Malfi'* (New York: Chelsea House Publishers, 1987). If you sample the critical views in these collections, you can then follow up your own interests by reading the extracted books or articles in full.

There are several other full-length studies of Webster's plays which are of interest. M. C. Bradbrook's *John Webster: Citizen and Dramatist* (London: Weidenfeld and Nicolson, 1980) examines the plays within Webster's political and intellectual context. Charles Forker's *The Skull Beneath the Skin: The Achievement of John Webster* (Carbondale: Southern Illinois University Press, 1986) summarises previous critical views on Webster. Jacqueline Pearson's *Tragedy and Tragicomedy in the Plays of John Webster* (Manchester: Manchester University Press, 1980) discusses Webster's dramatic form, an argument which is complemented by Christine Luckyj's *A Winter's Snake: Dramatic Form in the Tragedies of John Webster* (Athens, Georgia: University of Georgia Press, 1989). A good students' introduction is Rowland Wymer's *Webster and Ford* (Macmillan, 1995).

Recent feminist accounts of Renaissance drama which have addressed Webster's plays include: Catherine Belsey, *The Subject of Tragedy* (London: Routledge, 1985); Lisa Jardine, *Still Harping on Daughters: Women and Drama in the Age of Shakespeare* (Brighton: Harvester Wheatsheaf, 1983); Kathleen McCluskie, *Renaissance Dramatists* (Brighton: Harvester Wheatsheaf, 1989); and Alison Findlay's *A Feminist Perspective on Renaissance Drama* (Oxford: Blackwell, 1999).

There is an excellent short account of recent performances of the two plays by Richard Cave, *Text and Performance: The White Devil and The Duchess of Malfi* (Macmillan, 1988).

Index